THE THEORY OF WAGES

THE
THEORY OF WAGES

BY

J. R. HICKS
Fellow of All Souls College

MACMILLAN

© *J. R. Hicks 1963*
First Edition 1932
Second Edition 1963
Reprinted 1963, 1964 (twice), 1966, 1968,
1973

Published by
THE MACMILLAN PRESS LTD
London and Basingstoke
Associated companies in New York Dublin
Melbourne Johannesburg and Madras

SBN 333 02764 7

Printed in Great Britain by
LOWE AND BRYDONE (PRINTERS) LTD
Haverhill, Suffolk

HD
4900
H5
1973

PREFACE TO THE SECOND EDITION

THIS is only the second (regular) edition of a book which was first published in 1932 and which has been out of print in the United Kingdom for more than twenty years. I let it go out of print because my own views upon its subject had changed so much that I no longer desired to be represented by it. It has, however, been made clear to me that there is still a demand for it; not, I hope, because anyone wants to use the greater part of it as a source of direct instruction, but because there are several parts of it which are still alive in the sense that they provide convenient starting-points for much more modern discussion. References to it have indeed become too frequent for it to be left unavailable. That is the reason why I have finally decided that it ought to appear in a new edition; it also explains why the new edition has had to take so peculiar a form.

The change in my own views since 1932 has been too drastic for it to be possible to produce a new edition in the usual way, by changing this and that, and adding extra passages. Besides, it is the old book which is wanted for the purpose mentioned above; so it is this which must be reproduced. I have decided to deal with the situation in the following way.

Section I of this new edition is simply a reprint

v

of the first edition. Section II, entitled "Documents",
includes a couple of articles of my own, written within
a few years of the book's first appearance, which
serve to illustrate the kinds of change which I felt
impelled to make, even in the first stages of further
thinking on the subject. To these I have added an
important work by another author. This is the review
of my book written in 1933 by Gerald Shove—one of
the very small number of published works by that
excellent economist. It is included here as a statement
(I have come to think it to be a most admirable
statement) of the Case for the Prosecution. I am very
anxious that any readers (I am afraid there may be
some) who even now are tempted to take the 1932
volume too literally should read Shove's criticism.

Section III, entitled "Commentary", has been
specially written for this new edition. It begins with
an introductory section, which attempts to tell the
story of the book (its pre-natal as well as its post-natal
vicissitudes) in more detail than is appropriate for
this preface. I then go through the various chapters,
reviewing them (more or less as Shove did) from the
standpoint which I would myself take today. There
are of course some chapters on which there is little to be
said; but there are others (I., VI. and IX.-X. in
particular) on which I have had to sketch out a
different, and I hope more constructive, treatment.
I end with a set of "Notes on the Elasticity of Substitution", corresponding to the Appendix to the
first edition. When I wrote that Appendix, I had no
idea of the fruitful use that Mrs. Robinson was so

soon to make of what proved to be identically the same concept. Professor Lerner's simple proof of the "relative shares" proposition, proceeding from Mrs. Robinson's definition, is given in the "Revised Version" paper which appears in Section II; other ways in which my treatment could have been clarified by that alternative approach did not appear until much later.

ACKNOWLEDGMENTS

THE author wishes to acknowledge his indebtedness to the following, who have kindly given permission for the use of copyright material: the Editor of *Oxford Economic Papers*, for "Marshall's Third Rule", which appeared in the October 1961 issue in a slightly different form; the Editor of *The Review of Economic Studies*, for "Distribution and Economic Progress: A Revised Version", which appeared in the October 1936 issue; the Royal Economic Society, for "Wages and Interest: The Dynamic Problem", which appeared in the September 1935 issue of *The Economic Journal*; and the same Society and His Honour Judge R. S. Shove, for Gerald Shove's review of the first edition of this book, which appeared in the September 1933 issue of *The Economic Journal*.

PREFACE TO THE FIRST EDITION

THE task which is attempted in this book is a restatement of the theory of wages in a form which shall be reasonably abreast of modern economic knowledge. It is thus an undertaking which seems to need little apology. Periodical reconsiderations of each of the main departments of economic theory are an important part of the duty of economists; since, for one thing, one field is often illuminated by advances which have been made in others, and for another, the events of contemporary history make it necessary to examine possibilities, of which earlier writers may have been aware, but which they naturally regarded as not worthy of special attention. Such a reconsideration of wage theory seems long overdue. For the most recent comprehensive statements of a positive theory of wages in English—of anything more than an elementary character—are now thirty or forty years old. We have to go back for them to Marshall's *Principles* and Clark's *Distribution of Wealth*. Since that time important work on the subject has indeed been done, but it is nearly all special studies; even Professor Pigou's treatment of Labour, in the *Economics of Welfare*, ought probably so to be reckoned for our purposes. Of these works much use has been made in the following pages: to them this book owes a great debt; but they have not removed the need for some undertaking like the present.

The historical fact which dominates the wage-history of the present century—both in Britain and in other countries—is the growth of Trade Union power and the development of State Regulation of Wages. This fact, which is due to a complex of causes, and which could not have been wholly foreseen by economists thirty years ago, alters very considerably the range of problems with which we have to deal. It might even appear at first sight as if it ought to change the whole structure of our theory—that we ought to treat the regulation of wages as the normal case, and take its consideration first. But this course does not prove satisfactory. The same forces which determine wages in a free market are still present under regulation; they only work rather differently. It is therefore best for us to begin in the traditional manner with the determination of wages under competition; though at a later stage we must examine regulation in more detail than the traditional theories do.

By proceeding in this way, we secure the great advantage of being able to build directly upon familiar doctrines; and we naturally start with a consideration of that principle which was regarded by the economists of Marshall's generation as the basis of their theory of wages—the principle of Marginal Productivity. The validity and the importance of this principle we shall see no reason to question; but its very importance has one awkward consequence. For we shall get into endless difficulties if we allow any obscurity about so essential a principle to persist; and it is unfortunately the case that its original propounders did leave it—or at least its application—in some obscurity. We are therefore faced at the start with the hard task of trying to make clear something which Marshall and J. B. Clark did not make altogether clear; and we cannot hope to do this if we shirk difficulties. The reader must therefore be asked to follow Chapter I. with attention and some patience; but he may be assured that relatively smooth waters lie beyond.

One very important aspect of the theory of wages it has unfortunately been necessary to leave undiscussed —the relation of wages to general industrial fluctuations or trade cycles. In this branch of economics recent years have certainly seen striking advances; it does seem probable that in a few years' time we shall possess the main lines of an established theory of fluctuations; but that time is not yet. Thus to discuss trade fluctuations from any angle is hazardous, since nothing useful can be said unless one is prepared to take sides on the critical issues. And most of these lie altogether outside the theory of wages, although they have a direct bearing upon it.

Thus I must confine myself here to stating a personal opinion. It is my own belief that some parts of this book—particularly the last chapters—have considerable relevance to the theory of fluctuations, although they are not stated with that particular reference. But I shall make no attempt to defend this view at present.

I have to acknowledge a great debt of gratitude for

the help I have received in the preparation of this book. I work in an atmosphere which is very conducive to the making of such studies as the present, and I know what I owe to it. Professor Lionel Robbins, Professor Arnold Plant, and Dr. F. C. Benham, of the London School of Economics, and also Professor W. H. Hutt of the University of Cape Town, have all read the whole, or large parts, of my manuscript, and made most valuable suggestions—which I fear I have not always accepted. I have also to acknowledge the valuable criticisms which, at more than one stage in the development of my ideas, I have received from Mr. D. H. Robertson; and the generous assistance of Professor F. A. Hayek, in connection with those difficult points where the present enquiry begins to abut on the theory of Capital.

CONTENTS

xiii

PART II.—THE REGULATION OF WAGES

Chapter VII. The Theory of Industrial Disputes

Chapter VIII. The Growth of Trade Union Power

B

CONTENTS

TEXT

CHAPTER I

MARGINAL PRODUCTIVITY AND THE DEMAND FOR LABOUR

I

THE theory of the determination of wages in a free market is simply a special case of the general theory of value. Wages are the price of labour; and thus, in the absence of control, they are determined, like all prices, by supply and demand. The need for a special theory of wages only arises because both the supply of labour, and the demand for it, and the way in which demand and supply interact on the labour market, have certain peculiar properties, which make it impossible to apply to labour the ordinary theory of commodity value without some further consideration.

The demand for labour is only peculiar to this extent: that labour is a factor of production, and is thus demanded (as a general rule) not because the work to be done is desired for and by itself, but because it is to be used in the production of some other thing which is directly desired. Personal services are indeed an exception to this rule; but apart from this exception, the demand for labour is a derived demand, and the special properties of derived demand may thus reasonably be considered a part of the general theory of wages. It is true that these properties are important, not only in the theory of wages, but also in other departments of economics; most of what has to be said about the demand for labour applies equally to the demand for other factors of production. Yet the matter is so important for an understanding of wages that it has to be given serious attention here.

The supply of labour raises issues of an altogether different character. Most of the special difficulties of labour supply arise from the fact that "labour" is a two-dimensional quantity, depending both on the number of labourers available, and upon their "efficiency"—the amount of labour each is able and willing to provide. It is the task of manipulating these two dimensions simultaneously which has at times caused some confusion.

However, the very nature of this difficulty suggests at once the way in which we had best deal with it. In the earlier part of our discussions (Chapters I.-IV.) we shall assume the amount of work each man is prepared to do—the individual supply of labour—to be given. It will be found that we can explain most of the more important phenomena of the labour market without reference to the complication introduced by these variations. At a later stage (Chapter V.) we shall take these variations into account, and see what difference they make.

This assumption does not altogether remove the difficulties of the supply side, but it very substantially reduces them. For the question of the total number of labourers available in a community is one which modern economists are content to treat as lying outside the theory of wages (differing in this from their predecessors of a century ago). It may be regarded as belonging to the theory of population. For our purposes the total number of labourers available is given.

The distribution of this population between occupations is a problem of the theory of wages, but it is one of the easiest problems of the whole theory. We shall have something to say about it, but not much; for the general tendency for the wages of labourers of equal efficiency to become equalised in different occupations (allowance being made for other advantages or disadvantages of employment) has been a commonplace of economics since the days of Adam Smith, and little needs to be added here. The movement of labour from one occupation to another, which brings it about, is certainly a slow one; but there is no need to question its reality.

One difficulty of the supply side does, however, still remain. Unless our theory is to remain very unreal for an unduly large part of the process of its construction, we have to take into account the fact that the efficiencies of different men differ. We can continue for some time to neglect differences in the efficiency of the same man under different circumstances, without thereby making it impossible for us to grasp the more obviously important phenomena of the labour market. But we cannot neglect the differences in the efficiency of different men under the same circumstances without much more serious trouble.

However, in the present chapter we shall do even this, though the deficiency must be repaired as soon as possible. Most current theories of the demand for labour do work under the simplifying assumption that "all men are equal"; and while we are examining the demand for labour, it is therefore best to proceed under that assumption. But it will be dropped in Chapter II.

The interaction of supply and demand on the labour market is a problem which will have to occupy a good deal of our attention. All buying and selling has some features in common; but nevertheless differences do exist between the ways in which things are bought and sold on different markets. Organised produce markets differ from wholesale trade of the ordinary type; both of these differ from retail trade, and from sale by tender or by auction. The labour market is yet another type. It has been the usual practice of economists to concentrate their attention on those features of exchange which are common to all markets; and to dismiss the differences between markets with a brief reminder that markets may be more or less "perfect". There is little doubt that in doing so they did seize on the really significant thing; the general working of supply and demand is a great deal more important than the differences between markets. But this course meant the almost complete neglect of some factors which appear at first sight very important indeed; the fact that they are really less important than those aspects which were discussed was rarely demonstrated clearly.

When an attempt is made to apply to the labour market the ordinary principles of price determination —without making allowance for the type of market— the result appears at first sight very odd. Wages, say the text-books, tend to that level where demand and supply are equal. If supply exceeds demand, some men will be unemployed, and in their efforts to regain employment they will reduce the wages they ask to that level which makes it just worth while for employers to take them on. If demand exceeds supply, employers will be unable to obtain all the labour they require, and will therefore offer higher wages in order to attract labour from elsewhere.

Now this, as I hope to make abundantly clear, is quite a good simplified model of the labour market. So far as general tendencies are concerned, wages do turn out on the whole very much as if they were determined in this manner. It is therefore not in the least surprising if valuable results have been attained by this sort of reasoning. But, since it is a simplified model, it is extremely likely to be misconstrued by those who take it to be an account of how the real labour market works. One of the most obvious features of the real labour market is the fact that at all times there is a certain amount of unemployment. Now it is easy to say—and of course it has often been said—that this means that there is a permanent excess of supply over demand; and that in consequence wages have a permanent tendency to fall. The answer which is most frequently given to this line of argument is a mere appeal to facts. Facts certainly do disprove it; unemployment is undoubtedly sometimes coexistent with rising wages; but such an appeal is surely insufficient. If the conclusion to which an argument leads is false, then it is our business to show just at what point the reasoning was fallacious.

It is extremely unlikely that the unemployment which does occur in a free market has no effect on the determination of wages; and this, it is evident, many of the most orthodox economists would have admitted. But the traditional way of allowing for unemployment, as we find it in Marshall and Edgeworth and others of their contemporaries, is, to say the least, peculiar.[1] In effect, they use alternative models. Sometimes they

---

[1] Marshall, *Principles*, bk. vi., chs. i. and iv.; *cf.* also bk. v., ch. ii.

treat the labour market as a purely competitive market, working under the action of supply and demand—and then they leave unemployment out of account. But elsewhere they allow for unemployment, only to make insufficient allowance for competition. Marshall was perfectly well aware that the simple apparatus of supply and demand schedules does not make sufficient allowance for unemployment; but his further steps are uncertain. His extended theory of wages is a mere torso—an examination of one special case where the absence of competition may make the wage-bargain indeterminate. This is altogether insufficient.

The problems of the nature of the market are almost entirely problems of change. If no one was ever dismissed, and if no one ever had an incentive to change his employment, there would be no problem here. And this suggests a way by which we can postpone consideration of these questions—just as we decided above to postpone the problem of labour supply. We can begin by confining our attention to a labour market in equilibrium. Let us suppose that a level of wages is fixed so that demand and supply balance, and thus there is no tendency for wages to rise or to fall. Let us suppose, further, that this balancing of demand and supply is brought about, not by compensating fluctuations of the demand from particular firms, but by the demand from each firm being stationary, because no employer has any incentive to vary the number of men he takes on. It is necessary for us to adopt this abstract and rigorous conception of equilibrium, since otherwise we should not be effectively ruling out the difficulties of change, but should still be faced with very much the same kind of problem which confronts us in the case of a rise or fall in wages.

We have thus to examine the conditions of full equilibrium in the labour market, assuming the supply of labourers given, and their efficiencies given and equal. This enables us finally to isolate the pure problem of demand. It is true that we only achieve this isolation at the expense of a series of highly artificial assumptions; but in economics, as in other sciences, abstraction is usually the condition of clear thinking. The complications created by the things we have left out can be reintroduced later.[1]

II

The first of the necessary conditions of equilibrium is that every man should receive the same wage— subject at any rate to allowances for "other advantages" and possibly for costs of movement (but these things also we neglect at present). If wages are not equal, then it will clearly be to the advantage of an employer who is paying a higher level of wages to dismiss his present employees, and to replace them by other men who had been receiving less. If he offers a wage somewhere between the two previously existing levels, he will both lower his own costs (and consequently improve his own situation) and successfully attract the new men, since he is offering them a higher wage than they received before. So long as such transfers can be made advantageously to both parties entering upon the new contract, there is no equilibrium; since someone can always disturb it to his own advantage. Equal wages are a necessary condition of equi-

---

[1] See below, chs. ii.-v.

librium in a market governed by our present assumptions.

The second condition is much more critical. The only wage at which equilibrium is possible is a wage which equals the value of the marginal product of the labourers. At any given wage it will pay employers best to take on that number of labourers which makes their marginal product—that is to say, the difference between the total physical product which is actually secured and that which would have been secured from the same quantity of other resources if the number of labourers had been increased or diminished by one—equal in value to the wage. In this way the demand for labour of each employer is determined; and the total demand of all employers is determined from it by addition. Since in equilibrium it is necessary that the total demand should equal the total supply, the wage must be that which just enables the total number of labourers available to be employed. This must equal the value of the marginal product of the labourers available.

The conventional proof of the marginal productivity proposition is simple enough. It follows from the most fundamental form of the law of diminishing returns that an increased quantity of labour applied to a fixed quantity of other resources will yield a diminished marginal product. Thus if the employer were to take on a number of labourers so large that their marginal product was not worth the wage which has to be paid, he would soon find that the number was excessive. By reducing the number he employed, he would reduce his total production, and therefore (under competitive conditions) his gross receipts. But at the same time he would reduce his expenditure; and since the wage was higher than the marginal product, he would reduce his expenditure more than his receipts, and so increase his profits. Similarly, he would not reduce his employment of labour to such a point as would make the wage less than the marginal product; for by so doing he would be reducing his receipts more than his expenditure, and so again diminishing his profits. The number of labourers which an employer will prefer to take on is that number which makes his profits a maximum, and that number is given by the equality of wages to the marginal product of the labour employed.

It is thus clear that the wage at which equilibrium is possible will vary in the opposite direction to changes in the total number of labourers available. If the number of labourers available on the market had been larger, the wage must have been lower; since the additional product secured by the employment of one of these extra labourers would be worth less than the previously given wage, and consequently it would not pay to employ these men unless the wage-level was reduced. If the number had been less, employers would have had an incentive to demand more labourers at the given wage than would actually have been available, and their competition would therefore force up the level of wages. The only wage which is consistent with equilibrium is one which equals the value of the marginal product of the available labour.

This "Law of Marginal Productivity" is regarded by most modern economists as the most fundamental principle of the theory of wages. Nothing will be said here to contradict that view. Nevertheless, care has been taken in framing the above statement of the law to bring into clear relief the extremely abstract assumptions on which alone it is rigorously true to say that wages equal the marginal product of labour. A long road has to be travelled before this abstract proposition can be used in the explanation of real events.

We shall have to tread that road in future chapters; but it must first of all be pointed out that the difficulty of applying the law is considerably increased by the conventional method of proof. The proof which we have just given is theoretically valid, and it has its uses; some of the broadest and most far-reaching deductions which can be drawn from the theory are reached most easily if we look at the proposition in something like the above manner.[1] But other applications come out much more clearly if we adopt another way of looking at it (which is quite consistent with the first); and these are among the most important in the detailed study of reality.

The number of men employed by a firm depends directly upon two things: the quantity of product it desires to turn out, and the method it decides to adopt in production. Some methods use a large amount of one factor, some use less of that and relatively more of another; and though no entrepreneur in his senses would ever use a method which needed a large amount of all factors, when a method which needed a smaller quantity of each of them was available, a very real choice does arise between methods, one of which uses relatively more of factor A and relatively less of factor B, while the other uses less of A and more of B. If the method of production is given, then the quantity of labour employed varies directly with the output; the larger the output, the more men will be employed. If the output is given, then a variation in method

[1] See below, ch. vi.

will still vary the quantity of labour employed to some extent, since some methods need more labour than others.

In equilibrium, both the scale of production and the method of production must be chosen in such a way that no opportunity remains open for employers to benefit themselves by a change. Thus if for the present we work under the assumption that the methods of production are fixed, the amount produced in each firm (and consequently the demand for labour) is determined by the condition that the price of the product should equal its cost of production— including an allowance for "normal profits". These normal profits are genuinely an element in costs; for they are simply the price which has to be paid for the resources—the capital and managerial skill—which are contributed by the employer himself, in order just to induce them to stay in the branch of production in question. If the wages which have to be paid in a particular industry were higher, costs of production would be raised relatively to selling prices, and the profits of employers would consequently be reduced. These employers would therefore find that the employment of their own resources in the industry in question had become less advantageous relatively to the employment of similar resources in other industries, so that they would tend to turn their attention to other industries, and production in the first industry would contract. And under our present assumptions, the contraction of production would lead to a roughly proportional contraction of the demand for labour in that industry.

In exactly the same way, a fall in wages, other things remaining equal, would make the industry concerned a relatively profitable one for the investment of other resources; new capital would flow in, new firms would set up, and the demand for labour would expand. If the industry is to be in equilibrium, there must be no tendency for an expansion of this kind, or for a contraction; the cost of production must equal the selling price.

This particular relation (which, as we shall see, is not by any means the only one which we have to take into account) received particular attention from Marshall at one stage of his development. The wages of labour, Marshall declared, tend to equal "the net product of a man's labour"—"the value of the produce which he takes part in producing after deducting all the other expenses of producing it".[1] It is this which appeared in the first edition of Marshall's *Principles* as the main part of his theory of the demand for labour, although there is appended to it the celebrated warning that it is not "an independent theory of wages, but only a particular way of stating the familiar doctrine that the value of anything tends to equal its expenses of production".[2]

It is interesting to enquire whether "net produc-

---

[1] *Principles*, 1st ed., p. 548. It should be observed that as it stands this is not the same thing as the marginal product.

[2] Of course, even in the first edition, Marshall did not leave out of account the variation of methods, although he had not yet fully developed his characteristic way of dealing with it. This was to conceive of entrepreneurs as choosing between blocks of resources, each organised in a technically given manner (a man with a spade, to take the simplest case). Such a block would be taken on only if its marginal product was worth more than its cost; but it would not be taken on even then if another block was available, which offered an equivalent product at smaller cost. Marginal productivity sufficed to determine the total value of the block, but in order to discover the price which would be paid for one only of its components, the prices of the other components must be subtracted. Thus we have the "marginal net product".

The results of this approach do not seem to be appreciably different from those of the analysis in the text—though that is based on Walras rather than Marshall. But it may perhaps be claimed that the present version achieves a greater simplicity, and is not much less realistic.

tivity " is simply a determinant of the equilibrium
level of wages in a particular trade, or whether it is
also a sufficient determinant of the level of wages in
general. At first sight it would appear that if wages
were raised throughout all industries to a uniform
extent, there could be no tendency to a contraction of
the demand for labour from this cause. The withdrawal of capital (or land) from a particular industry is
due to the fact that other investments have become
more profitable; if profits are simultaneously reduced
elsewhere, this incentive seems to be removed. But this
is not the 'case. Since different industries are making
different products, it is almost certain that the proportions in which labour and capital are combined will
be different in different industries; and thus a given
rise in wages will diminish profits more in some industries than in others. There will thus still be an incentive for the other factors to move, capital, for instance, moving out of the trades which use relatively
much labour and little capital, into those in which the
proportions are reversed. In the less capitalistic industries there will be unemployment; in the more
capitalistic industries there will be a rise in the demand
for labour. But since in those industries which use a
high proportion of capital the amount of labour
required to use a given amount of capital is relatively
small, the transferred capital in its new employment
will absorb less labour than had been thrown out by
its withdrawal. There is net unemployment.

Similarly, a fall in the general level of wages will
lead to a transference of other factors in the opposite
direction, and so to a rise in the demand for labour.

Thus, even if we suppose the technical methods of
production in every industry to be fixed, it is still true

C

that there is a determinate rate of wages which will make demand equal to a given supply. If wages are higher, the supply will exceed the demand; if wages are lower, demand will exceed supply.[1]

The difference between the marginal productivity theory and this "net productivity" doctrine lies simply in a difference of assumptions. "Net productivity" assumes the methods of production to be fixed; marginal productivity assumes them to be variable. In fact, there can be very little doubt that they nearly always are variable to some extent; and consequently the marginal productivity theory has a deeper significance than the other. But this does not mean that the particular relation which is distinguished in the net productivity doctrine loses its importance. Even if the methods of production are variable, it is still true that in equilibrium "the value of anything equals its expenses of production". Thus the demand for labour will react to changes in wages through the consequent change in the relative profitability of investment in different industries—even if it reacts in other ways as well.

When an entrepreneur has to choose between two

[1] This extension of the "net productivity" doctrine to cover all industries together is due to Walras (*Eléments d'économie politique pure*, particularly Leçons 20 and 21).

The effect on the demand for labour which arises from the redistribution of other resources between industries ought to be distinguished from another closely similar effect, not discussed in this chapter. It is not improbable that the reduced (or increased) price which is paid for other factors of production (even after they have been transferred), as compared with their situation before a change in wages took place, may have some effect on their total supply. If, as the result of a rise in wages and consequent fall in profits, the supply of capital falls off, then the demand for labour will contract still further. And vice versa if wages fall.

But this effect on the total supply of other factors involves quite different considerations than the effect through changes in the application of a fixed supply of the other factors. Here, therefore, we concentrate on this latter effect. But the question of consequential changes in the supply of other factors will have to concern us later in this book (see Chapters VI. and IX.).

different methods of producing a given output, he may be expected to choose that which costs least. For, at any rate in the first place, anything which reduces his costs will raise his profits. If employers are not using the cheapest method of production available to them, they have an incentive to change; and so there is no equilibrium.

It is this condition of minimum cost of production per unit of output which leads us directly to the law of marginal productivity. For if we suppose the prices of all the factors of production to be given, the "least cost" combination of factors will be given by the condition that the marginal products of the factors are proportional to their prices. If the

$$\frac{\text{marginal product of factor A}}{\text{price of A}} \text{ is greater than } \frac{\text{marginal product of B}}{\text{price of B}},$$

then this means that it will be to the advantage of the entrepreneur to use a method of production which uses a little more of A and a little less of B, since in that way he will get a larger product for the same expenditure, or (what comes to the same thing) he will get an equal product at a lower cost.

This condition of the proportionality of marginal products is simply another means of expressing the necessity that the method employed in a position of equilibrium should be the cheapest method of reaching the desired result. No new principle whatever is introduced; so that in practical applications we can work with the condition of minimum cost, or with the condition of the proportionality of marginal products— whichever seems more significant in the particular case.[1]

---

[1] The proportionality of marginal products is simply the mathematical condition for minimum cost of production—or maximum production from a given expenditure. It is thus easy to see why it takes the same form as the law of equi-marginal utilities—the condition for maximisation of satisfactions.

It must, however, be observed that the above condition only states that the marginal products are proportional to the prices of the factors—it does not say that the prices *equal* the values of the marginal products. So far as the choice of methods of production is concerned, it appears that the prices of the factors might all exceed, or all fall short of, the values of the marginal products—so long as they do it in the same proportion. But if this were to be the case, it would be possible for the entrepreneur to increase his profits by expanding or contracting production without changing his methods. The condition of equality between price and cost of production would not be satisfied.[1]

When we allow for the variability of methods of production, there is thus another way in which changes in wages may affect the demand for labour. A rise in wages will make labour expensive relatively to other factors of production, and will thus encourage entrepreneurs to use methods which employ less labour and more of these other factors. And this evidently applies in exactly the same way to industry as a whole, as it does to particular industries. The more extensive the rise in wages, the more substitution will take place. For exactly the same reason, a fall in wages will lead to substitution in the reverse direction.

The law of marginal productivity, in its usual form, is simply a convenient means whereby the statement of the two tendencies we have been discussing can be combined. On the one hand, the returns to other resources than labour tend to equality in their different applications (the tendency which alone is taken account of in the formulation of "net productivity"); on the other hand, employers can modify the methods which

---

[1] For a further discussion of this point, see Appendix, sect. 1.

they employ in their businesses, and the relative profitability of different methods depends on the relative prices of the factors of production. For some purposes it is convenient to use the conventional formulation, which brings together the two tendencies, and enables us to manipulate them together; but for a good many other purposes it is convenient to treat them separately.[1]

[1] Some remarks may usefully be inserted here about the conception of "discounted marginal productivity" as we find it in the work of Professor Taussig (*Principles of Economics*, vol ii., p. 214 *ff.*). This conception is intermediate between "net productivity" and "marginal productivity", as we have defined them; just as they are consistent with each other, since they describe the same phenomenon under slightly different assumptions, so "discounted marginal productivity" is consistent with them.

One of the factors of production which is required to co-operate with labour in almost any employment is circulating capital; the amount of circulating capital needed for the employment of labour being equal to the wages paid, multiplied by the length of time elapsing between the payment of labour and the sale of the product. If now we suppose that this length of time—the period of production, in the familiar English sense—is given and constant, but that the proportions of labour to other factors of production except circulating capital are independently variable, then, although the amount of these other factors of production may be supposed constant when the amount of labour employed slightly increases, circulating capital cannot be kept constant; we have to allow for a small increase in circulating capital parallel with the increased employment of labour. In order to maintain the condition of equality of selling price and cost of production, the cost of this additional circulating capital must be deducted from the marginal product, *i.e.* the marginal product (estimated in this manner) must be "discounted."

However, there is no reason why, in general, we should not assume that the period of production is variable; and once we do this, we get a true marginal product of the kind described in the text. The employment of more labour with the same amount of circulating capital will generally involve a shortening of the period of production; but the additional product created by the additional labour under these circumstances is a true marginal product, which in equilibrium must equal the wage, without any discounting.

Professor Taussig's preference for this perfectly valid way of stating the theory springs no doubt from his conviction (so properly shown in all his work) of the extreme importance of circulating capital and of a right understanding of its functions. A full understanding of this important aspect of the determination of wages can, however, probably only be secured if we make use of some kind of modernised "elastic" wage-fund theory, such as has been elaborated in the works of Böhm-Bawerk, Wicksell, and Professor Taussig himself (see his *Wages and Capital*). Such a modernised wage-fund is perfectly consistent with marginal productivity; and I have often been tempted to use it on a considerable scale in this book. But I have concluded that the advantages of such a treatment would not compensate for the

III

There can be no full equilibrium unless the wages of labour equal its marginal product; since, if this equality is not attained, it means that someone has open to him an opportunity of gain which he is not taking. Either employers will be able to find an advantage in varying the methods of production they use, or investors and other owners of property will be able to benefit themselves by transferring the resources under their control from one branch of production to another. But we cannot go on from this to conclude that this equality of wages and marginal products will actually be found in practice; for the real labour market is scarcely ever in equilibrium in the sense considered here. In actual practice changes in methods are continually going on; and resources are continually being transferred from one industry to another, or new resources being put at the disposal of industry, which are not uniformly distributed among the various branches of production. This ceaseless change is partly a consequence of changes in the ultimate determinants of economic activity—those things which we have to take as the final data of economic enquiry—changes in tastes, changes in knowledge, changes in the natural environment, and in the supply and efficiency of the factors of production generally. As these things change, so the marginal product of labour changes with them; and these changes in marginal productivity exert

---

obstacles it would probably place in the way of readers brought up on the English tradition.

On this question of the relation of circulating capital to marginal productivity, see Barone, "Studi sulla distribuzione " (*Giornale degli economisti* 1896).

pressure, in one direction or the other, upon the level of wages.

It does not follow, however, that because the marginal product of labour has changed, therefore the level of wages will change in the same direction at once. There are several processes which have to be gone through first; and most of these are by no means instantaneous. Some of these processes (those which concern the reaction on the wage of an already effective change in the demand for labour) will have to be considered in detail in future chapters; for the present, it is only necessary to point out that a rise in the marginal productivity of labour with constant wages (or a fall in the wage with constant marginal productivity) does not necessarily lead employers to expand their demand for labour at once. Similarly, the fact that the employment of certain men has become less advantageous does not always lead to an immediate contraction in the demand for labour.

The principal reason for this "lag" is to be found in the fact that one of the co-operating factors—capital—is, at any particular moment, largely incorporated in goods of a certain degree of durability. It may have become more advantageous to use other methods, or to invest capital in other directions, than those which are currently practised; but if the capital is at present invested in durable goods, the change in conduct which follows from the change in relative profitability cannot immediately be realised. At the moment, only a small portion of the total supply of capital is "free"—available for investment in new forms—and although this portion will be reinvested in ways more appropriate to the new situation, that in itself may make very little difference to the demand for labour. But, as time goes on, more and more plant will wear out and have to be renewed; more and more half-finished goods will come to fruition, and the money they bring in become available for reinvestment in other ways; larger and larger will therefore become the possibilities of adjustment.[1] In the short period, therefore, it is reasonable to expect that the demand for labour will be very inelastic, since the possibility of adjusting the organisation of industry to a changed level of wages is relatively small; but if time is allowed the elasticity grows very considerably.

Since the whole conception of marginal productivity depends upon the variability of industrial methods, little advantage seems to be gained from the attempt which is sometimes made to define a "short period marginal product"—the additional production due to a small increase in the quantity of labour, when not only the quantity, but also the form, of the co-operating capital is supposed unchanged.[2] It is very

[1] The fact that the existing plant is now no longer the plant which best suits the existing situation will of course have its effect on the time of replacement. Suppose an entrepreneur to possess a machine A, while, owing to a change in conditions, a machine B which has the same original cost has become more productive. If his capital were free, he would thus invest in B rather than A. If, however, he has already acquired A, which is normally due for replacement after a certain number of years, then his replacement fund only amounts to a sum corresponding to the number of years A has already been in use; it is short of the total cost (of A or B) by a sum corresponding to the rest of A's normal life. Thus a decision to scrap A and replace it by B now involves the use of new capital—borrowed or drawn from some other part of the business—to an amount equal to this deficiency in the replacement fund. Now if the difference in the net productivities of B and A exceeds the interest on this extra capital, it will pay to scrap A; not in the contrary case. The older A is, the less is the extra capital required; and therefore at some point in the life of A, which is earlier than the normal time of replacement, the change will take place.

The lower the rate of interest, the sooner will a change in the fundamental conditions of equilibrium lead to an actual change in the structure of production.

[2] The ambiguity of this conception comes out clearly when we realise that the difference to total production made by the addition of a single man with form and quantity of co-operating capital supposed unchanged

doubtful if this conception can be given any precise meaning which is capable of useful application.

It seems much best to restrict the term "marginal product" to the sense in which we have used it in defining the conditions of full equilibrium. If we accept this view, then it is not true to say that a man's wage must always (or even normally) equal his marginal product. The changes in employment which go on every day in the most settled industries are themselves due to variations in the marginal productivity of the labour in question, and are set up by divergences between the marginal product and the wage-level. If wages are below the marginal product of labour, entrepreneurs have an incentive to expand production, and expand it in a way which uses more labour relatively to other factors than the methods which they have been using. If wages are above the marginal productivity of labour, entrepreneurs have an incentive to contract employment; they will contract their output, and contract in such a way as to use less labour proportionally to other factors than they have previously been doing. This may not be feasible at once; it may have to wait until machinery comes to be replaced; however, an incentive to the dismissal of labour exists, and the employment of a certain number of labourers is so far precarious.

The normal condition of the labour market is one in which there is a tendency to an expansion or a contraction of the demand for labour; this tendency is the way in which the forces described in the marginal pro

---

will be much less than the true marginal product (form supposed variable); while the subtraction of a single man when the forms of capital have been adjusted to the previous supply of labour will give a difference in total production much greater than the marginal product.

ductivity theory exercise their pressure upon the level of wages.[1]

[1] For a critical discussion of some current theories bearing on the subject-matter of this chapter, see my article, "Marginal Productivity and the Principle of Variation" (*Economica*, February, 1932). See also Valk, "The Principles of Wages"; Robertson, "Wage Grumbles" (in "Economic Fragments"); Schultz, "Marginal Productivity and the Pricing Process" (*Journal of Political Economy*, October, 1929); Schultz, "Marginal Productivity and the Lausanne School" (*Economica*, August, 1932); and my reply to Professor Schultz in the same number of *Economica*.

CHAPTER II

CONTINUITY AND INDIVIDUAL DIFFERENCE

WHEN the marginal productivity theory is stated in the form which has been adopted in the preceding chapter, it seems to be free from most of the objections which have been brought against it by its critics. Taken as a condition of full equilibrium in the labour market, it is immune from the criticism so often made against it—that the existence of fixed plant makes the free variation of the proportions in which factors of production are employed impossible. Once we realise that fixed plant has to be replaced, and that if the relative prices of the factors have changed, it is likely to be replaced in a different form, this objection collapses; leaving behind it, however, the important conclusion that the full effects of a change in wages on the demand for labour must not be expected to reveal themselves at once.

Nor can we take very much more seriously the possible objection that a small change in the relative prices of the factors will not be enough to lead to a change in methods. Naturally the most spectacular changes in method proceed from relatively large changes in the prices of the factors; small changes are little noticed except by those whom they immediately concern. After all, the making of small changes in method—well within the present meaning of the term —is one of the chief functions of the entrepreneur; and businesses do not only require management during Industrial Revolutions.

23

I

There is, however, still one further criticism—in itself of still less importance—which is not so directly met by the formulation we have offered. It is indeed no objection against the marginal productivity theory in general; at the most all it claims is that the determination of wages by marginal productivity is somewhat rough, so that there is in fact a certain "range of indeterminateness", within which wages can change without there being any reaction in the demand for labour. No one would seriously suggest that the range is a very wide one, so that the practical significance of this contention, even if it is accepted, is small. But since one of the principal objects of this book is to attempt a precise definition of the possibilities and probable consequences of interference with the competitive course of wages, we must not allow any opening for completely harmless interference, even a small one, to appear available, if it does not really exist.

As the number of men employed by a firm increases their marginal product diminishes. The marginal product of 15 men (the difference between the total product of 15 men and the total product of 14) exceeds the marginal product of 16 (the difference between the products of 16 and of 15). These two quantities give the limits between which the wages of a single man must lie, in order that 15 men, no more and no less, should be the most profitable number to employ. The wage cannot rise above the first figure, since otherwise it would not be profitable to employ as many as 15; it cannot fall below the second, since otherwise it would be profitable to employ more. These two marginal products—the internal and the external, we may call them—set limits to the wage which is consistent with equilibrium. Now it seems possible that the internal and external marginal products may differ by an amount which is not negligible; and if that is so, we are only possessed of upper and lower limits within which the wage must lie—limits which may not be close enough for us to be able to use the marginal productivity law as an exact determinant of the equilibrium level of wages.

The smaller the units in which a factor of production can be measured, the nearer together its internal and external marginal products are likely to be. If we were to plot the marginal products of varying quantities on a diagram, then the successive ordinates, in the case of a factor which can only be measured in large units, would differ quite appreciably, and we should get the familiar "stepped" figure; but the smaller the units can be made, the nearer we should approach a continuous curve, until ultimately the difference between successive ordinates became altogether negligible.

Thus in the case of capital, the problem of continuity presents no difficulty. Free capital, at any rate, is almost indefinitely divisible. And, as we have seen, it is free capital, not capital which has been locked up in fixed plant, which matters when we are examining the conditions of equilibrium.

Labour, however, is not indefinitely divisible. In a very large number of cases it is practically impossible to engage anything less than a whole man; even if we mean by a fraction of a man, a man for less than the whole of the time which is conventionally devoted to wage-earning employment. For, so long as we are concerned with conditions of equilibrium, we cannot

suppose that he remains unemployed for the rest of
his time. He will want to find another employer for
that; and although it is of course a familiar fact
that many men (gardeners and window-cleaners, for
example) do divide their time between a number of employers, this is not a practical proposition over the
greater part of industry; probably for the very good
reason that such division is incompatible with any
high degree of efficiency in organisation.

The indeterminateness which could conceivably
arise from this cause has perhaps received more attention from Edgeworth than from any other economist.
He showed (and it is certainly a very beautiful piece
of abstract analysis) that the fact that two employers
cannot easily "share" one workman, while two workmen can very easily share one employer, "constitutes
a positive advantage to the workpeople in their deal-
ings with entrepreneurs."[1] Yet all this means is that,
so far as there is a range of indeterminateness, wages
are more likely to lie at the higher than at the lower
end of the range. It is only if there is an appreciable
range that Edgeworth's proposition becomes of any
practical importance.[2]

The possibility of there being an appreciable range
depends to some extent on the elasticity of the demand
for labour. And that largely depends on the degree to
which substitution (or variation of method) is possible.
The more easily it is possible to substitute other factors
for labour, the greater the elasticity of demand for

[1] Edgeworth, "The Determinateness of Economic Equilibrium" (*Papers*, vol. ii., p. 318).
[2] Edgeworth did not himself imagine that his proposition was very important in practice. For a discussion of this matter, more precisely in terms of
Edgeworth's argument, see my article "Edgeworth, Marshall and the Indeterminateness of Wages" (*Econ. Jour.*, June, 1930).

labour becomes; and the less probable it is that any appreciable indeterminateness will arise from the indivisibility of the human unit.

However, it would be unsafe to rely on this very far, and it happens that we have other resources. It is only reasonable to assume that the various employers who are competing for the services of the workmen in a particular trade are differently situated in many respects, and are themselves of varying capacities. And once we make this assumption, it becomes clear that the internal marginal products of the labour employed by different firms are not likely to be exactly equal. If the same wage rules throughout the market, that wage must lie between the internal and external marginal products of the labour employed by each firm; but that is all we can say about the conditions of equilibrium. Now if the wage were slightly raised, it is quite possible that the increase might not be sufficient to give an incentive to every firm to reduce its demand for labour. The new wage might still be lower than the internal marginal product in many firms; but the rise would have to be very slight indeed to leave the demand of *every* firm unaffected. And similarly for a fall in wages. When there are a large number of firms competing for a particular kind of labour, it is safe to say that the range of indeterminateness due to the indivisibility of the workman will be too small to be perceptible.

II

Thus Edgeworth's "curiosum" disappears beyond the limits of vision; but only to leave behind it a much more disturbing problem. If we are to call to our assistance the individual differences of entrepreneurs, we cannot any longer leave out of account, as we have tacitly been doing hitherto, the individual differences of labourers. And it is impossible to allow for their differences without making considerable modifications in our statement of the marginal productivity formula.

If the labourers in a given trade are not of equal efficiency, then, strictly speaking, they have no marginal product. We cannot tell what would be the difference to the product if one man were removed from employment; for it all depends which man is removed. There would be a larger difference if a more efficient man ceased to work.

The only way in which it is possible to overcome this difficulty is to treat each man as a separate factor of production. His internal marginal product is then easy enough to identify—it is the difference which would be made to the total produce of the firm in which he is engaged if *his* labour were to be removed. That clearly sets a maximum to the wage he can get, and still remain undisturbed in employment. If he were to get more than this, his employer would soon be seeking to find a way of dispensing with his services.

With homogeneous units, the external marginal product is the productivity of a unit of the factor in that use which is just excluded, because there is not a sufficient supply of the factor to satisfy that particular unit of demand; or, otherwise stated, it is the productivity in that use which just does not pay at the current wage. With units that are unique, the external marginal product is still the productivity in that use which just does not pay. If the wage were slightly lower, some other employer would be willing to take on the man in question. The highest bid which is not satisfied sets the lower limit to the wage.

In order that the market should be in equilibrium, every man's wage must lie between limits defined in this manner. But these limits, set by a literal application of the marginal productivity law, are not the only ones which must be observed. It is true that if a man's wage rises high enough, his employer will prefer to do without him, even if it is impossible to replace him in any manner. Yet before this alternative comes to be seriously considered, other adjustments may be possible.

First of all, although we ought in strictness to treat the work of every individual labourer as a separate factor of production, the different labourers in a single trade are factors that can be readily substituted for one another. They are highly "rival" factors. It is precisely this possibility of substitution which ensures that a more efficient man will always tend to get higher wages than one who is less efficient; for if he does not, he will always be preferred to the less efficient man, and the less efficient man will find it impossible to get employment.

This gives us a second pair of limits within which the wages of any particular man must lie; he cannot be paid more than the man who stands next to him in the order of efficiency, but is just more efficient than himself; he cannot be paid less than the man who stands next below him. These limits are very likely to lie nearer together than the first set, and thus they are more likely to be effective, but they in their turn do not exhaust the list. In order that the wage should be in equilibrium, other conditions must be satisfied as well. It is possible that a wage could be

D

named at which it would not be profitable to replace a
man by one who is more efficient, since more efficient
men are very expensive, but at which it would be
profitable to replace him by a less efficient man at an
appreciably lower wage. Similarly, a man might be
receiving a wage at which other employers would find
it profitable to substitute him for men more efficient
than himself. Neither of these situations is compatible
with equilibrium. We have thus a third set of limits,
which is perhaps rather less likely to be the effective
set than the second pair is, because in most cases these
limits may well lie outside the second pair, so that a
wage which is capable of provoking the third kind of
adjustment would have an even stronger tendency to
provoke the second. But in at least two cases the third
pair is very likely to be effective; for in the cases of the
most efficient and the least efficient men in the trade
one member of the second pair of limits is absent; and
it must therefore be either the first or the third kind of
adjustment which is responsible for setting a maximum
to the most efficient man's wages, and a minimum to
the wages of the man who is least efficient.[1]

Suppose the number of men available for employment in a certain trade to increase by one; and since
that extra man must have some definite efficiency, let
us assume that his efficiency is indistinguishable from
that of the man who took the 400th place on the
original list when the men were arranged in descending
order of efficiency. Now the best job open to the new
man is the job which the original 400th man just turned
down, the job whose existence sets the minimum limit

[1] In the special case to which consideration of the marginal productivity law is generally limited, where the units are homogeneous and indefinitely divisible, these three sets of limits all merge together and become
indistinguishable.

to that 400th man's wage. But the new man can only get that job if he accepts something less than this minimum limit; *a fortiori*, something less than the 400th man had been getting. Now if he accepts that job, as he must do if he wishes to get the best possible employment open to him, the market is at once in a position of instability. For the old 400th man's employer will find that he can get the new man to come to him for a wage less than he had been paying to the 400th man, and since the new man is of the same efficiency as the 400th man, the employer will clearly benefit by the exchange. And the old 400th man can only regain employment by accepting lower wages than he used to get, since the old most favourable employment is now closed to him. (Of course it is unnecessary to suppose that the change round actually takes place. The threat of a change would be quite sufficient to compel the 400th man to accept lower wages.) And so the wage corresponding to that degree of efficiency which was represented by the 400th man is reduced; but the process is unlikely to stop here. If the new wage of the 400th man is less than the old wage of the 401st man (and that is very likely to be the case), then it will be profitable for the employer of the 401st man to replace him, either by the 400th man or by the new man, at a wage at least as high as the 401st man had been earning. And if this happens, the 401st man goes unemployed, being able to regain employment only at lower wages, which in their turn have a tendency to reduce the wages of all those below him in efficiency.

On the other hand, the fall in wages of the 400th man, by increasing the gap between his wages and those of the men whose efficiency is greater than his, will start a movement towards the substitution of more efficient by less efficient men, which can go on so long as the economy in wages outweighs the loss in efficiency. Just as the wages of those who are less efficient than the new man will tend to fall, so will the wages of those who are more efficient. An addition to the supply of labour will undoubtedly reduce the average wage paid in a trade, whether it is possible to assume that the differences between the efficiencies of workers engaged in that trade are negligible or not.

It does not follow, however, that it will reduce every wage. In the majority of cases it will affect the limits within which a particular wage must lie. But if the limits are not close together, then it is possible that a wage which was consistent with the old limits may still be consistent with the new. If it still lies between the limits set for it, it will be unaffected.[1]

We are thus brought back to the "range of indeterminateness". If a man's wage rises above a certain point, there will be a danger of his employer preferring to replace his labour by that of another man, or of a machine, or deciding to do without him altogether. If his wage falls below a certain point, there will be a danger of another employer tempting him away. How far can we assume in fact that these points are close together?

We have already seen that if the abilities of the various men in the trade were equal, it would be fair

---

[1] Since the limits to the wages of any particular man are largely dictated by the wages actually received by men whose efficiency does not differ very greatly from his, the immobility of any particular man's wage will help to insulate the wages of those round him on the scale of efficiency. But this only leads to the rather obvious conclusion that a change in the supply of labour of normal ability is somewhat less likely to affect the wages of exceptionally efficient or inefficient men than it is to affect the wages of "average" workers.

to assume that the range was negligible. Differently situated employers would be prepared, some to take on more men, some to dismiss men, as a result of very slight changes in the level of wages. And this conclusion proves to be applicable, to a very considerable extent, to the circumstances of reality. The abilities of the men in a trade may differ, but they are likely to differ in such a way that the number of "average" men is very large. In fact, the abilities of the different labourers in a trade are probably distributed according to something not far removed from the normal curve of error. There will be some who are well above the average—and perhaps quite distinctly spaced out above it—and there will be some who are distinctly below. But the majority probably differ in efficiency to no very marked extent.

Thus, so far as the majority are concerned, our earlier conclusion applies. The wage of any "average" workman cannot be changed appreciably (while the fundamental conditions of the market remain the same) without giving opportunities for substitution and displacement. His "range of indeterminateness" is so narrow that it is not worth considering.

With the exceptional men (whether they are exceptionally good workers or exceptionally bad) things may conceivably be different. The difference in efficiency between one man and those who are most like him may be sufficiently great for his wage to be only determinable—so far as the tendencies we are describing are concerned—within fairly wide limits. The exceptional man is in a position something like that of a monopolist; he has to look out for substitutes, but they give him a certain amount of elbow-room.

Yet it is not with the exceptional man that the

study of wages, for very good reasons, has generally been concerned. We need not be disturbed in our application of the marginal productivity theory to wages in general by our discovery that it does not tell us much if we try to use it in the cases of Charlie Chaplins and Sir John Simons. We can rest content with the knowledge that there may possibly be an important element of "bargaining technique" in the determination of the wages earned by their humbler counterparts, the superlative bricklayer and the engineer with a gift for his job. The wages of the "average workman" cannot be in equilibrium unless they are equal to his marginal product; and that is what matters.

III

Up to the present we have assumed that the efficiency of a workman is something which depends solely on the workman himself; but this is again one of those convenient simplifications which are not tenable on a last analysis, although they do not often lead us into serious error. Efficiency is not really the simple one-dimensional magnitude we have hitherto assumed it to be; it is a complex of various qualities, so that to say directly, without further precision, that one man is more efficient than another may sometimes be impossible. But it is an objective fact that, under given circumstances, a particular employer will prefer to take on one man rather than another; although the preference may not always rest purely on grounds of "productivity". If the technical qualities of a workman are such as to make him specially useful to a certain small class of employers, then the mutual competition of those employers will raise his wages above the level paid to other workmen of his grade (if his "grade" is established by referring to the preferences of employers who do not have this particular need). But if, say, the man happens to be a Communist, and the particular employers who would otherwise be specially appreciative of his qualities have an objection (however irrational) to Communists, he cannot expect to obtain the advantage he would otherwise have secured. Unquestionably this sort of thing may have a considerable influence on the wages of individuals; and it is sometimes desirable to interpret "marginal productivity" in a manner wide enough to include it.

The forces whose action has been described are sufficient to generate a tendency for men with particular qualities to move towards those employers who can make the best use of their qualities. But of course the demand of employers for particular qualities of labour (like their demand for other things) is satiable; and if a particular quality is not highly uncommon, some of the possessors of it will find that the demand of the employers to whom they are best fitted has been satisfied by the labour of men even better fitted than themselves; so that they, rather than force themselves into an employment where they could only be absorbed at a considerably lower wage than they could get elsewhere, will go elsewhere and offer their services on the basis of some productive capacity other than their special qualification.

The dependence of a man's efficiency on the efficiency of his employer has a significance which is not confined to the case of special qualifications. A workman A may be unquestionably more efficient than another workman B, so that, other things being equal, every employer in the trade would prefer to take on A rather than B. But even in this case differences may arise if other things are not equal. Simply because A is so unquestionably superior to B, he will ask a higher wage than B; and if the wages asked by the two men are different, two employers, who both wish to take on an extra man, may decide differently between A and B. An employer who is himself highly capable is more likely to prefer A, because he can make such use of A that A will be worth his higher wage; an employer who is less efficient himself would be wiser to prefer B, to pay lower wages, and to be content with the inferior workman whom alone he could get at those lower wages.

It is impossible to doubt that a very large part of the validity of that "Gospel of High Wages" which was preached so vigorously a few years ago springs precisely from this source. If an employer is of very superior ability, it will pay him to offer higher wages than his competitors, in order to have the "pick of the market". Such a policy, in his hands, may well be abundantly successful. But like so many economic panaceas, it does not bear generalisation. For an employer of less ability to follow in the footsteps of his successful competitors would be to court destruction. He cannot use men to such good purpose; in his hands the best workmen are not worth as much as they are worth under the direction of his rivals; to pay them more than they are worth will bring not gain but loss.

IV

The forces making for equilibrium in the labour market are for the most part rather slow in their action; and this is as true of those which have been the special subject of this chapter as it was found to be of those which were described in its predecessor. Although there is always a tendency for substitutions of the kind we have just been examining to take place —although any considerable opportunity for them to be carried through profitably is likely to be acted on sooner or later—it cannot be pretended that they are easy, or that we shall not expect an immense number of unused opportunities of this kind to exist in the labour market at any moment. The adjustment of wages to individual efficiency involves each employer in a series of difficult estimates—appraisals of the relative abilities of two men, one of whom he knows, but the other of whom he can only know in a much more superficial way. At engagement, the knowledge on which an exact estimate of a man's efficiency can be made will usually be lacking. This will not prevent a rough approximation of wages to efficiency, for something can be told from a man's record, or indeed, on occasion, from his mere appearance. But if it is not very clear indeed that the change will be advantageous, a perfectly rational conservatism will usually forbid it to be made.

Nevertheless, the adjustment is often made appreciably easier by the tendency of efficiency to cluster about an average. Save in very small businesses, a "standard rate" will naturally emerge. The majority of the employees are likely to differ so little in efficiency that it will not generally be worth while for a sensible employer to distinguish between them. To them the standard rate will be paid, since discrimination would involve a labour altogether disproportionate to the end in view. It might involve detailed supervision of a kind likely to annoy the men supervised, and make work under such an employer less attractive to them. Finally, it would open up a serious danger of disagreement between employer and men as to the basis of estimation, and consequent accusations of favouritism. On all these grounds it would not be worth while.

But there will probably be a small proportion who are obviously of superior ability, and if their ability becomes sufficiently well known outside the firm for them to have an opportunity of moving advantageously employers must pay them better. Since, even in this case, there may be room for disagreement about merit, such payments will often be made without much advertisement.[1] The same end can also be reached in a more straightforward way by promotion into a higher wage-grade. Here, too, there may of course be disagreements and discontents, but there is the countervailing advantage that a firm which is known to have a system of promotion will attract the better men, who will know that they will get better wages when they have proved themselves. It is even possible that something of the same sort is occasionally achieved if promotion goes only by seniority. The better workmen are less likely to be discharged when trade is bad; they will therefore earn promotion sooner, and charges of favouritism are less likely to be encountered when promotion is, at least apparently, automatic.

Men whose capacity is definitely inferior to the

---

[1] The "something extra in the pay envelope" which is so upsetting to wage statistics.

average will not get employment, save as a form of charity, unless they are prepared to accept something less than the standard wage. At all events, this will be the case if their inferiority is an obvious one, resulting from infirmity or a bad record that cannot be concealed. If it is due to some less obvious cause, they may get taken on at the standard rate, but they will be unable to maintain these favourable terms of employment. Sooner or later they must choose between staying with an employer at lower wages, or the only alternative—chronic unemployment.

Thus there is no reason to suppose that standard rates are in any way a particular product of Trade Unionism. And this deduction seems wholly borne out by inductive evidence. According to Mr. and Mrs. Webb, "the most autocratic and unfettered employer spontaneously adopts standard rates for classes of workmen, just as the large shopkeeper fixes his prices, not according to the higgling capacity of particular customers, but by a definite percentage on cost".[1] However, the standard rates of free competition are not in any sense minima; exceptional cases are always likely to be paid less.

A closer approximation to the "individual wage" of theory is probably secured by piece-work than is possible by time-work methods. A slow worker gets less; and a fast worker gets more (so that his employer can more easily retain him). And the adjustment can be carried out with less trouble and with less danger of discontent than would be possible with time-work. There is a definite objective measure of efficiency.

But it is not altogether a good objective measure;

[1] *Industrial Democracy*, p. 281.

and this is natural enough, for efficiency is a complicated thing and does not readily lend itself to objective tests. It is only in those trades where quantity of work done matters more than quality (or where the quality can be looked after satisfactorily in some other way) that piece-work is possible at all. If quality is likely to suffer from speeding-up, to pay merely for speed of work would be thoroughly bad economy.[1] Further, even where quantity is almost the only thing aimed at, a fast worker will get more out of his tools and machines, and will in consequence be worth a higher wage in proportion to his output than a slow worker is. But even when these things are allowed for, there is more to come.

Different men cause all sorts of varying amounts of trouble to their employers; some are very "reliable", they are never ill, never want a day off, are always content and on good terms with the management. Others are always causing expensive temporary adjustments for such reasons. In all these ways there may be variations in efficiency, of which piece-rates take no account, and indeed may make it more difficult to take account, since it is more difficult to pay more or less than standard piece-rates than to vary from standard time-rates. The more obvious and easily accepted excuses are absent.

In these last pages we have already forsaken the marginal productivity theory, and the slow moving forces determining "normal wages". We have entered upon the study of the labour market as it actually is, with the fundamental conditions of equilibrium con-

---

[1] Of course, since discrimination among workmen is only one object of piece-work, the general speeding-up which would follow from its introduction would not pay if the sacrifice of quality was serious, and reflected itself seriously in selling prices.

stantly changing, and entrepreneurs so busily occupied in adjusting their businesses to these more important changes that they have only a limited amount of time to spend on the finer adjustments. They have to content themselves with rough-and-ready devices to ensure that the more delicate relations do not become so considerably out of adjustment that the loss to them is serious. But the rough-and-ready devices are only means to an end—the making of those adjustments whose theoretical perfection was set out in the earlier pages of this chapter. If opportunities offer for their successful use, new means are always likely to be invented.

CHAPTER III

On the threshold of a more extended study of the competitive labour market must stand the problem of unemployment. What is the effect of unemployment on wages? How is it possible to reconcile the fact of unemployment with the simultaneous existence of rising wages? These are not the only new questions raised by the fact that the labour market of actuality is not in a state of equilibrium; but they are the most obvious questions, and we may conveniently begin by examining them.

It is now a commonplace that unemployment has many causes; the classification into seasonal, cyclical, casual, and so on, has become familiar. But it is precisely in this commonplace that the clue to the paradox of wages and unemployment is found to rest. Some kinds of unemployment do tend to pull down wages; others do not. When wages are rising, it is an indication that the first kind of unemployment is not present, but the second may be present all the same, and account for a considerable percentage of unemployed.

I

One kind of unemployment we have already had cause to mention in our discussion of individual differences. We have seen that the adjustment of wages to efficiency is unlikely, under any conceivable circumstances, to be perfect. The readiest means of partial adjustment is the adoption of standard rates, which are suitable to the average workman, but exceed the value of the least competent. There must always be some men in every trade who cannot earn the standard rates paid even by the least efficient and least well-situated employers within their reach; and although they may be able to get regular employment by accepting less than standard rates, there is no certainty either that they will readily consent to do this, or that employers can be found who are prepared to take the trouble involved in finding a wage which suits them.

When we remember that the things which drag down a man's efficiency below the ordinary level are particularly likely to be things not easily estimated— that they are less likely to be low direct productivity than carelessness or unreliability or bad temper—then it is very easy to see how unemployment of this kind may well be of no inconsiderable importance. It is not that the man's direct productivity is low, but that his net product is low—allowance being made in assessing his net product for the indirect costs involved in employing him. In such a case, his net product is likely to prove lower after he has been working with an employer for some time than it appeared at first; and so on experience his employer will either dismiss him or offer him lower wages. But for several reasons the first is rather likely to be the alternative taken; if lower wages are offered and accepted, the man may very well feel that he has a grievance, and as a result may prove to be worth even less than he was before; and again, from his own point of view, it may be advisable for him to go elsewhere, since he may find an employer who attaches less weight to his particular disabilities, or at the worst, he may find one from whom he can conceal his disabilities for a time. Even if lower wages are offered, quite probably they will not be accepted; and employers are thereby less likely to offer them.

Men whose efficiency is subnormal are thus peculiarly liable to find their disqualifications resulting in exceptionally long periods of unemployment rather than in exceptionally low wages. The most inefficient of all, the indirect cost of whose employment is extremely high, may find that there is no employment at all in the market where they can continue to receive a wage high enough to support life unassisted. So far as these men do get jobs, they will retain them only for short periods, and for the greater part of their existences they must depend on the support of relations, or on poor relief, or on charity.

These are the "unemployables"; their *net* product falls below the level of subsistence. Although in any community there probably are a certain number of these unfortunate people, it is generally recognised that they do not form a seriously important part, numerically, of the general unemployment problem.[1] What has to be recognised is that there is a much larger class of those whose efficiency is high enough for them to be able to earn—somewhere—a wage sufficient to support life unassisted, but who are exceptionally difficult to fit into the industrial system, so that they are likely to suffer from unemployment to a special degree.

This is one kind of "normal unemployment"; it accounts for part, perhaps the most important part, of that unemployment which persists even when a trade is neither expanding nor contracting, even when the demand and supply of labour are constant. Most of

[1] Beveridge, *Unemployment*, p. 138.

these "normal unemployed" are likely to be of sub-normal ability, unemployed because of the difficulty of fitting them in. But probably they will not all be sub-normal. For although the industry as a whole is stationary, some firms in it will be closing down or contracting their sphere of operations, others will be arising or expanding to take their place. Some firms, then, will be dismissing, others taking on labour; and when they are not situated close together, so that knowledge of opportunities is imperfect, and trans-ference is attended by all the difficulties of finding housing accommodation, and the uprooting and trans-planting of social ties, it is not surprising that an in-terval of time elapses between dismissal and re-engage-ment, during which the workman is unemployed.

Between them, these two causes account for most of "normal unemployment" as it is found in the majority of industries—the unemployment which is consistent with constant supply and demand for labour. But for completeness, we should add a third kind—which is unemployment, although it is voluntary, and raises no social problem; the unemployment of the man who gives up his job in order to look for a better. He may believe that he could get higher wages elsewhere, or he may merely desire to work in some other place for private reasons.

If the supply and demand for labour are constant, any attempt by an employer to take advantage of the existence of unemployment by cutting wages must ultimately prove futile. If he lowers the standard rate he pays, some of his men will soon be looking for jobs elsewhere; and though he can replace them, for the most part it will be with inferior men. It is conceivable that by careful selection, and a good deal of luck, he

E

might succeed in getting men of as good quality as those he lost; but even so, these in their turn are likely to drift away. By reducing wages, he has reduced his chance of getting good workmen; and sooner or later he will find that he suffers.

Sooner or later; for it is no use to pretend that in this, any more than in other processes of the labour market, the forces making for equilibrium are particularly rapid in their action. There is a temptation for unwise employers to snatch temporary gains by making wage-cuts that do not correspond with the fundamental conditions of the market. As long as they can retain at the lower wages men who came to them because they were offering higher wages, they can gain what is really a monopoly profit at the expense of their employees. But when those men go and are replaced by less efficient men, the employer's profits are likely to be smaller than they were at first. He has, in fact, degraded himself to a lower and less well paid class of entrepreneur. The retribution is definite enough; but it may not always be sufficient to prevent the action.

But usually it will be difficult for employers to cut wages without being able to offer some excuse; and so unjustified wage-cuts are most probable, not in a stationary condition of trade, but when there is a real change in demand or supply. It is possible that the existence of normal unemployment may result in the changes in wages which would, under such circumstances, be made in the most perfect market, being less favourable to the workmen than they would be otherwise. Of course, at the most, such an effect could be only temporary; and it remains to be seen whether it is not likely to be neutralised in another way.

II

Before passing on to the consideration of changes in demand and supply, we must turn aside to examine what may be reckoned as yet another kind of "normal unemployment"—although it differs in degree rather than kind from those already mentioned. There are certain industries in which the shifting of the demand for labour between firms is not the result of the slow rise and decline of those firms, but is due to chance day-to-day fluctuations in their activity. All firms, of course, undergo continual variations in activity, but it is only in certain industries that the smallest variations express themselves directly as fluctuations in employment. In most cases it is possible to find some less urgent work that can be done on slack days, so that, although employment may vary from year to year, or from month to month, it will not vary from day to day.

But where all the work which comes must be done at once, or where technical reasons do not provide any appreciable incentive to keep together a permanent labour force, the number of men employed by a particular firm may undergo daily fluctuations. The most marked cases of this are the docking, building, and contracting industries—the industries of casual labour.

When the amount of employment given by particular firms fluctuates daily, a large surplus of unemployed labour is inevitable. By the time a man has discovered that the firm he worked for yesterday does not want him, it may be too late for him to get employment elsewhere today. The time which it takes to find a job becomes closely comparable with the time a job lasts when it is found. Even if the total amount of work to be done remains unchanged, the place where it has to be done is continually changing. The total number of men "occupied" in the industry is divided into those who are working and those who are looking for work. Every month, and usually every week, nearly all the men attached to these industries get some work, but their work is not continuous.

The conditions of employment in these trades are such that one cannot help asking the question: Why are men drawn to them? Today they are for the most part relatively high-wage trades; and there is little question that high wages have a more powerful influence in attracting labour than a high chance of unemployment has in repelling it. But they were not always high-wage trades; and still they got their labour. It is true that a certain number of men do manage to make their abilities clear to their employers; they get regular employment and their earnings are good. But the majority? To a large extent the lower grades of casual employment must have attracted those who had failed elsewhere; they offer jobs where little skill is required and little reliability—for a man is unlikely, on this system, to stay long enough with one employer for his deficiencies to be found out. Partly they attract the lazy; the prospect of being able to take a day off when you choose outweighs for some people the chance of not being able to get work when you choose that. But the advantage is dearly bought.

How will these variations in employment affect wages? So long as the total demand for labour in the area remains steady, they are very unlikely to affect wages at all. It would be senseless for a firm to raise wages on days when its business was good and to lower them when its business was bad. The high wages

would not be effective in attracting labour until the
exceptional demand was past. And to lower wages
would indeed have a repellent effect on the supply of
labour to that firm—yet not on the day when business
was bad, but subsequently, when it might be expected
to have improved.

A firm which maintained wages steady would have a
definite advantage over one which was always changing
the wages it offered. To go for a job which was offered
at 12s. yesterday and find that today only 8s. was
being paid would be an experience enough to discourage applications in that quarter for a long time.
It would by no means be set off by occasional windfalls
in the opposite direction. So long as the activity of the
trade is unchanged, casual unemployment is most unlikely to give an opportunity for lowering wages.[1]

III

When unemployment is due to a fall in the demand
for labour, or to an increase in the supply, then, of
course, it is far more likely to affect wages than in any of
the cases we have considered up to the present. But
even here it is necessary to distinguish.

Take, first of all, the case of seasonal fluctuations.
A considerable number of trades vary largely in their
activity according to the season of the year. Some of
these fluctuations are due directly to the meteoro-
logical differences between summer and winter; agriculture and trades connected with it are most active
about harvest time, building operations are most easily
carried out in the summer, the demand for coal is
greatest in winter. Others depend more directly on

[1] But see below, p. 68.

social causes, such as the Christmas activity in the distributive and clothing trades, and the mysterious and complicated rhythm of printing.

Now the significant fact about these fluctuations is that they can be foreseen, and are foreseen, by employer and workman alike. This makes their effect on wages purely a matter of policy. It is perfectly possible to maintain wages at a fixed level throughout the year —a level which is sufficient to attract the right kind of labour in sufficient amounts, even when the probability of a certain amount of unemployment is reckoned in. Extra labour (of a sort) can generally be obtained in rush periods, simply because it is widely known that temporary employment is available in these trades at these times. There is no need to raise wages in order to get labour, at any rate to get "general" labour; it would be too much to expect that even a distinctly high rate would attract labour which was specially well suited to the occupation, since it is known that the engagement is most unlikely to last.

On the other hand, there may be certain advantages in varying the rates. This was generally done in the building trades before the war, in order to reduce the costs of building in the winter, and make it rather less disadvantageous to undertake building operations then.[1] If a firm varies its rates, that means that the terms it offers to permanent employees are, on a long view, rather less attractive; and it may find that as a consequence it gets less good workmen than it would get if it paid the same average rate regularly throughout the year. But if the difference in summer and winter rates appreciably reduces the extra cost of

[1] Since the war, as a result of Trade Union action, hours have been varied instead of wages.

working in the winter, it will be profitable to take on more business in the winter than it would otherwise have been. When a small variation in rates can be effective in transferring demand to an appreciable extent, it may easily outweigh the deterrent effects of variation on the supply of labour. The employer will vary rates, because it increases his profits; and it is certainly desirable that he should do so, because, by reducing the fluctuation of trade, it diminishes un-employment.

There is indeed nothing to prevent the two systems existing together for a considerable time. Some firms may adopt one, some the other. So long as the wage paid by the "steady-wage" firms lies between the "slack" and "busy" wages paid by the rest, in such a way as to make the terms offered for a long period of employment about equally attractive, men will not readily move from one to the other in order to snatch a gain that they know to be fleeting. In the long run, it is true, one system is likely to prove better fitted to the industry than the other, and it will slowly push the other out. The victorious system will then appear as a "custom of the industry".

The more the extent and duration of a fluctuation in trade can be foreseen, the more are its effects on wages a matter of policy. Seasonal fluctuations can be very clearly foreseen, but there are other kinds where some foresight is possible, though it is much less definite and reliable. In these cases the element of conscious policy will be less important; more play is given to "natural" economic forces.

An example can be taken from those little temporary slumps to which many industries (but particularly ex-

port industries) are subject, as the result of harvest
variations or political disturbances. Suppose an industry finds one of its markets closed by a revolution.
The firms particularly specialised to that market will
find themselves faced with two alternatives (once the
possibility of making for stock has been exhausted)—
either they must close down, or they must cut prices
and try and force their way into the markets of other
firms. This second alternative will take time, and if the
disturbance is expected to be brief, it will not be worth
while. It is no use to go to the trouble of building up a
new connection when your own market will soon be open
and you will then be exposed to retaliation by competitors. Thus so long as a rapid end to the disturbance
is expected, the stricken firms will probably refrain
from cutting into the markets of their more prosperous
rivals.

Now the prosperous firms, although not directly
suffering from the disturbance, will be in a position to
take advantage of it by lowering wages. But it does not
necessarily follow that they will do so. For the moment
they could get sufficient labour at a lower rate of wages;
but only for the moment. Once trade recovered they
would have to raise wages again. Employers in these
firms are therefore confronted with a choice: either
reduce wages and snatch this temporary advantage,
but with the compensating disadvantage of worsened
relations and a possible exodus of good workmen,
determined to seek better remuneration and security
even though they know circumstances to be unfavourable. Or on the other hand maintain wages, sacrifice a
temporary profit, but avoid these more lasting dangers.
The decision between these courses will depend in large
measure on the expected duration of the depression.

The longer it is likely to last, the more advantageous reduction becomes.[1]

The transition between this case and the next is gradual. When trade undergoes a permanent or prolonged decline, owing to a change in the character of demand, or to credit or currency deflation, the first instinct of employers is, as usual, to take the line of least resistance and assume the decline to be temporary. Wages may thus be maintained after unemployment has set in. But with a continued depression, wages cannot be maintained indefinitely. Sooner or later some employers will come round to a more pessimistic view, and to the action which is prompted by pessimism. Either some of those who have closed down will reopen at a lower rate of wages, or some of those who have remained open will see an advantage to be gained, on balance, by cutting rates. Once this has happened, the rest may delay for a time, but cannot avoid coming into line in the end. For if they maintain wages, they must either maintain prices and so lose trade, or cut prices and so incur direct losses. Continued optimism may lead them to do this for a while, but they cannot go on indefinitely with limited resources.

The wage policy of entrepreneurs in a period of depression is very largely a question of circulating capital. Selling prices will fall steeply if production is maintained; and therefore to continue to employ the same number of men at the old wage-rates would involve them in direct losses. If, instead of using their

---

[1] It is to the days before the growth of Trade Unionism to which we have to go for an inductive verification of these conclusions. It is thus interesting to read in Thornton's celebrated essay on " Paper Credit " (1802): "A fall (in price) arising from temporary distress will be attended probably with no correspondent fall in the rate of wages; for the fall in price, and the distress, will be understood to be temporary, and the rate of wages, we know, is not so variable as the price of goods" (1st ed., p. 82).

capital to pay wages, they put it in a bank, it will yield a positive profit, however small, and not a loss; consequently, if wages are maintained, there is an obvious incentive to reduce the number of men employed. But if a man is dismissed, it may not be possible to recover him again when he is wanted in the future; and thus, if the employer looks to the future, he may well think it worth while to retain some of his men (those whose services are specially useful to him) even if their present employment involves him in losses. And it may be technically necessary to keep on some of the others so that the men who are still employed should be able to do some useful work; so that the losses of continued employment should be as small as possible. Further, if he can afford to keep on those men whom he does retain without cutting their wages, he has a stronger claim on them in future; and the same reason which prompts him to keep them employed, prompts him to refrain from cutting their wages. But since his total net returns on his capital (when fixed charges have been met) are probably negative, he cannot maintain this policy indefinitely. As time goes on, present losses pile up, and future profits become more and more problematical. The advantages of maintaining wages grow steadily less, and finally he cannot avoid a reduction.

But since even at this stage the future advantages of maintaining wages will not altogether have disappeared, there will still be a check to the reduction which is likely to be made. If employers looked merely to the moment, they might cut wages to "subsistence level"; but it is fairly clear that the reductions made, even when employers are unhampered by Union opposition, are generally far less drastic than this.

In part, their moderation is simply the result of a desire to maintain good relations; but when large cuts are being made—have to be made—this cannot count for very much. There is also the possibility that some workmen may possess reserves, or chances of taking themselves off to other trades; so that the supply of efficient labour may be contracted if wages are cut too far. But these are surely not the main consideration. If an employer cuts wages too far in a period of depression, he will probably still get a sufficient supply of labour then; but the time may come when he is short of labour, and then he will be shunned. He will get the reputation of standing out for the last penny when he gets the chance; and so, when he wants labour, he will be unable to get it, because, although he offers good wages for a time, he does not offer security.

This is a potent check on the cutting of wages, but it cannot prevent a fall of wages altogether, if the depression is serious. At the very latest, a time must come when particular firms are faced with a choice between cutting wages and closing down altogether; and then, so long as it is possible for them to get labour at lower wages at that moment, they must choose that alternative. As soon as some firms have cut wages, they become thereby more serious competitors to the rest; and they hurry forward the date when the rest must cut wages too, however much they desire to gain the advantages which would follow from keeping wages steady.

It is impossible to resist the conclusion that we have here a good deal of the explanation of that distinction between "good" and "bad" employers which figures so largely in labour history. "Bad" employers, it appears to the workman, are people who seize every chance of

cutting rates; "good" employers have not this bad
habit, and consequently maintain better relations.
But if the foregoing analysis is correct, the distinction
is not merely a question of character. If it was, it
would be a far less important matter than it is, for bad
employers would be much less of a danger to their
work-people. Their action would always tend to lead
to their own destruction. The distinction is to a very
large extent one of financial resources, and of judgment; since naturally the pessimist will cut rates before
the optimist does so. And pessimists do not abolish
themselves by the foolishness of their actions; not infrequently they are right.

If a labour market could be found which was
genuinely in equilibrium, so that every employer could
go on employing the same men, and every man could
go on working for the same employer, without either
party having any incentive to make a change; and if
then the employers' opportunities of profitably employing labour were suddenly reduced, or the number
of labourers available suddenly increased, unemployment would result. If the new conditions remained
unchanged indefinitely, then, under competitive conditions, this unemployment must lead to a fall in wages,
going on until the excess of labour was absorbed. But
these artificial conditions, although they may serve as
a convenient model for analysis, are not a description of what really happens. Even in a stationary
trade, when there is no appreciable change in the
general activity of business or in the supply of labour,
the position is not sufficiently near to theoretical
equilibrium for unemployment to disappear. Men
grow older, and their efficiency changes. Luck (or

what is very nearly luck) brings about continual changes in the activity of different firms. But the reserve of labour produced by these minor changes can stay practically unchanged without its having any tendency to depress wages. At the worst it offers opportunities for foolish employers to snatch transitory gains at the expense of ultimate loss—it induces an element of instability.

Against this factor of instability to the detriment of the labourer must be set an element of rigidity due to the desire of employers to maintain good relations and safeguard the future. If the presence of normal unemployment has some tendency to make the labourer's position less secure than it would appear to be on the basis of pure equilibrium theory, his wages are likely to suffer less from the presence of abnormal unemployment than a hasty application of pure theory would lead us to expect. A sensible employer will not reduce wages until he is convinced that men at least as efficient as those he is employing will come, and will continue to come for an appreciable time, at lower rates. And it is likely to take a considerable amount of unemployment before he can be sure of this.

Whether this rigidity atones for the first instability, or whether it is another evil superimposed on the first, is a matter on which the reader will be able to form an opinion from his study of later chapters.

CHAPTER IV

THE WORKING OF COMPETITION

I

IT has become clear that the effect of unemployment on wages can only be explained if we allow very fully for two general circumstances which do not receive much attention in equilibrium theory—the time and trouble required in making economic adjustments, and the fact of foresight. Even in equilibrium theory the importance of these things is not quite negligible; but their significance is immensely enhanced when we come to deal with "economic dynamics"—the theory of change. It is by considering them that dynamic analysis can best begin, to whatever part of the economic field that dynamic analysis is to be applied. Naturally they are the most convenient means of approach to the dynamic enquiry which is necessary to complement an equilibrium theory of wages.

It is true that in equilibrium theory the importance of the facts that workmen cannot move from one employment to another without cost and trouble, and that similar costs are imposed on entrepreneurs when they change their methods of organisation, is not altogether negligible. Such costs of transference influence the conditions of equilibrium; for an entrepreneur, or indeed any individual, may sometimes be satisfied with a particular system of production or particular contracts, even if there is another system which he would prefer if he could move to that other system without costs.

But if the advantage in "income" which he would gain on that other system is less (when capitalised at the current rate of interest) than the cost of getting to that new position, he will not move there.

However, in the majority of those cases with which we are concerned, costs of transference are not great enough for the interest on them to be a quantity of outstanding importance in determining the conditions of equilibrium. (And sometimes, as we have seen in the case of technical change by entrepreneurs, these costs can be reduced very appreciably by selecting a favourable moment for the change.) So long as the cost can be spread over an indefinite period, it very frequently becomes negligible.

When a market is not in equilibrium, costs of transference cannot be spread over an indefinite period. Even if it is certain that the change will be a change for the better, it is not certain (and indeed it is highly improbable) that the new position will long continue to be the best attainable. It would be highly imprudent to change unless the cost of changing would be covered by the gain within quite a brief period. Costs of change, therefore, become a vastly more important influence on action that they would be under conditions of stationary equilibrium.

The increased importance of foresight is more obvious. Elementary economic analysis, which culminates in the determination of the conditions of equilibrium, assumes, when it does deal with change, that the change has not been foreseen, but that, when it takes place, everyone can count on the new conditions being maintained. Such an assumption naturally leads to paradoxes. In fact, everyone does foresee changes to some extent, and the effects of a change differ, according as it is expected to continue or not. Suppose an entrepreneur receives a sudden increase in orders. This may mean any one of four things: (1) It may mean merely that ordinary orders have been brought forward, so that the exceptionally great demand of today will be matched by an exceptionally low demand at some future date; (2) it may be a special demand for some special non-recurring purpose, so that after it has been met demand will return to normal; (3) it may be an indication that demand will henceforth settle down to a new and higher level; (4) it may be the beginning of an expansion, so that demand will not only maintain the new level, but rise above it. It may mean any one of these four things, and it will be met in a profoundly different manner according as it is interpreted to mean one or another of them.

Further, the effects of today's actions are not ended today; and action is always liable to be influenced by the remoter consequences which are expected to flow from it. But the importance attached to these remoter consequences depends on what the situation is expected to be in which they materialise; and thus any action depends on all the consequences which are expected to flow from it, and also on general expectations of the relevant future. Neither can be foreseen perfectly; but both can be foreseen to some extent, and both must be allowed for.

II

When the economists of the late nineteenth century wished to concentrate their attention on the imperfections of the labour market caused by costs of movement, they usually contented themselves with the analysis of one special case, where costs of movement are sufficient to shut out competition over a considerable range.[1] In normal circumstances, wages are determined by competition on both sides; if labourers compete for jobs, employers at the same time compete for labourers. But where there is only one employer whom a particular labourer can work for, save at great sacrifice and expense of transference, and where there is only one man, or one set of men, whom that employer can secure to work for him, it is perfectly evident that there is a possibility of great indeterminateness in the wages paid. The lowest wage which can be paid is the wage which will just not induce the labourer to go elsewhere; the highest is the wage which will just not induce the employer to do without him. Where costs of movement are considerable, the difference between this maximum and minimum may be large; and since it may be thought that employers are likely to be the better bargainers (that is to say, employers are more likely to be able to guess the workman's minimum than workmen to guess the employer's maximum), the wage actually paid is more likely to be near the lower end of the "range of indeterminateness" than near the higher.[2]

This is all very well; but as an argument to be used in serious analysis of the labour market it is presented far too much *in vacuo*. What are the circumstances to which it is meant to be applied? If to stationary

---

[1] For a discussion of the history of this argument, this particular kind of "indeterminateness", see W. H. Hutt, *The Theory of Collective Bargaining*. Professor Hutt is sometimes rather hard on the authors he criticises.

[2] Stated in this way, the argument does not need any great theoretical refinement. It only becomes interesting as an exercise in pure theory when account is taken of variations in the amount of work the labourer may be willing to do at different levels of wages. But although the intricacy of the argument may easily be increased in this way, its significance is not appreciably changed.

F

equilibrium, it is formally valid; but if we are dealing with stationary equilibrium, the costs of movement can be spread over so long a period of time that, in the majority of cases, the "range of indeterminateness" becomes very narrow. If we are not dealing with stationary equilibrium (and it is hard to believe that the importance attached to costs of movement by many of those who have used this argument does not arise from an appreciation of the much greater importance of these costs in a changing world), then we must allow, not simply for the costs themselves, but for the fact of change, and for the anticipation of change. When we make this allowance, the picture changes appreciably.

It is true that there do take place a certain number of labour contracts (generally contracts of personal service) where a particular job of a practically unique character has to be done. The particular job will not recur again, or, if it does recur again, it will only do so after a considerable interval of time, and perhaps at a very different place. It is impossible to get labour which is specialised to such work as this, and the man who desires to become an employer must take such labour as is available, often from a very narrow circle. The difference between the lowest terms on which some available labourer will do the work and the highest terms which the employer will consent to pay may often be very considerable. Unquestionably there is here a "range of indeterminateness". But no one would expect any important conclusions about such cases from a theory of wages.[1]

[1] Of course it is impossible to base a defence of wage control on the sort of indeterminateness which arises here. Where neither employer nor employee is specialised, there is no reason why "bargaining advantage" should be on one side rather than on the other. Further, where jobs are not generally repeated, control, which must relate to future contracts, is evidently impossible.

Where contracts are not repeated, no foresight on the part of either party can have any influence on the terms of the contract. Indeterminateness is rife; but the case, from our point of view, is supremely uninteresting and unimportant. It is only when a trade is continuous, when bargains of the same kind are being continually struck, that the major problems of wage determination arise. It is only at this point that economic analysis can really get to grips with the matter. And it is at this point that foresight begins to be important.

The repeated contracts of a continuous labour market can conveniently be divided into two classes: (1) Those in which a labourer normally expects to be re-engaged by the same employer when his first contract has expired; (2) those in which he does not. The second class is evidently that of casual labour in the widest sense. In both of these foresight is important, though it is more important in the first class—"regular" employment.

If we could conceive a "casual" market in which employers were generally specialised to a particular trade or branch of production, but their labourers were altogether unspecialised, in the sense that, having completed their service with one of these employers, they passed on out of the trade altogether; and if, at the same time, those who had passed through held little or no communication with those who were to follow after; then these employers would not have to look to the future at all, and provided it was not easy for men to go about hawking their services to different employers, costs of movement and the time taken being too great, each employer could beat down each man to the very lowest level that man would take. Wages would be fixed at "subsistence level" because of the "bargaining power" of the employers. The traditional "indeterminateness" analysis would fit perfectly. But there is no need to enlarge upon the absurdity and improbability of these conditions. It is practically impossible to conceive of employers beginning to exert a fairly regular and continuous demand for labour, without some labourers very soon becoming specialised to some extent to the performance of the service required.

The opposite case to this is a much more real one. There are certain services (those of porters, for instance)[1] for which there is a fairly regular demand, but a demand which does not come continuously from the same people. The demand is regular enough for it to be worth while for people to become specialised to that occupation, but nevertheless they work for a particular employer for a very short space of time; they can never count on seeing him again, and he never has to reckon on seeing a particular workman, or an associate of that particular workman again.

The conditions under which such labour is sold are very similar to those of retail trade. In an undeveloped community, where opportunities for the profitable employment of time are strictly limited, it may be worth while for a seller (of labour or of goods) to spend some time "higgling and bargaining" to get as good a price as he can. If this procedure is followed, the terms are almost as indeterminate as with the isolated bargain. But as economic activity increases, haggling over small sums becomes a more and more uneconomic way of spending time. Both in the retail market and in the labour market its use diminishes. It becomes more

---

[1] Some professional services do not depart very far from this type.

convenient for the seller to fix a definite rate and to stand by it.

The labour market has developed in this direction to a much less extent than the retail commodity market. The reason for this backwardness is probably to be found in the fact that the continual change of employers makes it impossible for each man to be continuously at work. The retail shopkeeper often has a second customer waiting to be served, when his business with the first is finished; but the retail seller of labour expects to spend an interval, of minutes or of hours, between his jobs; and he will often be willing to spend part of his time trying to better the terms he gets.

The influence of "bargaining advantages" in this market is all on the side of the wage-earners. They can, and undoubtedly do, demand higher wages from employers who appear to be more wealthy; to this extent they act as discriminating monopolists. Their monopoly arises because they know the market better than their employers do; because their employers generally cannot spare the time to seek another source of supply; and because direct undercutting, by other workmen offering themselves at lower terms, is hindered by its probably unpleasant personal consequences.

But although this market is one of the most imperfect with which we have to deal, demand and supply do influence wages even here, in however halting and irregular a fashion. An increase in demand will raise wages; for the workmen, finding that their more ambitious suggestions are accepted with greater alacrity than before, are likely to advance their claims. A diminution in supply has the same effect, for it will be felt as an increase in demand by each individual workman. Wages, however, will fall less easily than they rise. An abnormal surplus of supply over demand will be felt as an increase in unemployment. Each man gets fewer jobs; and earnings fall, while wages per job may be less easily affected. Nevertheless, some effect on wages per job there will probably be; some potential employers are being excluded by the high rates demanded; those wage-earners who are more moderate in their claims find that they get more employment; slowly, very slowly perhaps, the news will spread that moderation is a more paying policy; and competition does its work.

No one will pretend that the working of such a market is a pleasing spectacle from any point of view, social or economic; yet it is significant that in this market, the most imperfect with which we have to deal, the danger (once it is given that men will come to this sort of work) is not that they will be exploited by low wages, but that by refusing to reduce the wages they will accept, when a reduction is called for, they will cause themselves to suffer unnecessary unemployment.

III

We pass now to the case of the casual market proper, which is distinguished from these last by the fact that both employers and employed are continuously attached to the trade. But though the demand of these employers is continuous, in the sense that practically every day each employer has some men working for him, it is not regular, since the number of men he employs fluctuates incessantly. A large proportion of the labourers, therefore, cannot count with any assurance

at all on being taken on again by the same employer
when their period of contract has expired.[1]

We have already seen that the unemployment,
which is inevitably a serious matter in such a market,
may be a "normal" unemployment, perfectly consistent with stationary wages. For although each firm's
demand for labour fluctuates continually, a change in
wage-rates would affect, not the present, but the
future supply of labour. So long as each firm expects
to want labour, on the average, as much in the future
as it has done in the immediate past, it would be
obvious folly to change the rates it pays.

By its very nature, a casual labour market is a
highly competitive market. Since men do habitually
move from one establishment to another, the costs of
movement can be no obstacle to mobility.

This intense competitiveness, combined with the deferred action of wage-changes on the supply of labour,
must make for stability in wage-rates. Wages cannot
be affected by the day-to-day variations of the market;
and they are likely to resist even more serious fluctuations to some extent. For if the activity of trade increases, and a firm finds it difficult to get labour, it may
well postpone raising wages as long as possible. It
knows that the higher wages cannot in any case exert
their full effect in attracting labour to it for a little
while, and by that time the end of the pressure may be

---

[1] The precise boundary-line between "casual" and "regular" trades is
of course impossible to define strictly. In every trade a certain number of
men leave their employers at the end of every contract period (day, week,
month, etc.). The "casual coefficient" of a trade could be defined as the
proportion which the average number of men leaving employers at the end
of a week bears to the total number employed in the trade during that week.
It is impossible to say how these coefficients would be distributed among
different trades; there may be a regular progression from the most casual
to the most regular. But it is only necessary to examine the extreme cases.
The reader will have little difficulty in deducing the working of those between.

in sight. It knows, too, that its action is likely to compel similar action on the part of its competitors, and that this will follow so quickly that the efficacy of the rise in drawing labour from them will be seriously diminished. The principal hope is to draw labour from outside the industːy, or from another area, but then much of what can be hoped from this quarter may very well be secured simply by the prospect of more assured employment (which follows in any case from the activity of trade) without a rise in wages. It may be only when this source dries up that firms will be forced to raise wages, with the object, at bottom, of compelling their weaker competitors to relax their demands on the labour market.

A similar (though possibly less prolonged) lag is probable when demand falls off. A firm will not lower wages until it feels sure that it can get at a lower rate all the labour it expects to require for a considerable period in the future. This implies, not only that the firm in question expects a period of quiet trade, but that it can rely on its competitors' demands also being lower than they have been in the past. If it lowers wages before this, it will have to reckon on the likelihood of its low-wage policy picking out the least efficient men in the market, who will know that they have a better chance of employment with the low-wage firm than with its competitors. So long as any attention is paid to the quality of labour (and even in the lowest grade of casual market some rudimentary selection is usually practised[1]) this is a risk which will not easily be invited.

But although wage-rates, even in casual trades, are capable of resisting for a little while an abnormal ex-

---

[1] Beveridge, *Unemployment*, pp. 83, 86.

cess of supply over demand, they probably do fall
more easily than they rise. This is mainly due to the
familiar fact that while it is very easy to become a
casual labourer, it is much more difficult to stop being
one. The gate into casual employment stands wide
open, and can always be entered by the unemployed of
other trades. The way out is much harder. The casual
labourer has often acquired habits which diminish his
usefulness to the employer of regular labour; he is
usually unlikely to have acquired savings which enable
him to move into localities of developing industry.
Thus, although a considerably increased demand for
casual labour must raise wages, the effect may well be
belated, and possibly small.[1]

IV

"Regular" trades—those in which a man does not
frequently change his employer—are regular because
for them there is an economy in regularity. This
economy must be found in the fact that experience in
working for a particular employer makes a man more
useful to that employer; he gets to understand the
particular sort of work his employer needs, and also
the personal idiosyncrasies of his employer (or, in a
large works, the manager or foreman under whom he
works directly). Simply because a man has worked
for a time with a particular employer, he becomes

---

[1] If other industries share to a wide extent in the activity of the casual
industry, the delay may be much reduced. General unemployment is low;
the reserves which can be drawn into the industry are much harder to find;
even an exodus out of the industry is not impossible, since in times of boom
employers are less particular whom they employ, and the ex-casual labourer
may find it more possible to get a footing elsewhere. Some delay in raising
wages there may be still; but it will not be more marked than the delay in
reducing wages when trade falls off.

more useful to that employer than another man would
be, even a man whose initial qualifications were just
as good, so that, if neither had been engaged before,
it would be indifferent to the employer which he took.
This special advantage of maintaining the same men
in the same business is, of course, most marked in
the higher, more responsible, and more skilled grades
of labour; but it is not altogether negligible even in
lower grades.

If "regularity" is associated with, and is largely
due to, an advantage which accrues to employers if
they can maintain the same men in their employment,
it also brings about a similar advantage to workmen
if they can continue to work for the same employer.
If a workman is to continue long in the same employment, he will find it convenient to live near his work,
and once he has come to live in a place specially chosen
so as to be near some particular employer, he is likely
to incur quite significant costs if he moves. On both
sides, therefore, there is an economy in maintaining
the mutual relationship; and this economy appears
to reintroduce into the most regular and settled trades
those elements which we saw to make for indeterminateness in the isolated bargain.

But this "indeterminateness", instead of making
the determination of wages haphazard, has precisely
the opposite effect. It greatly enhances the stability,
or "rigidity", of wage-rates. If an employer's need for
a particular labourer falls, he is the more chary of
reducing his wages, because he would be unable to
carry out a threat of replacing this man by another
without considerable inconvenience. If a workman
hears that he could get better wages elsewhere, he is
the less likely to use this opportunity as a lever to

demand higher wages from his employer, because he
knows that he cannot take action to back his claim
without considerable trouble and expense. Once,
therefore, a wage is established, it is likely to stand up
to minor fluctuations of demand and supply; it is only
when the pre sure passes a certain point that wages
will be altered.

It is convenient to analyse the working of a regular
labour market by taking the case of a rise in the
demand for a particular class of labour, and examining
in detail its probable effect on wages. (The contrary
case of a fall has already been discussed in the previous chapter, and so needs less attention here.)
Suppose the demand for the product of that labour
to increase; the new demand is likely to be concentrated at first on a limited number of firms, who
find more orders coming in. Now the action of these
firms will depend on their expectations, whether they
expect the change to be temporary or permanent. If
an entrepreneur interprets an increase in orders to
mean that ordinary orders have been anticipated, he
will make no serious attempt to speed up production
to meet the new demand. A short oscillation may thus
have no effect on the demand for labour. If he interprets it as an additional demand, but an addition
which he does not expect to last long, he will probably
work overtime, or, if this is not enough, he will pass on
some of the orders to other firms, either directly, or
indirectly, by raising prices. In some cases, of course,
he will take on extra labour, but since he requires it
only temporarily, he will not trouble much about its
quality, but will take any unemployed man who will
come, and who is more or less fitted for the work.

It is probably the case that any increase in demand will be met at first in one or more of these ways. To assume that a change is temporary involves less adjustment than to assume that it is permanent. These are the lines of least resistance. But if the increase continues, these methods will usually be abandoned. Overtime is expensive; no one likes to lose trade which could have been secured; to use labour of inferior quality is often expensive too. Once an employer looks for a continuance of good times, he will normally reorganise his works, and expand his demand for labour of normal quality, which is what matters.

This reorganisation itself may take time. If the firm has been working at full capacity, an expansion may involve building operations or the installation of new machinery. We have to reckon with a probable delay between an employer's decision to expand his works, and the increase in labour force which follows from it.

Now whether this increase in labour force involves a rise in wages depends, not on the circumstances of the particular firm, but on those of the whole industry, or at least so much of the industry as is within fairly easy reach of the expanding firm. Particular firms may expand even when the whole industry is in a stationary condition, but their expansion need not force up wages if they merely absorb those men who have been thrown out by others. Probably the normal process is for an expanding firm to seek labour through the usual channels, telling foremen to tell their friends, and such haphazard methods, by advertisement, or (nowadays) through Labour Exchanges. At first it will not be difficult to get men of reasonably good quality, but after a time the supply at the old rates will dry up. At this point the expanding firm may take the initiative in offering higher rates, but more probably applicants for work, realising the market is now getting tight, will demand higher rates. Indeed, the applicants may very well prove to be men who already have a job, but are willing to move if it is made worth their while. In one or other of these ways the wages paid by an expanding firm must ultimately rise.

The next stage is for the rise to be diffused throughout the industry. The attraction of high rates will set in motion a gradual flow of labour from less active to more active centres of trade. But before a man moves to seek work on the better terms offered elsewhere, it is reasonable for him to try and get better terms without moving. His first step will be to demand a rise in wages from his present employer.

If that present employer is also doing well, the rise is very likely to be conceded. A time of active trade is the last moment when he wants to lose good workmen. But once the adventurous, who have really considered moving, have been given the increase, it must generally be extended to other workers in their grade. For although an employer may guess that some of his men are not in a position to carry out a threat of moving, he will hardly be able to examine their cases in detail and distinguish between them. Further, such discrimination would lead to extremely bad feeling. The "unfairness" would almost certainly diminish the efficiency of those men who were left out.

Thus, once one or two firms have found it necessary to raise wages, the rest of those who are in a prosperous condition must follow. But what of those firms who have not shared in the general prosperity? They will presumably refuse to raise wages, or will try to make the rise as small as possible. This involves losing some of their men, who can only be replaced, if at all, by others less efficient. Here there will be a real movement of labour, due, of course, to a real shifting of demand from one set of firms to the other. The less prosperous firms will be faced with smaller profits if they raise wages—with less efficient labour, and so again smaller profits, if they do not raise wages. In any case their position becomes progressively unfavourable.

V

Since the general rise in wages depends upon the action of workmen, on their moving from one employer to another, or on their consideration of the possibility of such movement, it is easy to see that the transmission of an increase must be a slow process. Indeed, it is so slow that it is not by any means confined to periods of spectacular development of the demand for labour in particular trades or areas, but is going on all the time. There can be little question that this slowness is largely responsible for those local differences in wages which present a picture of such bewildering complexity in many trades.

Even in a position of equilibrium, some local differences indeed would probably persist. Some are due to differences in the cost of living, some to the indirect attractions of living in certain localities, some are simply due to differences in efficiency. The conditions of equilibrium postulate no more than that the "net advantages" of employment in different places must be equal for labour of equal efficiency.

It is extraordinarily difficult, when examining

actual statistics of wage-rates, to disentangle the
effects of differences in "other advantages" from the
effects of immobility. Yet sometimes it can be done.
The way in which agricultural labourers' wages used to
be "zoned" round a developing manufacturing centre
in the early days of the Industrial Revolution has been
worked out by Dr. Redford. This is exactly what we
should expect under conditions of incomplete mobility.
"In Lancashire it had been observed, so early as 1794,
that the rate of agricultural wages was in inverse
proportion to the distance from the manufacturing
centres. At Chorley a common labourer got 3s. a day
with ale; at Euxton 2s. or 2s. 6d.; at Eccleston 1s. 6d.
or 2s.; whilst at Mawdsley and Bispham labourers
could be got, even in harvest time, for 1s. 2d. or
1s. 4d".[1]

The same tendency can be traced, though rather
less clearly, in the apparently bewildering confusion
of varying local rates which marked the building trades
before the war.[2] London rates were higher than the
rates anywhere else in England, and although this is
partly accounted for by the high cost of living, that is
certainly not the whole explanation. For the regular
influx of building-trade workers into London is a well-
known phenomenon. It is an ancient custom of the
London builders to train relatively few apprentices, and
to rely on the influx to keep up their supplies of skilled
labour.[3]

Throughout the country there was to be noticed a
high degree of correlation between the number of men

---

[1] Redford, *Labour Migration in England*, p. 59.
[2] Of course these were Trade Union rates, so that the elements of Trade
Union strength and Trade Union policy cannot be neglected.
[3] Dearle, *Unemployment in the London Building Trades* (1908), p. 104.

employed in a district and the level of wage-rates there. Where much building was going on, many workmen were required, and wages were high.

These two examples will suffice to illustrate a very obvious and simple thing. The movement of labour from place to place is insufficient to iron out local differences in wages. But the movement does occur, and recent researches are indicating more and more clearly that differences in net economic advantages, chiefly differences in wages, are the main causes of migration. The labour market is not a perfect market; the equalising forces do not act quickly and easily, but nevertheless they do act.

Just as wages within a single trade are subject to the equalising force of movement in search of betterment, so are wages throughout a nation. Even within a trade, the equalisation is not completely effective; between trades it is much less effective. For between trades the obstacles to movement are much greater; and also the probability that differences in wages correspond to differences in ability is much more serious. Wages may rise very high in one occupation because of large demand for the kind of service there given; and they may remain high indefinitely, because the number of people with natural aptitudes for that kind of work is limited. The earnings of doctors are higher than those of postmen, largely because of the long training which is required of doctors and which comparatively few people can afford; but probably also because comparatively few postmen would make good doctors even if the costs of training were removed.

And so we cannot expect that the movement of labour between trades will be very effective in equalising wages, or even in equalising the net advantages of different occupations. Even if movement was easy, it would not iron out all the differences. As it is, movement is far from easy.

The supply of labour can adjust itself to exceptional differences in wages between trades in two ways: by an actual transfer of adult workers, or by a deflection of the supply of juveniles. Every year a certain number of the people working in each industry pass out of employment on account of old age and death; and in a normal industry their places are taken by juveniles fresh from school. The least wasteful way to meet a shift in demand from one industry to another is to cut off the supply of juveniles to the first industry and direct it to the second. Any other way involves a sacrifice of acquired skill and experience.

But although this is the least wasteful way, it does not follow that it will naturally be adopted unless special encouragement is given to it. Young people entering industry are probably less influenced by wage-rates than adults are. A kind of work which is attractive and easily accessible from their homes may easily get recruits even if the wages it offers are relatively low. Even the question of wages itself does not always present itself to them in a form which corresponds closely with the true demand. A trade may require labour badly and so promise high rates—ultimately; but if it is a skilled trade, it will not offer them at once. A boy may easily prefer a less skilled "blind-alley" occupation which promises relatively high rates in early years although the ultimate prospects are far inferior.

Actually, although in normal times the deflection of juveniles is probably the principal way of adjust-ment, there can be little doubt that the supply of labour to different trades is adjusted to a very con-

G

siderable extent by a transfer of adult workers. In the case of the less skilled trades, where the period required for a new man to work up to full efficiency is short, such transference is fairly easy. And these are, after all, the great majority.

Again, some of the more skilled trades fall into groups. Within such a group the trades are distinct, but the kinds of skill they require have much in common. If a man moves from one to another of these trades, he forfeits some elements of his special acquired skill, but other elements he can still put to useful purpose. He is in a favourable position to learn the new trade more quickly than other men would do. If a considerable divergence between the wages paid in different trades, which are allied in this way, were to develop, movement would undoubtedly take place to some extent. Thirdly, transference from a skilled to a less skilled trade is always possible. In one sense, indeed, this sort of transference is always happening, and is a regular, if unfortunate, characteristic of the labour market. A certain proportion of the men who have been trained for a skilled trade usually prove unsuited for it. They find it difficult to earn standard rates, and drift into intermittent unemployment. Sooner or later they see that they would do better by flying lower, and they go over to some less skilled occupation, where they have a better chance of regular employment.

But this sifting-down of the failures has little relation to the forces determining standard rates. However, when a skilled trade undergoes a permanent or long-continued decline, the road does stand open for men of normal efficiency to move into less skilled, but more urgently needed, occupations.

In all these ways, then, there is in a free market some considerable degree of mobility between trades. And since there is mobility, we shall expect to find (to a lesser degree, no doubt) the same sort of relation between rates as we found within an industry. If wages rise in one industry, the possibility of movement towards it will usually exist. And this possibility, hardly realised, perhaps, but vaguely present, will set on foot demands for a rise in wages elsewhere. If other industries are sharing in the prosperity of the first, they will concede the rise. If not, they will refuse it, and therefore tacitly assent to a beginning of the transference of labour.

Activity in one trade often leads to activity in others. All industries share to some extent in times of good trade, and all alike suffer from bad. Thus while wages may rise in one trade from causes peculiar to it alone, this is not often the case; and similarly for a fall. If the possibility of movement sets on foot demands for a rise in wages, the fact of simultaneous activity often makes it possible for the demands to be granted. If the fact of simultaneous depression sets on foot demands for reduction, the possibility of movement towards that trade makes it more necessary that the demands should be conceded.

Potential mobility is the ultimate sanction for the interrelation of wage-rates. But it is a sanction that need not be continually used. If, when movement is possible, wages do not move together, the sanction will, slowly and ponderously indeed, begin to operate. But it is improbable that the sanction is always in the minds of those who are actually concerned with changing rates. That certain rates move together—or, at least, that the change of one gives a *prima facie* case for a change in the other—becomes a matter of custom.

"Before the war the economic changes to which wages had to be adjusted were gradual. Rates of wages, therefore, had a high degree of stability, and the relations between wages in allied or neighbouring occupations were equally stable. Wages, it may fairly be said, constituted a system, since there were well-understood rates for most occupations; the relations between these were stable and generally accepted, and a change in any one rate would prompt demands for a change in other rates."[1] This is just what we should expect.

The "system" was not by any means simply a product of Trade Unionism. Even in a perfectly free market wages must work in something like this way. Demands for a rise in wages come, in the first place, because a rise appears to be "fair". And the principal motive in an employer's mind when he concedes such a rise may be a desire that his wage-policy should not appear to be an "unfair" one. The same argument which is used by the workmen to support their claims for a rise is used by employers to justify a reduction.

But although this appears to be the motive for a very large proportion of wage-changes, it is not their real reason. These rules of fairness and justice are simply rough-and-ready guides whereby the working of supply and demand is anticipated. That they are not perfect guides is shown by the fact that they are so often broken. If an employer is not doing well, his men may indeed demonstrate to him that a rise would be "fair", but he will nevertheless refuse it, and compel them to have recourse to their further

[1] Clay, *Problem of Industrial Relations*, p. 74.

sanction—to leave him. If an employer wishes to expand his business, he will have to pay higher wages in the end, however much *he* may grumble that the rise is "unfair". It is only in an equilibrium market, or in a market so nearly in equilibrium, that its changes can leave wages unaffected, that perfect "fairness" of wages can always be preserved. Any change, even those most desirable changes of a progressive community, must always create a certain amount of "unfairness."[1]

VI

If an employer refuses a demand for a rise in wages made on the ground of fairness, because he does not consider that it would be profitable to go on employing the workman in question at the higher wage, then, although his conduct may be grumbled at, it is not susceptible of valid economic criticism. It is perfectly open to the workman to leave him; if he does not do so, the presumption is that costs of movement (which may be quite personal to the workman himself) prevent transference to the place of expanding employment. Thus if employers are in any way compelled to give way to claims of this kind, the result must be, at the best, that the man dismissed can only regain employment at a net sacrifice.[2] But although this

---

[1] We shall see later on that much of Trade Union policy is simply an attempt to carry these principles of "fairness" further than they will go in an unregulated market.

[2] *Cf.* Pigou, *Economics of Welfare*, 2nd ed., pp. 522-527. The term "fair wages" is used above in a much looser sense than Professor Pigou's. His precise definition is devised with the object of defining an "optimum" distribution of labour, but since this is not our present concern, it seems better to preserve the wider connotation given to the term in actual practice.

Professor Pigou's approval of "interference to raise unfair wages", when the unfairness is due to ignorance, is irrelevant to our hypothesis.

means that a certain amount of "unfairness" is a necessary concomitant of economic change, this is not to say that it is impossible for "unfairness" to arise which has less excuse. It is conceivable that an employer, faced with claims for a rise on the ground of fairness, might refuse, not because he could not grant the rise without dismissals, but because he believed that he could retain a considerable number of men without raising wages, and the gain to him from the low wages paid to these men would exceed the loss he would incur from the contraction in employment. In fact, he might prefer to act as a monopolist with respect to the labour he employs, and "exploit" that labour.[1]

This is a real possibility which we cannot afford to neglect. But in estimating its importance there are two things which must be borne in mind.

1. Exploitation is just as probable, if not more probable, in better-paid as in worse-paid trades. It is, in fact, extremely improbable that exploitation has much to do with the grosser scandals of the labour market. The extreme cases of poverty and low earnings have usually arisen, not in regular trades, where the peril of exploitation is admittedly present, but in those trades which we have classified as casual, in the widest sense. But in casual trades, competition is generally quite sufficiently intense to prevent any possibility of exploitation. Casual labour is often badly paid, not because it gets less than it is worth, but because it is worth so appallingly little.

2. The loss of labour, which an exploiter must face, will not usually be a single disaster, over and done with as soon as the first loss is over. That first loss

---

[1] Pigou, *Economics of Welfare*, 2nd ed., pp. 527-534.

may indeed be quite small, so that his initial position may be distinctly favourable. But the loss will go on. The circumstances in which men live are continually changing, and everyone finds it easier to move at some times than others. Opportunities for movement will come to others of his men, and slowly his original labour force will contract. The places of these men can only be filled, if at all, by others less efficient, for, unless he is very lucky, these are all he will get at the wages he is offering. Besides this direct movement, there is the normal wastage of labour. Men grow old or leave him for other reasons than the wages offered. These again he will be unable to replace.

A point must come when the decline in the efficiency of his business outweighs the advantages gained from exploitation. And when this time arrives, it may be too late to save the situation by a change in policy.

Anticipation of this course of events must usually be sufficient to deter employers from any considerable use of the power to exploit which undoubtedly lies in their hands on occasion. It may sometimes even be sufficient to deter them from a quite temporary exploitation, which they expect to abandon after a short while. For when a man thinks of changing his employment, he looks, not only at the wages he is to receive at the moment, but at his prospects. And he judges his prospects on what has happened in the past.

The possibility of exploitation thus depends on two things: on the ease with which men can move, and on the extent to which they and their employers consider the future, or look only to the moment. The more difficult men find it to change their employment, and the less experience they possess on which to forecast the future, the more opportunity for exploitation there will be. Thus in earlier ages, when communication was bad, and when repressive enactments restrained the mobility of labour, the possibilities of exploitation were considerable; and the same is doubtless true of some of the more backward countries of the modern world. But communications have generally improved with the rise of industrialism; and direct legal impediments to mobility are so obvious a hindrance to the growth of wealth that they have generally disappeared—within national areas. In the first stages of industrialisation, improved mobility may conceivably have been offset by lack of experience of the conditions of an unfamiliar employment; but at the most this can have been only a passing phase. It is very hard to believe that the exploitation of labour, in the strict sense considered here, is likely to be a serious social evil in advanced industrial states.

There is, however, one kind of exploitation whose feasibility appears at first sight to have been increased, rather than diminished, by economic progress. Although (apart from institutional obstacles, of the kind we shall consider in our second part) the difficulties of movement from place to place have been diminished, the increased specialisation of labour has had some tendency to increase the difficulty of movement from trade to trade. (Of recent years this has to some extent been offset by the increased specialisation of machinery, which has reduced the need for highly specialised skilled labour.) At the same time, the increasing advantages of large-scale production have made it more possible than before for a single firm to monopolise a whole industry. If cases can be found where a particular skilled trade is specialised to the performance of labour required only by one firm, the members of that trade are peculiarly liable to exploitation.

Where an employer is a monopolist, not only with respect to labour, but also with respect to his customers, the limitation of the supply of labour which will follow from an attempt to pay specially low wages is particularly likely to pay him. Yet simultaneous exploitation of customers and employees is a peculiarly dangerous policy. So long as the monopolist is exposed to any sort of potential competition (as what private monopolist is not?) exploitation of skilled employees is so likely to drive them away, when they may offer themselves as a most convenient basis for the expansion of a rival, that it will be worth his while to go some distance to avoid this danger. In fact, it is much more likely that a private monopolist will feel it prudent to offer his skilled employees a share in his monopoly gains than that he will ask them to contribute.

When the monopoly is not a private "economic monopoly", maintaining itself by superior efficiency and the economies of large-scale production, but a legal monopoly, protected by the State, there is much less reason for such prudence. But when we come to State employment, or semi-State employment of this kind, criticism is baffled. The higher the wages paid, the better (on the whole and in the long run) will be the service rendered; and vice versa. Yet there is no direct means of telling whether the better service to the community is worth the extra cost. Since the benefits are obvious, and the costs are indirect and for a long while much less obvious, democratic States are peculiarly liable to indulge in long periods of extravagance, and then, when the bill comes in, in fits of indiscriminate and often misdirected parsimony.

VII

The results of this chapter have reinforced and fortified the conclusion of our first: that there is no necessity whatsoever for the wage a man receives at a particular moment to equal his marginal product. In so far as that term "marginal product" can be given any sense at all in a changing community, it can only mean the wage a man would ultimately receive if the fundamental conditions of equilibrium—the number of people in the market, their tastes, their ability to labour, and the property they possess—were made eternal as they exist at the moment, and the process of settling down followed to its furthest limits. This marginal product is a regulator of wages, but it does not determine their precise magnitude. For the marginal product of a man's labour, defined in this way, changes incessantly, and wages do not incessantly change. Sometimes the wage must fall below the marginal product, sometimes exceed it. But any such difference, if it is maintained for long, slowly bends wages to meet the new situation. The forces elucidated by equilibrium analysis are the forces which, in nearly every case, cause wages to change.

Like Professor Clay, we must conceive the wages of labour (at least over a very large part of the labour market) as a "system," a system with considerable internal stresses of its own. As economic conditions vary, they bring about changes in the system, but external changes have to reach a certain magnitude and a certain duration before they can break down the internal resistance. Some of these variations in economic conditions are what seem fortuitous; changes in taste, for instance, are often fortuitous from the point of view of the economist, since their origins lie outside his field of vision. Some, however, are not fortuitous in this way, but arise from the fact that a particular wage-system has effects peculiar to itself on the slow-moving ground-swell of the economic world—that it influences the distribution of labour, and stimulates or discourages the accumulation of capital, in a way of its own. Any change in the wage-system must influence these slow-moving tendencies, and they in their turn react on the wage-system. In the freest of markets such actions and reactions go on; they are what we call economic progress. But to some extent it is possible to deflect the wage-system from this regular course, and make it follow a path, which is not the resultant of millions of separate desires, but the fruit of conscious policy. The working of such control will be our concern in later stages of this enquiry. .

Before we can pass on to that subject, there are still some respects in which our study of the competitive labour market needs to be extended. First, we must drop the assumption with which we have generally worked up to the present, that the amount of work a man does in return for his wages can be treated as given. It has not indeed always been possible to hold rigidly to this assumption, since we have been obliged (for reasons of convenience) to take into account the way in which personal relations between employer and employed (the content or discontent of workmen) may influence the efficiency of a business, and therefore the wage-policy of employers. But this is only one of the ways in which variations in the individual's supply of labour may affect the determination of wages. The other ways must be our concern in the next chapter.

Secondly, it is convenient to insert at this point an examination of the way in which we may expect the general forces of economic progress to affect the average level of wages. This is one of the most important sets of deductions which we can draw from the general marginal productivity theory; and in addition to the considerable intrinsic importance of the subject, it will be found a convenient background against which to place our later study of the effects of wage-regulation.

CHAPTER V

INDIVIDUAL SUPPLY OF LABOUR

I

WHEN an employer hires a workman, he buys work. The wage he is prepared to pay—the price he is prepared to give—depends on the amount of work—the amount of the commodity bought—he expects to receive in return. Other things being equal, a more efficient workman offers more "work" than a less efficient; and he receives higher wages in consequence. In our earlier discussions, we have assumed these other things to be equal, so that the amount of work offered by each man is something fixed, depending on the nature of that man, but not on the conditions on which he is employed. It is now time to drop this convenient simplification. The amount of work a man does is partly a matter of choice, and the amount he chooses to do depends on what he gets for it; if he works under superintendence, the conditions of this superintendence also affect the amount of work he does; and further, his ability to work may be affected by the wages he has been in the habit of receiving in the past. A change in the amount of work offered, arising from any of these causes, will affect wages; but it is not only for their effects on wages that we must examine these reactions through the amount of work performed. The amount of work a man does, and the conditions under which he does it, are themselves matters of independent interest. They are part of his wage-contract with his employer; they determine, simultaneously with his actual wage, the degree of benefit he derives from his employment. The improvement of the conditions of labour is as much a desideratum of social progress as the simple raising of wages.

But before we can go on to examine these reactions, there is one preliminary question which must be settled. What exactly do we mean by a variation in the amount of "work" or "labour" a man performs? How is it to be measured? A change in the effort a man puts into his work will affect the disagreeableness (or agreeableness) of that work to him; and it will also affect the value to his employer of the work he does. But it is by no means certain that it will affect these two things in the same direction; it is even less likely that it will affect them to the same extent.[1] Along which of these lines are we to seek for a measure of the quantity of labour supplied? There can be no question that it must be the second. The benefit derived by an employer from a particular man's work is a benefit capable of transference, since the work might have been done for another employer. It is the actual service performed by the labourer which is bought and sold, not the sacrifice he endures in order to perform that service, or the effort he expends in doing it.

Now the direct services performed by a single labourer are often very heterogeneous, and when he works "more," it is often not by doing more of a particular service, which could be added arithmetically to the collection, but by reassorting the services he has been doing in a complicated fashion, which, however,

---

[1] So far as the degree (as opposed to the direction) of a change in subjective cost is measurable at all.

results in a collection preferred by his employer. Even
in the case of those men who are engaged on repetitive
operations, with whom an increase in their supply of
labour does seem to reflect itself directly in an increase
in output, there is no guarantee that the increase in
labour supply can be considered to be proportional to
the increase in output; for, on the one hand, an increase in quantity may be accompanied by a fall in
quality, and, on the other, the increase in output is almost certainly due in part to the co-operation of other
factors of production.

This difficulty cannot be overcome without making
reference to the general system of prices; and since we
must make this reference, the validity of the solution is
inevitably narrow, and only to be made use of with
great care. The only way is to use the account given in
Chapter II of the determination of wages in equilibrium, when allowance is made for differences in
capacity among labourers. We assumed there that the
efficiency of each labourer (the amount of "work" he is
prepared to do) was given, and then showed how in
equilibrium a scale of wages would be constructed, so
that a man of higher efficiency would always get higher
wages. If we suppose a labour market to be in equilibrium, and consequently a scale of this sort to be
established; if now we suppose the ability of one
labourer to change (or the effort he expends upon his
work to change); then in the new position of equilibrium which results from this change, the position of
this labourer on the scale will be altered. We can best
define an increase in an individual's supply of labour
by its results; if he supplies more labour, while other
things (the remaining fundamental conditions of
equilibrium) remain the same, his equilibrium wage

will rise; if he supplies less, his equilibrium wage will fall.

So long as we are dealing with a strictly competitive system, so that the change in one man's conduct is insufficient to have an appreciable effect on the wages of other men, or on the prices of commodities, we can assert, without any danger of awkward consequences, that the change in that man's supply of labour is proportional to the change in his equilibrium wage. This, as an exact definition, does give us practical results of the same kind as the looser conceptions commonly in use. If a man's abilities increase, if he works harder (*successfully* works harder), or if he works longer hours which have no detrimental effect upon his efficiency, his equilibrium wage will rise, and in all these cases it is perfectly natural to assert that the quantity of labour he supplies has increased.

But of course this is not to say that if a large number of men simultaneously increase their supply of labour, then their equilibrium wages must rise. It is perfectly possible that separate individual action of a certain kind might increase a man's wages (at the expense, if we like, of an infinitesimally small reduction spread over the wages of many others), yet, if a large number simultaneously acted in this fashion, the loss would outweigh the gain.

In the case of repetitive work (provided that we can leave out of account the possibility of substitution, or change of method), the change in a man's supply of labour becomes proportional to his net output. This again is perfectly consistent with common usage.

If we remember these limitations, it is perfectly possible to treat "labour" as a commodity consisting of discrete homogeneous units, for which therefore

there are well-defined curves of supply and demand.
It is decidedly convenient to do this when treating
some special problems; but it is a method with very
considerable dangers, which can only be avoided if we
think back our arguments into a more cumbrous but
more realistic form as frequently as possible.[1]

II

Changes in the individual's supply of labour may
arise from any of three kinds of economic cause:
(1) they may result from a change in the conditions
of labour fixed by the employer or agreed upon between him and the labourer (of these the most important is a change in hours); (2) they may be the man's
conscious reaction to a change in the wage offered
(such as a change in piece-rates); (3) they may be the
unconscious result of his whole situation, including
the wages he has received and the work he has done in
the recent past. In modern industrial employment the
first type is very probably the most important. When
once the conditions of employment have been fixed, the
variations in supply of labour of which account still
has to be taken are relatively small. Nevertheless,
that they are not without importance is shown by
the advantages frequently derived from the use of
piecework. Piecework enables such changes to be reflected directly and rapidly in the wages earned; although in theory changes in the amount of work done

---

[1] It may conveniently be observed here that precisely the same kind of
difficulty arises with other factors of production, particularly capital. And
the same solution, for all its limited validity, is the only solution possible.

H

will affect wages under time-work, there can be no question that the adjustment there is extremely slow and imperfect. There are considerable theoretical advantages to be gained if we begin by ruling out these difficulties; if we suppose that there are no conditions of employment other than wages to be settled between a man and his employer (that is to say, we are in fact dealing with something like the "domestic system"); and further if we assume (what almost follows as a consequence of this) that wages are paid by the piece. The amount of work a man does is determined, then, partly by his ability, and partly by his relative demands for income and leisure. Both of these may be affected by his wages.

To take ability first. Higher wages may react favourably on a man's efficiency in several ways. They enable him to be better fed, and consequently stronger; they open up to him new opportunities for recreation and self-improvement; and, further, they offer indirectly many of those advantages of increased leisure with which we shall subsequently be more immediately concerned. Higher wages make a man's hours of leisure more genuinely hours of leisure, since many of the fatiguing things a poor man must do for himself, a better-paid man can have done for him by other people. A poor man's wife and family are often compelled to become wage-earners themselves. But a rise in wages sets more of their time free for household work.

The influence of this reaction upon wages (and the same of course applies to the other reactions which we shall have to examine later) depends on the elasticity of demand for labour. If for any reason wages are falling, this will reduce the efficiency of labour to

some extent, perhaps not at once, but at any rate
after a time. If the demand for labour is inelastic,
the reduced supply will actually check the fall in
wages per head; if the demand is elastic (the elasticity
greater than unity) reduced supply will accelerate
the fall in wages.

The case of falling wages to which attention has
generally been directed in connection with this reaction is the case of a "declining trade", declining because it has to meet some new kind of competition.
A new method of production, more highly mechanised,
or using a different sort of skill; the growth of industry
in other districts, or other countries, whose comparative advantages are greater—these are the kind of
things from which such a prolonged decline in wages
may arise. Now under these circumstances, just because
the decline is due to competition, we may be nearly
certain that the demand for labour will be elastic.
If the old trade can maintain its efficiency, it will fight
its battle better; if its efficiency is impaired, defeat
will come all the sooner.

Thus in this important case, the reaction of low
wages on efficiency will accelerate decline. But it
will not only accelerate decline; it will make movement
from the declining trade more difficult. Thus it is
undoubtedly a cause aggravating the difficulty of those
redistributions of labour which are inevitable in a
progressive community, but which too often result
in a prolonged exclusion of considerable sections of the
community from the benefits of progress.

But although the reaction of wages on efficiency
complicates adjustments, it must not be forgotten
that its general effect in a progressive community
is highly favourable. Once the first step out of sta-

tionary conditions has been taken, rising wages promote rising efficiency, and these again rising wages.[1] In this way, as in others, progress stimulates progress. Wealth facilitates further accumulation.

It should not be inferred, however, that such a cumulative process may go on indefinitely. The wealth of a community is determined not only by the efficiency of labour, but also by its capital equipment and technical knowledge. With given supplies of capital, and given technical knowledge, there is a definite limit to the possible rise in wages, and consequently a limit to the possible degree of efficiency of labour. If capital increases, or technical knowledge improves, the direct benefits of this improvement will be increased by an indirect effect through the efficiency of labour. But probably that is all.

Further, when wages are low, a rise in wages may improve efficiency very greatly; but there is in this matter a law of diminishing returns. The difference between a very low level of wages and one slightly higher will inevitably be spent to a very considerable extent on "necessities"—in the sense of things which are necessary to keep a man in a fully fit condition. At first, indeed, while he is becoming accustomed to a new standard of living, much of the increase may be "wasted", spent upon commodities with a merely meretricious attraction, much greater to people who have not been able to try them than to people who have. But if his standard of living has been so low that his physical condition has seriously suffered from privation, the greater part of an increase in wages

---

[1] So long as we are concerned with wages in general throughout a progressive community, there is no need to fear inelastic demand (see below, pp. 132, 246; also Pigou, *Economics of Welfare*, 2nd ed., p. 624).

is likely to be spent (possibly after an experimental period) on those things most needed to restore fitness. A large proportion of a low wage is inevitably spent on things which have an immediately favourable reaction on efficiency.

But as wages rise, this proportion must decline. It is true that, even when a man has as much food as he can eat, he can still spend money in ways that do increase efficiency. But he can also spend it in many ways that do not. It is a good thing that expenditure should increase the pleasure of existence, but pleasure and efficiency do not always go together. After wages have reached a certain level, only a few men will spend any further rise upon things which promote their efficiency as workers. If the wages of a large group of men are increased, there will nearly always be some favourable reaction on efficiency; but the higher the wage, the smaller is that reaction likely to be.

III

The other way in which wage-changes may react upon the productivity of labour is by affecting, not the workman's ability, but his willingness to work. In Marshall's terminology, a man will work up to the point where the marginal utility of the income he derives from his work equals the marginal disutility he incurs in the effort to acquire it. If wages are changed, the marginal utility of income will be changed, and so the amount of work done must be changed also in order to restore equilibrium.

It has sometimes been thought that a change in

wages will always change the willingness to work in an opposite direction; but there is no logical justification for this view.[1] If piece-rates fall, it does not inevitably follow that men will be willing to work harder. They may be inclined to work less hard. But it is possible to distinguish to some extent the cases in which we shall expect to find the one reaction or the other.

The expenditure of income is largely a matter of habit; and since there is a considerable amount of inter-relation among different expenses, the adjustment to a lower standard of living (apart from the direct loss of satisfactions) is not an easy matter to arrange. Some expenses, indeed, like housing accommodation, are arranged for over long periods, and a change often cannot be made here without considerable trouble and expense in the adjustment. The use of leisure time, however, once that time has passed a certain minimum, is much less a matter of habit. If leisure is to be used to advantage, it must yield a good deal of variety. Thus about the use of leisure there are fewer commitments, and if the work done becomes less remunerative, it is easier to sacrifice leisure than to sacrifice income.

But in applying this argument, there are two things which must be noted. First, although it suggests a probability that a fall in piece-rates will be followed immediately by an expansion of output, it is uncertain

---

[1] See Robbins, "Note on the Elasticity of Demand for Income in Terms of Effort" (*Economica*, June, 1930). In this article it is shown (by turning round the individual supply curve of labour so as to exhibit it as a demand curve for income in terms of labour) that the only natural deduction from the law of diminishing marginal utility is, not that the supply curve of labour must slope downwards, but that this demand curve for income must slope downwards. The elasticity of demand for income in terms of labour must be positive; but this means that the elasticity of individual supply of labour must be either positive or lie between 0 and − 1.

if this expansion will be maintained. As time goes on, it becomes more possible to adjust expenditure to the lower standard, and the attractions of increased leisure are doubtless more deeply felt. Secondly, although the argument applies to some extent to people with all sizes of income, it applies most strongly to those with low incomes. Larger incomes are less stereotyped in expenditure; and a considerable part of most large incomes is saved. Savings can usually be reduced without any immediately awkward reactions on the rest of expenditure; and other economies can often be made without any very great sacrifice. Thus although the reduction of a poor man's wages may generally make him willing to work harder (at least for the time being) this is less certain in the case of a rich man. Very remunerative work offers such prizes as to encourage a great expenditure of effort on it (it appeals to the imagination as well as to more commonplace passions); if work becomes less remunerative, it is not inconceivable that such men may become less, and not more, willing to exert themselves to any exceptional extent.

So long as a change in piece-rates affects the supply of labour in the same direction, no new problems arise. The case is precisely the same as that we have already studied when dealing with ability, and this reaction can only intensify the other. If demand is elastic, the change in wages will be accelerated yet further; if inelastic, it will be checked. But if, as seems very possible in the case of manual labour, the supply of labour is changed in the opposite direction, we do have a new situation. A fall in the demand for labour increases the supply, and piece-rates must therefore fall more than they would have to do if we could leave this reaction out of account.[1] But whether total wages will fall more than they would have done if the willingness to work had been unaffected, depends upon the elasticity of demand for labour. If demand is elastic, piece-rates indeed are lower, but income per head is not lower. If demand is inelastic, income per head will be further reduced by the increased output.

✳ Although increased effort will reduce income when demand is inelastic, it does not follow that the increased effort will not be made. For, at the piece-rates in existence at the moment, income will be increased by extra effort; it is only when it has proved impossible to absorb the increased supply of labour without reducing rates, that there is any danger of a reduction.✳

As we have seen, the most important case of falling wages with an elastic demand for labour is that which arises when a trade is being contracted by the force of some new kind of competition. Under these circumstances, the affected workpeople can maintain their weekly wages to some extent by working harder. But, this is not the end of the story. The increased effort, as well as the lower wages, are likely, after a time, to

---

[1] This appears to raise a disquieting possibility. With such a downward sloping supply curve, is stable equilibrium possible at all?

If equilibrium is to be stable, the sum of the elasticities of demand and supply at the point of intersection of the two curves must be positive. Thus, if the elasticity of supply is negative, the elasticity of demand must be greater than the elasticity of supply with its sign changed. All the elasticities of supply with which we are concerned must lie between 0 and −1; so that stability is certain so long as the elasticity of demand is greater than 1. It is only if the demand for labour is inelastic that a difficulty arises, and probably then only in cases of extreme inelasticity.

If time is given for readjustment, there can be no question that the demand for labour in general is generally elastic. There is therefore nothing in the downward slope inconsistent with general equilibrium. The possible instability is not a question of the general equilibrium of the economic system; it is essentially a question of short-period adjustment, when, owing to the lags in the redistribution of labour between trades, and owing to the obstacles to rapid reorganisation of businesses, inelastic demands for labour are certainly possible.

have unfavourable effects upon efficiency. The final level of weekly wages may therefore be rather lower than that which initially resulted from the change.

The most important case of falling wages in which we have good reason to expect that the demand for labour will be fairly inelastic is that which arises from temporary depressions in trade. If, in this case, falling piece-rates are met by increased output, the result will be to depress weekly wages still further. It is quite possible that if this tendency could continue indefinitely, there would be no limit to the extent to which wages could fall. But it must be remembered that a prolonged and sharp fall of this kind will almost certainly drive some workmen out of the trade; and even if this is ruled out, the fall will ultimately be checked (in a sufficiently miserable manner, it is true) by the reaction of the low wages on efficiency.

But of course there is not the slightest reason to suppose that this deplorable drama will be played out on any but very exceptional occasions. The adjustment of piece-rates to changes in the economic situation is itself not particularly rapid; and, although theoretically a similar adjustment should take place with time-rates, it will certainly be even slower. But it is precisely in the very short run (*while* such adjustments are being made) that an extremely inelastic demand is most probable. The depression must last long enough for considerable changes in rates (probably more than one change in rates) to be possible; and yet the longer it lasts, the more likely it is that it will be profitable to make adjustments in the organisation of industry to meet it; and the more adjustments which can be made, the less is the probability of inelastic demand.

Further, it is not at all unlikely that the expansion
of output will be checked by a suspicion on the part
of the workpeople that demand is inelastic—the superstition of the "work fund" may in this instance serve
a useful social purpose.[1] Finally, we have seen how in
times of depression "good" employers are likely to try
to maintain wage-rates; and we now see an additional
advantage which they may gain from doing so (whether
or not it has anything to do with their motives). By
maintaining the efficiency of their workmen, while
competitors are undermining the efficiency of theirs by
lower wages, they make up to some extent for the extra
cost imposed by their higher wages, and put themselves in a good position to reap further advantages
when trade recovers. Then their competitors will be
forced to raise wages again, but increased wages do not
at once lead to increased efficiency, and in the mean-
while the "good" employers are producing under a
definite advantage.[2]

It would be possible to go on for some time working
out special cases in which reactions through the individual's supply-curve of labour complicate wage-
problems. But there seems little to be gained from
doing this, since their practical importance does not
appear to be very great.[3] In the great majority of

---

[1] Both this reaction and the next are only genuinely advantageous if a
recovery can be expected from external causes, without any adjustment of
labour costs being necessary. How far general trade depressions are of this
type is a bitterly argued question, which cannot be examined here. But personally I incline to believe that they are not.

[2] The effects through willingness to work of a rising demand for labour
can be worked out in a similar manner. But it should be remembered in this
connection that, while an inelastic demand may remain inelastic till the
price falls downward to zero, the elasticity must ultimately increase if the
price *rises* far enough.

[3] One such reaction ought perhaps to be mentioned for a personal reason.
Just as past wages may affect the ability to work, and present wages the desire
to work, so it is conceivable that past wages may affect the desire to work,

cases, the magnitude of these reactions is probably small; in those cases where they do matter, they tend usually to intensify those precise effects which we had already detected by simpler lines of reasoning. Sometimes, indeed, they may increase the evil effects of fluctuations to a marked and important extent. Where that occurs, it only points the familiar moral of the need for mobility and adaptability if smooth working of the economic system is to be ensured. But on the whole, these reactions affect the shading, rather than the outline, of our picture. We should need far more accurate quantitative knowledge than we possess, or are very likely to possess, before we could derive much advantage from a more prolonged study of them.

IV

When a man works under supervision, it is still possible for him to vary to some extent the amount of work he does according to his own choice. To that extent the tendencies which have been described in the preceding pages will still operate. But there can be no question that his freedom is much more circumscribed than it would be under a "domestic system." The most important conditions determining changes in the individual's supply of labour are those which are laid down by the employer, or settled deliberately between

---

if any of those past wages are carried over or saved, to act as a reserve in the present period. This particular reaction I hold to be supremely unimportant; but since I was once led to express some views about it in the *Economic Journal* (in order to meet certain arguments of Mr. M. H. Dobb) it may be well to explain what is its place in relation to the present discussion (see *Econ. Jour.*, June, 1930, pp. 227-228).

the employer and workman; of these again the most important is the length of the working day.[1]

⚹A change in wages does not always influence the supply of labour in the same manner; and the same is true of a change in hours. It is indeed true that the immediate effect of an increase in hours must always be to increase the supply of labour, and the immediate effect of a reduction in hours must always be to reduce it. But here again immediate and ultimate effects are not always the same. Even if the hours worked have been excessively long, their reduction will reduce the supply of labour for the moment; but after a while it is reasonable to expect that there will be favourable reactions on the ability to work which will offset the first decline. Increased leisure means increased facilities for rest and recreation; rest and recreation improve physical strength and increase alertness; these in their turn react upon efficiency. In almost every case a reduction in hours will be followed by some favourable deferred action of this kind; and in certain cases the improvement may be great enough to restore in the end the former output, or even cause it to be exceeded. ⚹

⚹If, for the present, we leave out of account these transitional effects of changes in the length of the working day, and fix our eyes only on the supply of labour which will be reached when a given length of day has been in force for some time, we inevitably reach the conception of an "optimum." A man who is accustomed to working six hours will nearly always

1 The classical statement of the theory of "hours" in a free market is to be found in Sir Sydney Chapman's article, "Hours of Labour" (*Econ. Jour.*, September, 1909). His arguments have been restated by Professor Pigou (*Economics of Welfare*, bk. iii., ch. vii.). There is very little that needs to be added to the conclusions of these authorities.

produce a greater daily output than he would do if he were accustomed to working four; but on the other hand it is very likely that he would produce more at an accustomed ten hours than at an accustomed twelve. There will be some length of working day which, if it were maintained, would yield a greater supply of labour than any other, whether less or greater; and this we may describe as the "optimum" length of working day—from the output point of view. ✳

The position of this optimum will, in all probability, vary very greatly in different cases; it will vary with the individual, with the kind of work, with the circumstances of work (with such things as climate, for example). But a group of men working in a factory will have an optimum, just as a single man will have. Some men might turn out more if the hours were longer, some men more if they were shorter; but if the total output is maximised at a given length of day, that length is the optimum.

✳The length of day at which output is maximised will be the length of day for which employers will be prepared to offer the highest wages (assuming, as before, that the effects of any change on the general price system can be neglected). But although this "optimum" working day will yield the highest wages, it does not follow that this output optimum is the true equilibrium length. If the wage offered, although the greatest which could be secured by varying hours, were still very low, then it is hardly doubtful that workmen would look to that wage, and would be moved very little by any other consideration. But if the wage were not very low, then it is at least possible that a large number of people would prefer shorter hours and lower (weekly) wages to longer hours and higher wages, and since the regular and settled output would probably not be very greatly reduced by an appreciable reduction of hours below the output optimum, such terms could usually be found. Employers might find it easier to attract labour by offering shorter hours than by offering higher wages, so that the hours ultimately established might be below the output optimum. Of all the conditions within reach, these might best satisfy the wants both of employers and employed.

Now, although this arrangement would, in the long run, be the most satisfactory to all parties, it does not follow that it would easily be realised in practice. As industry develops, the strain to which workpeople are exposed probably increases; rest and recreation become more necessary; and thus the output optimum length of day probably falls. If output is to be maintained at the maximum possible, hours ought to be reduced. On the other hand, the development of industry brings with it higher wages and a raised standard of living. The desire for leisure and the willingness to sacrifice income for leisure almost certainly increase too; for without leisure the advantages which can be derived from a higher income are very limited. If the equilibrium length of working day is to be found, hours ought to be reduced below the output optimum.

History gives us no ground for supposing that the reduction takes place at all easily. The long hours worked in the early days of the Industrial Revolution are notorious; they were reduced, it is well known, mainly by State regulation and Trade Union action. It was found, after they had been reduced, that "the output of eleven hours' work might be greater than that of twelve".[1] Employers had been working at more than the output optimum, without realising it.

Probably it had never entered the heads of most employers that it was at all conceivable that hours could be shortened and output maintained. But it is clear that there were a few who had realised it.[2] Why did they not reduce hours by their competition, just as enterprising firms force up wages by their competition?

One reason, and perhaps not the least important, lies in the technical considerations which usually make it necessary for a change in hours to apply to a whole establishment at once. It must, therefore, spring from the employer's initiative. As we have seen, this is not the case with a rise in wages. That comes mainly from the initiative of workpeople, and may begin in a small way, with one workman finding an employer who is in great need of labour and from whom he can thus extract higher wages. It need not come into the light of day until it has gone too far to be stopped.

But a man seeking work in this way under such favourable conditions cannot ask for reduced hours. If he did, the employer would be likely to take it as an attempt to dictate how his works should be run, and his estimate of the man's *net* product would undergo a very rapid depreciation.

A reduction in hours must therefore come from the initiative of employers (if it is not imposed from outside). And there is a good reason why they should be rather slow to take it. The immediate effect of reduced hours must be to reduce output and increase costs,

---

[1] Hutchins and Harrison, *Factory Legislation*, p. 122.
[2] Robert Owen, for instance ; *cf. op. cit.*, p. 22.

unless the reduced hours are accompanied by reduced wages, and not only by reduced time-rates, but reduced piece-rates, since fixed costs will, for the present, have to be spread over a smaller output. But a reduction of wages in the period of adjustment has to meet all the objections against temporary wage-reductions which have been discussed in previous chapters. It has also to meet the further objection that the reduced wages will militate against an improvement in efficiency, the very thing to which the employer was looking for a large part of his gain from the reduction in hours. At the best, wage-reductions will lengthen the period of transition; at the worst, they will prevent the improvement in efficiency altogether. An employer who was sufficiently enlightened to undertake the change at all would be very unlikely to want to push the costs of the change on to the shoulders of his employees.

But if he does not reduce wages, he has to bear the cost of the transitional period himself. His losses during this period are a form of investment, from which he hopes to gain later. But they are a very risky investment, since it must always be extremely uncertain whether additional leisure really will improve output in the end, and if so to what extent. It is not surprising that the number of employers who are willing to undertake investments of this kind is limited. They can only be undertaken by those who are possessed of adequate capital (no one could raise a loan for such purposes) and they are at least only likely to be begun by people of a certain kind of temperament. Though doubtless when these have pointed the way, others will slowly follow.

There is, in addition to this, a further difficulty. When the transitional period is over, an employer has no guarantee that those men whose efficiency he has improved will stay with him. The terms he is offering to his employees are better than those offered by his rivals; at least, they are better to a man in ordinary circumstances. But a man's relative valuation of income and leisure may change; and if he is faced with misfortune (for example, an illness in his family) it often does change. Although under normal circumstances he may prefer the shorter hours to a rise in wages, he may not always prefer them. If he is in difficulties the temptation to go elsewhere, to work longer hours, but to offer his improved efficiency as a claim to higher wages than are generally being paid, may be irresistible. The first employer must then replace him with another man, whose efficiency has to be worked up; and instead of reaping his expected profits, he is faced with another period of loss.

In spite of all these difficulties, it must not be assumed that a purely competitive system is powerless to reduce the hours of labour, so as to give the labourer some of the fruits of industrial progress in the form of increased leisure. Even the darkest days of the Industrial Revolution had their Robert Owen; and there can be little doubt that since that time the number of employers who are highly competent and adventurous and at the same time sympathetic to the needs of labour, has been on the increase. They can be relied upon to do something to mitigate excessive hours; and their success must induce others to follow their example. However, the struggle is not an easy one. It does seem probable that there are occasions when interference to reduce hours may secure to large numbers of workmen an increase in leisure at the cost of a fall in wages, which, nevertheless, seems to most of them well worth it; and it is also probable that there are occasions, rarer indeed, but quite real, when no sacrifice in wages has to be called for. But, as we shall have cause to see in greater detail at a future stage of this enquiry, this is certainly not always the case.

Much of what has been said about hours applies in a similar way, but with less force, to other "conditions of labour." In many ways the work of a factory can be varied, and devices introduced, which themselves add to costs, but ultimately react favourably upon the productivity of labour. "Breaks" in working time, washing and recreation facilities, adjustments in work so that it can be done sitting instead of standing, all these things which are now considered to be the special domain of the Industrial Psychologist, react ultimately upon the efficiency of labour, and at the same time make employment in a factory where they are used more attractive. With them again there is usually some gap before they improve efficiency, and the uncertainty of retaining men whose efficiency has been improved by them. So that there will probably be the same delay in their application which is likely with the reduction of hours.

But in one way these changes are easier than a change in hours, for they can be carried out more gradually. Experiments can be made on a smaller scale, and thus the risk involved is less.

Protection against dangerous work, a matter which has bulked so large in Factory Legislation, stands of course on a different footing. Competition is here less effective than is desirable, but for a rather different reason. Until a man has had experience of a certain kind of work, he is unlikely to know that it is dangerous, and then the damage is often done. And even when the danger is known, most people are too inclined to suppose that they can escape dangers which overcome others.

CHAPTER VI

DISTRIBUTION AND ECONOMIC PROGRESS

I

THE subject of this chapter is one of the most venerable of economic problems. The effect of progress upon distribution was a question inevitably raised by the Ricardian theory of rent, and naturally it often engaged the attention of the classical economists. But we do not now need to go back to the classical economists; for we possess today, in the marginal productivity theory, a much superior line of approach to it. The marginal productivity theory is simply an extension of the Ricardian law of rent; and it suggests the problem as infallibly as its predecessor did.

Nevertheless, none of the modern treatments of the problem seem wholly satisfactory. The best account in English is undoubtedly that of Professor Pigou, in the *Economics of Welfare*.[1] Almost everything which is there said seems to be beyond criticism; but it must be remembered that his account does not profess to give a complete examination of the problem. He is simply concerned with one special question—whether anything which is to the advantage of the National Dividend as a whole is likely at the same time to be to the disadvantage of the poorer members of society. He concludes—rightly, it appears— that while it is possible for economic progress sometimes

[1] 2nd ed., bk. iv., chs. ii. and iii.

to make the poor poorer, while it makes the rich richer, this is highly unlikely.

So far as this goes, it is satisfactory; but this is not the only question to which a theory of distribution and progress ought to provide an answer. For example, there is the question of relative shares which was raised by Professor Cannan.[1] Is economic progress likely to raise or lower the proportion of the National Dividend which goes to labour? A complete theory ought to answer this question too.[2]

Before setting out a positive solution, it is necessary to make clear two assumptions on which the following argument rests. For one thing, although we are really dealing with a community in constant change, and comparing two stages of that change, we are obliged to assume that in each case the system is in equilibrium. The use of the marginal productivity method implies this.[3] But although this assumption is a grave weakness, it need not deprive our results of all usefulness. For some purposes, it is the equilibrium position which we want to know about; and for the rest, although we should have to introduce large qualifications if we sought to apply our results to the distribution of the National Dividend in two years quite close together, the error from this source will generally be quite small if we are comparing two fairly long periods separated by a considerable span of time.

The other assumption is more recondite, and at

---

[1] "The Division of Income" in *The Economic Outlook*, p. 215.

[2] Professor Cannan's aversion from the more abstract and rigorous methods of economic analysis probably prevented him from giving a final solution. An attempt at a solution on more abstract lines is, however, to be found in Dalton, *The Inequality of Incomes*, pp. 185-220. If it were possible to accept Dr. Dalton's argument, much of the discussion in this chapter would be unnecessary. But it appears to contain a flaw.

[3] See above, p. 21.

the same time its significance is much more doubtful. We have to ignore the possibility of increasing returns, using that ambiguous expression in the sense of economies of mere size, arising from an increase in the quantity of resources in general at the disposal of the community, independently of any variation in the proportions between the quantities of different kinds of resources available. Clearly the possibility of such economies has an enormous importance in the theory of Production and Economic Progress. It is not impossible that they have a bearing on distribution. This could conceivably be allowed for to some extent, but only at the cost of wrecking completely any simplicity which it has been possible to import into the following arguments. And it could probably be shown that the conclusions would be substantially unaffected.[1]

II

The kinds of "progress" which have to be dealt with in economic theory are four in number:

1. Increase in population.
2. Increase in the ability or willingness to work of a constant population.
3. Increase in capital.
4. Inventions and improvements.

To these there should perhaps be added changes in the tastes of consumers, as a fundamental cause of secular economic change, very similar, as we shall see, to invention, as far as their effects on distribution

[1] See Appendix, section (ii).

are concerned; but they cannot, by any stretch of the imagination, be classified as "progress."

From a purely analytical point of view, 1, 2, and 3 are the same problem. The consequences of a change in the quantity of labourers, of labour, or of capital, can all be treated as special cases of the general question of the effect on distribution of a change in the supply of one factor of production.

The answer to this question can be stated in the form of three rules, of which one is scarcely more than a definition, but is put in for completeness; the second is a generally accepted, but less obvious, proposition; the third appears to be new. Much the most satisfactory way of proving the validity of the second and third rules is to use the mathematical method set out in the Appendix to this book;[1] but an attempt at non-mathematical proof can be made, and will be set out here.

The three propositions are:

1. *An increase in the supply of any factor of production will increase the absolute share (i.e., the real income) accruing to that factor if the elasticity of demand for that factor is greater than unity.*

2. *An increase in the supply of any factor will always increase the absolute share of all other factors taken together.* If the increase in the variable factor is small, then the return to the additional units will approximately equal the addition which they have made to the whole product. But since the marginal product of the variable factor is now reduced, the units previously present will get a smaller return than they got before, so that the old total product will be divided between these units and the other factors in a ratio more

---

[1] See Appendix, sections (iii.) and (iv.)

favourable to the latter. The return to the other factors will therefore be increased.[1]

It is possible, however, that the increased return to the other factors may affect their supply. But in whatever way their supply is affected, whether it increases or diminishes, it is inconceivable that it should diminish to such an extent as to leave the total return to them smaller than it was before. The most extreme case conceivable is that in which the providers of these other factors have a completely inelastic demand for income in terms of the factor they supply; in this case the return to these other factors will of course be unchanged.[2]

Although the absolute share of all other factors taken together cannot diminish, this is not necessarily true of any particular other factor. For example, if the demand for bakers' services is inelastic, but bakers are easily transmuted into confectioners, then an increase in the supply of bakers will probably not increase the real income of confectioners. But we need not trouble ourselves with this difficulty so long as we are talking about groups which are reasonably distinct. In nearly any application which we are likely to want to make, it will be true that an increase in the supply of any factor will increase the real income of any other factor.[3]

---

[1] This is seen at once if we use the rent diagram, continually used by Clark in *The Distribution of Wealth* (*e.g.* on p. 366).

[2] See above, p. 98, note.

[3] Some of the conclusions which follow from this are very far-reaching and illuminating. It is always to the interest of a particular man that other people in the same trade as himself should not work too hard; for if he works with the same intensity as before, and they work harder, his wages will tend to fall. But it is nevertheless to his interest that people in other trades (at any rate in those which do not compete very directly with his own) should work as hard as possible, for by doing so they raise his real wages. Similarly, it is nearly always to his interest that as much as possible of the national

3. *An increase in the supply of any factor will increase its relative share* (i.e., *its proportion of the National Dividend*) *if its "elasticity of substitution" is greater than unity.* This is the new rule, involving a new definition. The "elasticity of substitution" is a measure of the ease with which the varying factor can be substituted for others. If the same quantity of the factor is required to give a unit of the product, in any circumstances whatever, then its elasticity of substitution is zero.[1] If all the factors employed are for practical purposes identical, so that the varying factor can be substituted for any co-operating factor without any trouble at all, then the elasticity of substitution is infinite. The case where the elasticity of substitution is unity can only be defined in words by saying that in this case (initially, before any consequential changes in the supply of other factors takes place) the increase in one factor will raise the marginal product of all other factors taken together in the same proportion as the total product is raised.

The proposition can thus be expressed in another way. In so far as the direction of change in the relative sharing of the National Dividend is concerned, secon-

---

income should be saved. In the short run, particular men may be displaced by an increase in saving; but in the long run, the accumulation of capital is always favourable to the interests of labour.

The following special case is particularly worth noting. Although it may well be to the interest of working men to work for shorter hours as their economic position improves (even if this involves a sacrifice in wages), it is definitely against the interest of the employing and capitalist classes that they should do so. And, looking at the same thing the other way round: if we seek for an economic policy designed to serve the long-run interests of the working class, it ought to be one which discourages the rich from taking out their privileged economic position in consumption and in leisure, but encourages them to work and to save. One cannot help feeling that the obvious change in this respect between the nineteenth and twentieth centuries is a sad comment on the success of progressive policy.

[1] In the terminology of Walras, this is the case where the "coefficient of production" of the varying factor is constant.

dary and consequential changes in the supply of the
other factors *do not matter*. If the conditions of technique and consumers' demand (which determine the
elasticity of substitution) are such that an increase
in the supply of a particular factor would increase its
relative share with constant supplies of the other factors, its relative share will still be increased in whatever way the providers of the other factors react to
the change in their fortunes. It is not too difficult to
show this—at least with some degree of plausibility.
If the elasticity of substitution is greater than unity,
the initial effect of an increase in the supply of one
factor will be to increase that factor's relative share.
But at the same time the real return to the other factors
will be increased, so that the supply of the other factors
is likely to change to some extent, upwards or downwards. If the supply of the other factors falls, the relative supply of the first factor is greater than ever, and
thus its relative share (under the present assumption)
is likely to rise still further. There is thus no danger
of our proposition breaking down in this case. The
dangerous case is the other one, where the supply of
the other factors *increases*. In order to prove that this
does not disturb the rule, it is best to take the most
extreme case. Suppose the elasticity of supply of
the other factors to be infinite, so that their supply
increases, as a result of their now more favourable
position, to such a point that their real return per
unit is unchanged. It cannot increase so far as to lower
their real return per unit, since otherwise the first
situation would not have been one of equilibrium.
If the real return per unit to the other factors (or
their marginal product) is unchanged, this must mean
that the relation between the supplies of the factors

is the same as before; for we are ruling out the possibility of increasing returns to all the factors taken altogether, and diminishing returns to all the factors taken together is obviously impossible. If the proportion between the supplies of the factors is the same as before, and their marginal products the same as before (which evidently follows), the relative shares of the factors in the distribution of the National Dividend must also be the same.

Thus in the most extreme case conceivable, the increase in the supply of the other factors can only just cancel out the effect of the primary change. In any less extreme case, the direction of the change in relative shares must be the same as if there were no secondary effect through the supply of the factors. And this could be proved in a similar fashion for an elasticity of substitution less than unity.

Another important consequence of our third proposition is that the condition for an increase in supply increasing a factor's relative share is symmetrical. If we classify all our factors of production into two groups—whether we label them "work" and "property" with Dr. Dalton, or "labour" and "capital" "supposing that land can be neglected" with Professor Pigou, the elasticity of substitution of labour for capital is the same as the elasticity of substitution of capital for labour. If the conditions of technique and consumers' demand are such that an increase in the supply of capital will increase capital's relative share, then an increase in the supply of labour will increase labour's relative share. And *vice versa*.[1]

---

[1] The startling conclusion put forward by Dr. Dalton (*Inequality of Incomes*, p. 204), that "the relative share of property will increase, as the result of increases in the supply of work and property, or in the amount of either alone", is therefore untenable. Some remarks on the detail of Dr. Dalton's argument will be found below (see Appendix, p. 247).

We may now proceed to examine more closely the things upon which the elasticity of substitution depends. Substitution, in the sense in which we are using it, may take any of three forms:

1. The change in the relative prices of the factors may lead simply to a shift over from the production of things requiring little of the increasing factor to things requiring more. If capital increases, the commodities in whose production capital had already been used to an extent above the average will become cheaper relatively to others, and presumably, therefore, more of them will be made.

2. Methods of production already known, but which did not pay previously, may come into use. This form will include, possibly as its most important case, the mere extension of the use of instruments and methods of production from firms where they were previously employed to firms which could not previously afford them.

3. The changed relative prices will stimulate the search for new methods of production which will use more of the now cheaper factor and less of the expensive one.

Partly, therefore, substitution takes place by a change in the proportions in which productive resources are distributed among existing types of production. But partly it takes place by affording a stimulus to the invention of new types. We cannot really separate, in consequence, our analysis of the effects of changes in the supply of capital and labour from our analysis of the effects of invention. To the theory of invention we must now turn.

III

Under the assumption of competition, it inevitably follows that an invention can only be profitably adopted if its ultimate effect is to increase the National Dividend. For if it is to raise the profits of the entrepreneur who adopts it, it must lower his costs of production—that is to say, it must enable him to get the same product with a smaller amount of resources. On balance, therefore, resources are set free by the invention; and they can be used, either to increase the supply of the commodity in whose production the invention is used (if the demand for it is elastic), or to increase the supply of other commodities (if the demand for the first is inelastic). In either case, the total Dividend must be increased, as soon as the liberated resources can be effectively transferred to new uses.[1]

But although an invention must increase the total Dividend, it is unlikely at the same time to increase the marginal products of all factors of production in the same ratio. In most cases, it will select particular factors and increase the demand for those factors to a special extent. If we concentrate on two groups of factors, "labour" and "capital," and suppose them to exhaust the list, then we can classify inventions according as their initial effects are to increase, leave unchanged, or diminish the ratio of the marginal product of capital to that of labour. We may call these inventions "labour-saving," "neutral," and "capital-saving" respectively. "Labour-saving" inventions increase the

---

[1] For a fuller elaboration of this argument, see Wicksell, *Vorlesungen,* vol. i., pp. 195-207. Also Kaldor, "A Case against Technical Progress?" (*Economica,* May, 1932).

marginal product of capital more than they increase the marginal product of labour; "capital-saving" inventions increase the marginal product of labour more than that of capital; "neutral" inventions increase both in the same proportion.

A labour-saving invention, according to this definition, need not actually diminish the marginal product of labour, and consequently labour's absolute share in the Dividend. It may do so, if it is very labour-saving; there is nothing to prevent the ratio of marginal products being changed to such an extent as to make the absolute size of one lower than it was before. But equally it may not. In every case, however, a labour-saving invention will diminish the relative share of labour. Exactly the same holds, *mutatis mutandis*, of a capital-saving invention.

It may be observed that the definition of a labour-saving invention just given is not identical with that given by Professor Pigou.[1] He supposes the technical change to take place in an industry which produces no wage-goods—*i.e.* none of whose products are bought by labourers. (This is, of course, a very unreal assumption if we interpret labour in the very wide sense which it has to be given in this discussion. The Attorney-General is a labourer.) However, taking this special case, he defines a labour-saving invention as one which diminishes the ratio of capital to labour employed in the rest of industry. Now if the ratio of capital to labour in the rest of industry is diminished, the marginal product of labour in terms of the products of the rest of industry (which is all that matters to labour) must be diminished. An extension of Professor Pigou's definition—and it cries out to be extended—would thus

[1] *Op. cit.*, p. 632.

make a labour-saving invention one which diminished the *absolute* marginal product of labour. Professor Pigou's case then becomes a useful illustration of this definition, but it is too limited to serve as a definition itself.

But even the extended Pigou definition appears on reflection rather unsatisfactory for our purposes. For if we were to call "labour-saving" inventions those which diminished the absolute marginal product of labour, and "capital-saving" inventions those which diminished the marginal product of capital, there would be a wide range of neutral inventions between—quite possibly including the great bulk of those inventions in which we are actually interested. But some of these "neutral" inventions would be more favourable to capital than labour and some the contrary. They would all increase both marginal products, but some would increase that of capital more than that of labour, and some the reverse. If we have any interest in relative shares, we do not want to leave this distinction in the dark. Thus it seems best to make the definition hinge upon relative shares; but it must of course be realised that any invention which is *very* labour-saving may diminish the absolute marginal product of labour; and similarly for capital.

Although this amendment of Professor Pigou's definition appears desirable, the definitions are still fairly close, and most of the things which he says about inventions can be perfectly well applied with the definition just given. In particular, there is no reason to question his view that inventions have a decided bias in the labour-saving direction. It is indeed difficult to find clear cases of important capital-saving inventions—wireless is, of course, the standard case, but beyond that, although there can be little doubt that capital-saving inventions occur, they are not easily identified. Obvious labour-saving inventions, on the other hand, are frequent. Not all those inventions popularly called labour-saving are labour-saving in the strict sense, but there can be little doubt that the great majority are.

This predominance of labour-saving inventions strikes one as curious. It may conceivably be the case that it is a mere "optical illusion"; labour-saving inventions cause more social friction than others, and so force themselves on the attention of the observer. There is probably some truth in this, but it hardly seems a sufficient explanation. It is also possible that the utilisation of fixed capital has a close relation to the particular kind of scientific knowledge which has been available for industry during the last two centuries: that it is to be connected with the special growth of mechanical and physical science. But this again does not seem very probable. For after all, wireless is the result of physics; and there seems no reason in the nature of physical enquiry why the growing complexity of industrial technique should not have been kept in check through the constant supersession of complex methods by simpler methods requiring less capital.

The real reason for the predominance of labour-saving inventions is surely that which was hinted at in our discussion of substitution. A change in the relative prices of the factors of production is itself a spur to invention, and to invention of a particular kind—directed to economising the use of a factor which has become relatively expensive. The general tendency to a more rapid increase of capital than labour which has marked European history during the last few centuries has naturally provided a stimulus to labour-saving invention.

If, therefore, we are properly to appreciate the place of invention in economic progress, we need to distinguish two sorts of inventions. We must put on one side those inventions which are the result of a change in the relative prices of the factors; let us call these "induced" inventions. The rest we may call "autonomous" inventions. We shall expect, in practice, all or nearly all induced inventions to be labour-saving; but there is no reason why autonomous inventions should be predominantly labour-saving. There is no obvious reason why autonomous inventions should incline, on balance, to one side more than to the other. In the absence of special knowledge we may reasonably assume a random dispersion. Then, since induced inventions are mainly labour-saving, both kinds taken together will give us a predominance of labour-saving inventions—precisely what we appear to find in practice. There is nothing therefore in observed fact inconsistent with the hypothesis that autonomous inventions are evenly distributed. But of course, this even distribution will, at the most, be a long-run affair; it is quite conceivable that scientific discovery may tend to produce inventions with a bias in one direction over quite long periods.

In order to complete this classification, one further distinction must be drawn—within the field of induced inventions. An induced invention is made as the result of a change in relative prices; but it may be such that its adoption depends upon the change in prices, or it may not. Capital increases, let us say, and in consequence a labour-saving invention is made and

K

adopted. But either this invention would have paid before capital increased—and would therefore have been adopted if it had been known—or not. If it would not have paid under the old circumstances, then it is simply a cause increasing the facility of adjustment to a change in circumstances—*i.e.* increasing the elasticity of substitution. The elasticity of substitution is greater than it would have been in the absence of such an invention; consequently the possibility of capital increasing its relative share in the Dividend is greater. But so long as the invention is of this type the second rule about absolute shares still holds; it is quite certain that as a result of the whole change the absolute share of labour will be increased.

But it is certainly quite conceivable that a change in relative prices will stimulate invention to do more than this—to discover methods which, if they had been known, would have paid even before prices changed. Now induced inventions of this type (if they are labour-saving, as we may suppose generally to be the case) may reduce not only the relative share of labour, but also its absolute share. Such inventions as these are perhaps not very common, but there is little reason to doubt their occurrence; they are the only kind which are really dangerous to the real income of labour.

The classification of invention just made is a purely economic classification; there is no reason to suppose that it corresponds to any kind of scientific or technical division. At times when scientific and technical activity is great it will probably manifest itself in a large crop both of autonomous and induced inventions. In the dark ages of science, both autonomous and induced inventions will be rare. Further, although the kind of induced inventions just referred to (those which are induced by a change in prices, but do more than adjust technical methods to the new economic conditions) may occur at any stage of development, they are perhaps most likely to be important when the accumulation of capital has been proceeding for a long while, but many kinds of production have retained conservative methods, and have not benefited by technical progress.

IV

The significance of this theoretical analysis can perhaps best be illustrated if we examine its working in two extreme cases. In both we shall assume population constant and capital increasing; but in one technical progress is very lethargic, in the other very rapid.

In the first case, where inventions of all kinds are almost wholly absent, substitution is practically confined to the first two lines mentioned above—the increased use of those commodities requiring much capital, and the more extensive use of known capitalistic methods. It is conceivable that in an early stage these may be sufficient to keep the elasticity of substitution greater than unity. In that case, the relative share of capital will increase, even though the absolute share of labour increases simultaneously. But as capital continues to grow, it is certain that the more advantageous applications will be used up; the elasticity of substitution must fall, and ultimately the relative share of capital must fall and that of labour rise. It is impossible to say how soon this stage will set in, but it must set in sooner or later. But of course this process involves a fall in the marginal product of capital and therefore of the rate of interest. Eventually the fall in interest will check saving, and the community whose technique does not progress will approach the "stationary state" of the classical economists.

In the other case, where invention is very active, the elasticity of substitution will be high and will remain high. Thus the relative share of capital will tend to increase, and that of labour to fall. But not only will induced inventions be active, autonomous inventions will be active too. If we are right in assuming that autonomous inventions have no particular tendency to stimulate a special demand for either factor, then the initial effect of autonomous inventions will be to increase the marginal products of both labour and capital in much the same proportions, and so leave the relative distribution of the Dividend unchanged. However, since an enlarged absolute return is more likely to stimulate an increase in the supply of capital than an increase in the supply of labour, autonomous inventions may have a secondary effect in encouraging the accumulation of capital. But under the supposed conditions, an increase in the supply of capital will increase capital's relative share, and thus activity in autonomous inventions will, indirectly, have a similar effect to activity in induced invention.

But although for both these reasons the relative share of labour will diminish, neither a great activity in autonomous invention, nor a high elasticity of substitution, has any tendency to reduce the real income of labour. The only kind of invention which is likely to have this effect is that which has already been mentioned—that which is inspired by a change in relative prices, but which would have been profitable to apply even before prices changed.

Some inventions of this kind doubtless occur fairly frequently, but if they are—as is probably usual— merely a small part of general inventive activity, then it is most unlikely that their influence will be dominant. For if they tend to reduce labour's marginal product, there are simultaneously at work other forces, derived from the increase of capital and the expansion of autonomous invention, tending to increase the marginal product of labour. There can be no doubt that these latter forces are usually far more powerful.

It may be suggested, very tentatively, that a fall in the general level of real wages is really likely to occur as the result of invention only on those rare occasions when invention breaks into a new and extensive field of industry that has long been conservative in its methods. Such "economic revolutions" always cause maladjustment, and social unrest arising from the maladjustment; but it may be useful to point out that in such times the malaise may go deeper. A fall in the equilibrium level of real wages is here a real possibility.

But it is difficult to feel that this danger is a very pressing one today. The generalised character of technical change is a considerable safeguard against it. Inventive activity usually makes itself felt quickly enough, so that a prolonged failure to adjust technical methods to new circumstances is unlikely on a large scale. Our continuous "industrial revolution" protects us from the discontinuous revolutions of the past.

Thus, so far as the absolute share of labour is concerned, a rather different line of enquiry does not lead us to modify in any way the optimism of Professor

Pigou. It is possible, but extremely improbable, that economic progress may cause a decline in the equilibrium level of real wages. And further, it should be remembered, even if this unlikely event should materialise, it would be temporary; enlarged profits would mean new saving; increased capital would raise the level of real wages again.

But it is difficult to feel the same degree of optimism in the matter of relative shares. For the chance of an elasticity of substitution greater than unity stands in an altogether different order of probability. Increasing capital, accompanied by stagnant invention, may very well raise labour's relative share in the Dividend; but increasing capital, with active invention, is very likely to do the contrary. And since the activity of invention is definitely favourable to the growth of the Dividend—and with few exceptions also favourable to growth in the real income of labour— it is highly probable that periods of most rapidly rising real wages will also be periods of a falling relative share to labour. It is clear that we have here a divergence of no small significance.

V

The application of these conclusions to historical fact is no easy matter; and what follows must be largely guess-work. But it seems worth while to state the most probable interpretation, if only to serve as a basis for future discussion. According to Professor Bowley,[1] the share of property in the National Income of Britain just before the war was about one-third;

[1] *The Change in the Distribution of the National Income*, 1880-1913, p. 25.

and it would seem to follow from this one ascertained
fact that there must have been periods in English
history when the elasticity of substitution between
labour and property was greater than unity. For it
is practically inconceivable that a few centuries ago
the share of property can have been anywhere near
this figure.[1] In the Middle Ages, capital was scarce;
but not only was the supply small, the demand was
undoubtedly small too, so that it cannot have made
up to any appreciable extent for its lack of quantity
by a high rate of remuneration. Nor is it possible that
the smaller share of capital can have been made up
by a larger share of land; for (if we exclude predatory
and monopolistic gains, as we are entitled to do, for
all the large part which they played in a pre-capitalist
economy) we cannot escape the evident fact that land
was far more plentiful relatively to the population than
it is today. Thus it seems clear that the equilibrium
relative share of property must have been much smaller
than it was in 1913; at some stage it must have risen
considerably.

On the other hand, it seems clear from Professor
Bowley's figures that it was not rising in the period
immediately before the war. He gives $37\frac{1}{2}$ per cent. as
the proportion of the National Income going to
property both in 1913 and in 1880, though these
percentages require some correction for our purposes.
Clearly income from property held abroad ought not
to be included; but when it is omitted, the results
are even more striking. For the proportion of home-
produced income going to property in 1880 was about
34 per cent.; in 1913 it was only about 31 per cent.

[1] See Cannan, "The Changed Outlook in Regard to Population" (*Econ.
Jour.*, December, 1931, p. 528).

On the whole this period seems to be long enough for us to be able to neglect disturbances arising from the fact that it is really unjustifiable to regard the situation of the economic system at these dates as being one of equilibrium—although it would be much more satisfactory if we had figures for an average of several years round about each date instead of figures for a single year. If we accept these figures, then it is clear that the elasticity of substitution must at this time have been rather less than unity. Not necessarily very much less; quite a small difference would be sufficient to give the observed result.

These facts, if they are correct, do not upset our theoretical conclusions; but the theory does suggest a clear interpretation of them. If capital is increasing more rapidly than the supply of labour (and it may be fairly supposed that this has generally been the case in modern English history[1]), a tendency towards a diminished elasticity of substitution will generally set in as capital grows. This diminution may be counteracted by invention—it is conceivable that it might be counteracted indefinitely—but clearly invention has a progressively harder task as the process goes on. Invention has generally been increasing in activity, but it is quite possible that this increase has failed to set off the fall due to the first cause. But because it failed to do so in the period under consideration, because in this period it is probable that the elasticity of substitution tended to fall, we should not be over-confident that in the future it may not rise again. And in many ways it would be good for us if it did

[1] This is indeed less certain than usual for the years which immediately preceded the War, in view of the extraordinary export of capital in that period, and its natural consequence, a great retardation in the rate of increase of real wages. (*Cf.* Taussig, *International Trade*, ch. 21.)

so; for it would probably be a mark of national prosperity.

Changes in the distribution of the Dividend since 1914 are harder to interpret; and it seems most unlikely that we can hope to do so if we leave out of account the regulation of wages.

VI

The theoretical conclusions of this chapter have considerable interest in relation to the question of the causes governing inequality of incomes; but there are other implications of hardly less importance. These are in connection with the theory of money wages. If we assume a monetary policy designed to stabilise the price-level of consumers' goods, and successful in that end, then, of course, no theory of money wages is necessary, for money wages and real wages are always directly proportionate. Recent investigations, however, have thrown doubt upon the feasibility of such a policy in a community where the fundamental determinants of economic wealth are in process of change; they suggest rather, that the price-level ought to fall with rising productivity, and rise with falling productivity; if it does not do so, there will be in the one case a boom in trade, leading to dangerous over-expansion, in the other case there will be monetary causes making for a depression.[1] Examination of this contention would be out of place here; but if we accept it provisionally, we can draw from it some consequences which do seem to belong to the theory of wages.

[1] See Haberler, *Der Sinn der Indexzahlen*, p. 112 *ff.* Hayek, *Prices and Production*, p. 23. Also Robertson in *The International Gold Problem*, pp. 21-24 and 45.

If stabilisation of the price-level is ruled out, as being in normal times more or less inflationary, our thoughts naturally turn to other less ambitious forms of stabilisation. One of these is stabilisation of the "money earnings of the factors of production" or of the money value of the Social Dividend. If we assume a monetary policy of this character, the conclusions about relative shares reached in this chapter begin to have some practical significance. If population is increasing, then it is true that this monetary policy must lead to a fall in the level of money wages— under all circumstances; while the level of money wages would rise with diminishing population. But if population is constant and capital increasing, then the trend of money wages depends upon the elasticity of substitution. If the elasticity of substitution is less than unity, the average level of money wages will rise; but in the contrary case it will fall. And as we have seen, it is this latter case which is likely to be associated with the most rapid rise in general economic prosperity, in the level of real wages.

Even if the elasticity of substitution is less than unity, it is unlikely, in any community that can genuinely be called progressive, to be much less than unity. If this is the case, it cannot be expected that the average level of money wages would rise much. But this would mean, in a world where men are specialised to particular trades, and do not move easily, that frequent cases of reductions of money wages in particular trades would be unavoidable. And it is useless to minimise the gravity of this conclusion.

For the raising of real wages through falling money wages with prices of consumption goods falling more rapidly could not be a smooth and painless process.

The reductions in wages would almost inevitably take place at intervals, which would not correspond exactly in time with equivalent falls in prices. There would thus certainly be temporary reductions in real wages; the trend of real wages might be upward, but there would be sharp fluctuations about the trend. It would thus not be in the least surprising if the reductions in money wages were strongly resisted. We shall see at a later stage what would be the probable effects of this.

There is no doubt that these unpleasant results could be avoided, initially at any rate, by a more elastic monetary policy. But whether this would be a real cure, or whether it would only put off the evil day, is one of the major unsettled questions of economics. It is possible that there is some third alternative, intermediate between stabilisation of prices and stabilisation of the social income, which would avoid intense fluctuations of industry and also avoid a downward pressure on money wages. But it seems improbable that in a period of increasing productivity, all, or nearly all, money wages could be exempted from such pressure.[1] Further consideration of this problem lies outside the scope of this book.

[1] *Cf.* Robertson, *op. cit.*, p. 24.

CHAPTER VII

THE THEORY OF INDUSTRIAL DISPUTES

I

IT IS now time for us to take a further step towards actuality. The equilibrium labour market, which we studied in the first chapters of this book, could never exist; it is merely a convenient abstraction, by which we can isolate for thorough examination some, but only some, of the fundamental factors at work. The free labour market, which we studied in Chapters III.-V., is, on the other hand, a real possibility; markets very similar in their working to this have existed and do exist. Yet it is hardly possible for a market to exist, as we have been supposing, in a condition of violent change, without competition being displaced to some extent by combination. The combination may be abortive, in which case the account already given is reasonably complete, apart from some rearrangement of motives; but if it is not abortive (and in advanced communities it is unusual for it to be so altogether) we have yet some significant strokes to add to our picture.

We have already seen how, in a regular trade, perfect plasticity of wages (immediate response of wages to a change in the value productivity of labour) is hindered, among other things, by employers' perception that a reduction in wage-rates is likely to impair efficiency by worsening their relations with their men. Even if we suppose (as it was convenient to do throughout that earlier discussion) that combination among the men is ruled out—because, let us say, no one has thought of it—there would still be present this consideration tending to slow down wage reductions. But in practice, of course, even in a market where labour is still unorganised, the principal check of this sort on the action of employers is generally their fear that reductions will stimulate combined resistance.

About the origin of such combination it is unnecessary to say much; where it is possible for men to snatch gains, real or apparent, permanent or temporary, from the abandonment of separate individual action, it would be surprising if they did not sometimes attempt it. Monopolistic combination is common enough in all parts of the economic system; very much the same motives which drive business men to form rings and cartels drive their employees to form unions. The one, as much as the other, is a natural product of a gregarious animal.

It will perhaps have been observed, in our analysis of a changing competitive market, that more than one situation came to our notice when a stimulus to combination must in real life have been present. When a man takes on a job in a regular trade, he generally begins to form habits of life and expenditure which are really based on the half-conscious assumprion that he will continue in that same employment more or less indefinitely. He has no legal guarantee that this will be the case; but it is not in the least surprising that he feels himself, with the flow of time, to have acquired a customary right to continue in that employment on much the same terms. If, after a time, his employer desires to reduce his wages, he feels, not only that his interests have been damaged, which is certainly true, but also that he has been cheated of a legitimate expectation. If a considerable group of men find themselves with the same grievance, it is not surprising that they should seize any weapon which lies to their hand to enforce what seem to be their rights. And a weapon does lie ready. The same thing is likely to happen if, instead of reducing wages, an employer merely refuses a demand for an advance made on the ground of fairness—because wages in similar firms, or associated trades, are rising. We have seen that the competitive system naturally gives rise to the belief that a rise in wages in one firm ought to be followed by rises in similar firms: this is the mechanism whereby advances are transmitted from firm to firm. But although the competitive system engenders this belief, and uses it, it cannot always fulfil the promise held out.   There are always firms which have not shared the prosperity of the rest, and which will refuse demands made upon them. But the grievance arising from such a refusal seems positively to ask for united pressure; and since united pressure will not infrequently attain the end which is outside the power of separate action, it is extremely likely to be employed.

Any attempt at wage-reductions, and any uneven rise in wages, is therefore likely to stimulate organised resistance; and since it is only in an extremely static economy that such things are not likely to be frequent, static conditions are probably a necessary pre-requisite of a perfectly free labour market. But though change itself is sufficient to supply a stimulus to organisation, it is a long way from this to the successful formation of Trade Unions. For that other conditions are re-quired: a legal system not too unfavourable to the growth of voluntary corporations, and a supply of organising ability competent to overcome the very considerable administrative difficulties inherent in the establishment of associations with any degree of stability.

The absence of these latter conditions is enough to explain the long series of failures which marks the early history of British Trade Unions; while the final elaboration of a technique of Union government explains the spread of Unionism at home and abroad in the later years of the nineteenth century. Over the whole world, Trade Unionism has generally followed upon the tracks of capitalist industry and the distur-bance of ancient habits which accompanied indus-trialism; but where, as in America, more attractive opportunities long remained open to the men who would have been the Union organisers, the develop-ment of Unionism has been somewhat held back.

When once a Union has been formed, a repetition of the original stimuli will not necessarily be needed to spur it to action. It is likely to resist wage-reductions, certainly, and to demand increases in line with those granted elsewhere; probably these will be the objects for which members' enthusiasm will be most easily roused. But when once it has been discovered that a prosperous firm can generally be induced to grant advances without great difficulty, the mere sign of prosperity may prompt claims; under Socialist in-fluence a Union may take action without even this excuse. Trade Unionism has been found a convenient weapon whereby militant Socialists can threaten the overthrow of Capitalism; and it is consistent with revolutionary principles to demand advances even when it is obvious that the advances cannot be given without the collapse of the firms in question—for the collapse of the firms (in their existing form) is in fact the end in view. But such extreme doctrines have rarely dominated any powerful Unions for long, since the ordinary man is naturally reluctant to stake his livelihood upon so dangerous a gamble; to protect the customary standard of life (which may be conceived as a money wage or, in times of monetary disturbance, a real wage), to maintain fair wages, and to secure to the workers a share in exceptional profits, are the usual aims of the wage policy of Trade Unions.

II

The weapon by which Trade Unions endeavour to secure more favourable terms for their members than competition would give is the strike: the concerted withdrawal of considerable bodies of men from employment.[1] Even in the absence of combination an employer who offers less favourable terms than others must expect to find difficulties in retaining labour; but when his men combine, he is faced by a more immediate danger, the withdrawal of most or all of his employees, not into other jobs, but into voluntary unemployment, with the object of forcing him to re-employ them at the terms they dictate.

When a Trade Union demands an advance in wages,

---

[1] I shall use "strike" to mean "stoppage of work arising out of an industrial dispute", whoever "began it". The distinction between strike and lock-out is useless for our purposes.

or resists a reduction, it sets before the employer an
alternative: either he must pay higher wages than he
would have paid on his own initiative (and this generally means a prolonged reduction in profits) or on the
other hand he must endure the direct loss which will
probably follow from a stoppage of work. In either
case he is less well off than he would have been if his
men had not combined, but one alternative will generally bring him less loss than the other. If resistance
appears less costly than concession, he will resist; if
concession seems cheaper, he will meet the Union's
claims.

We can learn a great deal about TradeUnion action,
its possibilities, and its limits, by examining the circumstances which are likely to make an employer
incline towards one alternative rather than the other.
First of all, it is obvious that the higher is the wage
demanded, the greater will be the cost of concession;
and therefore the more likely he is to resist. On the
other hand, the longer he expects the threatened strike
to last, the more likely he is to give way. Now, for the
present, let us leave out of account all the other things
on which his choice will in fact depend; let us assume
"other things equal" and concentrate upon these two.
We can then construct a schedule of wages and lengths
of strike, setting opposite to each period of stoppage
the highest wage an employer will be willing to pay
rather than endure a stoppage of that period. At this
wage, the expected cost of the stoppage and the expected cost of concession (accumulated at the current
rate of interest) just balance. At any lower wage, the
employer would prefer to give in; at any higher
wage, he would prefer that a stoppage should take
place.

L

This we may call an "employer's concession schedule"; we can express it graphically by an "employer's concession curve". It will leave the y-axis at the point Z, where OZ is the wage which the employer would have paid if unconstrained by Trade Union pressure. (It may be the same or different from the wage which he had been paying when the dispute arose.) The curve cannot rise higher than some fixed level, since evidently there is some wage beyond which no Trade Union can compel an employer to go. If wages are to swallow profits completely, he will prefer to close down his works and leave the industry.

Now just as the expected period of stoppage will govern the wage an employer is prepared to pay to avoid a strike, so the wage offered will govern the length of time the men are prepared to stand out. They, in their turn, are making a choice between present and future evils—present unemployment and future low wages—and thus the length of time they are prepared to stand out will vary according to the prospect of gain from doing so. Since the sacrifice involved in accepting a wage of 60s. a week instead of 65s. is greater than the sacrifice of accepting 65s. instead of 70s., an extra period of stoppage which might not be borne for the sake of the second may be borne for the first. In order that their wages should not be reduced below 65s., they are likely to put up with greater temporary privations than they would endure to stop the wage going below 70s. So in their case, too, we can draw up a schedule, a "resistance schedule", giving the length of time they would be willing to stand out rather than allow their remuneration to fall below the corresponding wage. This again can be translated into a "resistance curve".

At its lower end, the resistance curve must cut ZZ′
at some finite distance along it, for there must be some
maximum time beyond which the Union cannot last
out whatever be the terms offered. At its upper end, it
will usually cut the *y*-axis, because, as we shall see,
there is usually, though not always, some wage beyond
which the Union will not desire to go, however easily,

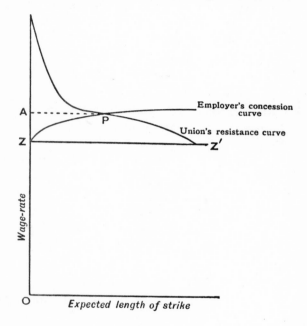

Employer's concession
curve

Union's resistance curve

A

P

Z   Z′

Wage-rate

O   *Expected length of strike*

in terms of striking time, it can be secured. Very often,
the resistance curve will be nearly horizontal over a
considerable part of its length, since there is some level
of wages to which in particular the men consider themselves entitled. In order to secure this level they will
stand out for a long while, but they will not be much
concerned to raise wages above it.

The employer's concession curve and the Union's

resistance curve will cut at a point P, and the wage OA corresponding to this point is the highest wage which skilful negotiation can extract from the employer. If the Union representatives demand a wage higher than this, the employer will refuse it, because he concludes that a strike, undertaken to obtain so high a wage as this, will not last long enough to make it worth while for him to give way. A strike is the lesser evil. If the Union demands a wage less than OA, the demand will be conceded without much difficulty, but the negotiators will have done badly for their clients. Naturally, Union spokesmen, more or less in the dark about how much the employer will concede, prefer to begin by setting their claims high, and only moderating them when they see that the first proposals have no chance of succeeding.

If the highest wage is to be secured, this is the inevitable method of negotiating, but it is easy to see that it is a dangerous method. The Union leaders are bound to set their initial claims high, in order to avoid the criticism of their supporters. In order to give their more ambitious proposals a chance, they have to pretend to be unwilling to make concessions, but at the same time they have to be prepared to retreat to a more defensible line as soon as it is clearly impossible to maintain the first. If they are not sufficiently obstinate in maintaining their first proposals, they may lose an opportunity of inducing the employer to accept them. If they do not moderate their demands in time, they may be forced to carry out their threat of striking, when more favourable terms could have been got without the sacrifice entailed by the strike.

For there is a general presumption that it will be possible to get more favourable terms by negotiating than by striking. The reason why an employer is prepared to pay higher wages than he would otherwise have done, as a result of Trade Union pressure, is that it pays him to offer a certain amount of "Danegeld" to buy off the loss which would follow from the strike. Once a strike has begun, all he can buy off is the remainder of the strike; the loss incurred as a result of the stoppage which has already taken place is a "bygone"—nothing can now be done about it. It is the further resistance of the Union which he has to dread; but once a strike has lasted (say) two weeks, the power of the Union to last a further five weeks is less than its power to last out five weeks at the beginning of the stoppage. Since it is only the further length of the probable stoppage which matters, we may say that, as the strike proceeds, the Union's resistance curve moves to the left, and the highest wage that can be obtained by negotiation consequently falls.

This is indeed subject to the condition that "other things remain equal." It is possible that while the strike is taking place, the prospects of trade may alter, and in consequence the employer's concession curve may be shifted. It is possible that the employer, or perhaps both negotiating parties, have anticipated the staying-power of the Union altogether wrongly. If the prospects of trade grow suddenly brighter, or the Union proves to possess undisclosed resources which make its power of resistance greater than had been expected, then it may indeed do better by striking than it could have done by negotiating. But even in this case it would be well to come to a settlement as soon as the more favourable factors appear on the horizon. To fight out to the bitter end can only mean going back upon the employer's terms.

And clearly it is most unwise to count on such favourable factors appearing subsequently. New unfavourable factors are just as likely to appear as new favourable factors, so that the odds are heavily in favour of negotiation being a more hopeful policy than striking. Although, by luck, it may sometimes happen that a better settlement (from the Union's point of view) is secured by striking than could have been secured without a strike, the general presumption is that a strike is a sign of failure on the part of the Union officials.

To this, indeed, there are some exceptions. Weapons grow rusty if unused, and a Union which never strikes may lose the ability to organise a formidable strike, so that its threats become less effective. The most able Trade Union leadership will embark on strikes occasionally, not so much to secure greater gains upon that occasion (which are not very likely to result) but in order to keep their weapon burnished for future use, and to keep employers thoroughly conscious of the Union's power.

Under a system of collective bargaining, some strikes are more or less inevitable for this reason; but nevertheless the majority of actual strikes are doubtless the result of faulty negotiation. If there is a considerable divergence of opinion between the employer and the Union representatives about the length of time the men will hold out rather than accept a given set of terms, then the Union may refuse to go below a certain level, because its leaders believe that they can induce the employer to consent to it by refusing to take anything less; while the employer may refuse to concede it, because he does not believe the Union can hold out long enough for concession to be worth his while.

Under such circumstances, a deadlock is inevitable, and a strike will ensue; but it arises from the divergence of estimates, and from no other cause. Any means which enables either side to appreciate better the position of the other will make settlement easier; adequate knowledge will always make a settlement possible. The danger lies in ignorance by one side of the other's dispositions, and in hasty breaking-off of negotiations.

This analysis suggests, what has in fact been the general practical experience of collective bargaining in England, that the best way of reducing the probability of strikes is the institution of joint meetings of employers and Union leaders, using sufficient formality to prevent hasty ruptures of negotiations, and meeting frequently enough for each side to gain some understanding of the circumstances of the other. It suggests Conciliation Boards and Joint Councils.

Yet conciliation, however intelligently operated, cannot prevent strikes altogether. There will still be some strikes necessary to keep the Union "in training", and further and more important, there remains the possibility of a difference of opinion between the Union leaders and their rank and file. The leaders may be convinced that they have got the best that could be got by any method, but they may fail to convince their supporters. Probably conciliation actually increases this evil; the closer the contact between Union officials and employers, the more the officials become negotiators instead of agitators, the easier it is to persuade the ordinary member that his interests are being neglected. The proportion of strikes into which officials are forced against their will is certainly very high.[1]

Conciliation generally works best when the board possesses an independent chairman, who can interpret the demands of one side to the other, smooth over misunderstandings, and make suggestions. His function is simply to facilitate the working of the board, and to prevent unnecessary disagreements. It is altogether different from the function of an arbitrator—although in actual usage the terms conciliation and arbitration have become hopelessly confused. The application of arbitration to industrial disputes is different, and of much more doubtful efficacy. It is indeed probable that cases arise in which excessive confidence on the part of the Union, or irritation on the part of the employers (leading them to under-estimate the cost to them of a strike) may offer an opportunity for independent valuation of the strength of the rival parties, so that an arbitrator could put forward proposals which would have a good chance of acceptance. Even when direct negotiations have reached a deadlock, it is nevertheless possible in almost every case for an arbitrator to put forward terms which it would be to the advantage of each side to accept; the Union because it is most unlikely to get better terms by striking, the employers because acceptance would be less costly than a strike would be. It may not be easy to find such terms, and still less to persuade the disputants that acceptance will really be advantageous; neverthe-

---

[1] This possible failure of leaders to carry their followers with them is of course the foundation of Marshall's claim that "strong Unions facilitate business" (*Economics of Industry*, 1907, p. 385). The more control over their followers the leaders possess—and formal organisation with the accumulation of funds gives a considerable amount of control automatically—the easier is it for employers to come to binding agreements with the Unions, and the less is the probability of strikes.

less the authority of a respected arbitrator may well induce a frame of mind disposed to concession. If the arbitrator has succeeded in inducing a belief in his genuine impartiality, it may be psychologically easier to yield to him than to the other party.

It makes very little difference to this argument whether the parties have pledged themselves to accept an arbitrator's decision before he gives it, or not; in either case a wise arbitrator will proceed upon the same lines. In either case he ought to seek for a settlement which it will be to the advantage of each side to accept; for even if a previous pledge makes it possible to enforce a decision "against" one party, to do so will certainly have the effect of disgusting that party with arbitration. The present dispute is only settled at the expense of making settlement more difficult in the future by ruling out one possible method of solution.

Many arbitrators do indeed proceed on these lines; but the general usefulness of arbitration as a method is diminished by the fact that an alternative line of approach presents fatal attractions. It is difficult to get out of the minds of arbitrators the notion that their function is in some way judicial—and this in its turn induces a legalistic approach, which has remarkable consequences in the field of industrial relations.[1] For lawyers think in terms of rights, and so do Trade Unionists. A legally-minded arbitrator cannot fail to be impressed by Trade Union claims, couched in terms of rights, to a customary standard, or to fair wages.

---

[1] Sir Rupert Kettle, one of the early English enthusiasts for arbitration, imagined that he had found the laws for which he was looking in the laws of economics. When acting as chairman of a conciliation board, he used to refer "from time to time to any well-settled economic laws bearing directly on the question" (see my article, "The Early History of Industrial Conciliation," *Economica*, March, 1930). Kettle's notions about the difference between conciliation and arbitration were very vague.

Unless he is uncommonly perspicacious, he is likely to
be more affected by his feeling of the justice of such
claims, than by any apprehension of the consequences
of successful Trade Union pressure, of which, too often,
he has only a dim idea. It cannot be too clearly recognised that in an arbitrator, legalism is a bias; the
arbitrator's job is to find a settlement that the disputants can with advantage accept, not to impose a
solution that seems to him fair and just. If he is influenced by considerations of justice (based nearly
always on very limited conceptions of where justice
lies) he cannot expect that party, whose procedure he
is inclined to consider unrighteous, to be very ready to
bring disputes for his decision.

If legalism generally implies a bias in favour of the
Union, it may perhaps be suggested on the other side
that class prejudice (arbitrators being rarely working-
men) provides a countervailing bias in the other
direction. Now the fear of class prejudice is certainly
a reason which makes Trade Unions loth to submit to
arbitration, and in consequence it is one of the things
which diminishes the usefulness of arbitration. But it
may be doubted whether the fear is justified, whether
(for this is the decisive test) the alleged class prejudice
of arbitrators can ever have any significant influence
in encouraging employers to use the method. In
practice, the danger of class prejudice is such an
obvious one that arbitrators are inevitably on their
guard against it; no arbitrator who took his job at
all seriously could fail to discount such a bias
fairly thoroughly. The bias of legalism is less easily
recognised, and so more insidious. It supplies a good
reason why employers should naturally be on their
guard against arbitration; if employers have a good

reason, and unionists a bad reason (though one which inevitably weighs heavily with them) why they dislike arbitration, it is not surprising that the history of Industrial Arbitration is not very glorious.[1]

When arbitration, instead of being simply one of the methods of dealing with disputes, so that disputants can go to arbitration or not as they choose, is made by law the method which must be applied to any intractable dispute, a different situation arises. Compulsory arbitration (at least in its extremer forms, as practised in Australia, or over a considerable part of British industry during the war) has many of the characteristics of State regulation of wages through Wages Boards. The sanction for the wage fixed is the power of the State, not the power of the Unions; but since it is much easier to exercise State power against employers (who are relatively few in number, and whose property can be confiscated) than it is to exercise it against Unions (fining Unions large enough sums to act as an effective deterrent is politically difficult, and strikers cannot be sent to gaol, for that would prolong the withdrawal of their labour), arbitrators on a compulsory system are driven to make large concessions to Union claims. Indeed, so far as the immediate objects of the Unions are concerned, compulsory arbitration is the best system conceivable, since the Unions are likely to get whatever they can persuade the State, or coerce the employers, to grant

---

[1] In her valuable survey of the work of the Industrial Court, the principal official organ of arbitration in Great Britain since the war, Miss M. T. Rankin shows that this body has been as much concerned with establishing a system of quasi-legal principles on which wages *ought* to be fixed, as with settling disputes. It is hardly surprising that these principles turn out to be nothing else but the living wage and fair wages, the traditional principles of Trade Unionism (*Arbitration Principles and the Industrial Court, passim* ; see also Amulree, *Industrial Arbitration*, ch. xix.).

them—whichever is the higher. But this, as we shall have abundant cause to see, is not the end of the story.[1]

III

The problem of Industrial Peace is only one, and not by any means necessarily the most important, of the economic problems raised by Trade Unionism. Within wide limits, the more pacific is a Union's policy, the greater its economic influence—in particular, its influence on wages—is likely to be. Thus, in studying the potential influence of Unionism on wages, it is best to assume that we are dealing with Unions whose officials are highly competent, and in which there is a spirit of confidence between officials and members. Such Unions will strike rarely, and when they do strike they will quickly come to a settlement with the employers. We may now examine what are the circumstances which favour the establishment by such Unions of wages considerably higher than the wages which would have been paid if combination had not been present. This will give us a maximum value for Trade Union gains; the Unions of actual fact cannot generally be expected to do as well as this.

In our diagram (p. 143) this maximum level to

---

[1] The direct regulation of wages by the State, in the absence of Trade Unions—through Trade Boards, or Wages Boards of whatever description—does not concern us here; but not only because it falls outside the title of this chapter. The level of wages fixed by such boards is a matter of public policy, and there is no economic reason why they should not in the first place fix any level they choose. Of course, some sets of wages would be so obviously ruinous to the industry in question that they would only be fixed by a Government or board which had altogether taken leave of its senses; but this is a matter of consequences, and the consequences of wage control are reserved for consideration in a future chapter.

which wages can be raised by Trade Union action,
when executed with the greatest possible degree of
skill, is given by OA; and it is the causes which determine the level of OA, or rather ZA (the extra wage
due to combination) which we must now examine.
This level clearly depends upon the shape and position
of the two curves.

About the form of the Union's resistance curve
there is not much that has to be said. It has already
been suggested that in many cases the resistance curve
may be horizontal for an appreciable portion of its
length; for example, in times of bad trade, a union may
resist a reduction in wages with all its might, but
suggestions for an advance, if they are made at all, are
not meant seriously. When the dispute arises originally
out of the men's claim for an advance, a horizontal
stretch is indeed less likely; but even in this case, some
new level may easily invoke a special attachment—
because it has been granted elsewhere, and is therefore
considered fair, or because it has been paid at some
earlier period, or for some similar reason. If now the
employer's concession curve cuts the resistance curve
on the horizontal part, the union will generally succeed
in maintaining its claim; but if it cuts it at a lower
point, compromise will be necessary, and it is over such
compromises that misunderstandings and strikes most
easily arise.

More or less sentimental considerations of this sort
evidently have a large influence on the willingness to
hold out for a given rate of wages; but the actual
duration of resistance depends on ability as much as
on willingness. Strikers' ability to hold out depends,
in its turn, partly on the size of the union's accumulated funds (the amount of strike pay it can give),

partly on the savings of the members (which enable
them to be content with a low rate of strike pay, or to
hold out when strike pay has disappeared), partly on
the attitude towards the strike of parties not directly
concerned (the willingness of shopkeepers to give
credit, the willingness of other unions or independent
well-wishers to give loans or donations to the union).
The greater the extent of such resources, the stronger
the union will be; and the more likely it is to be able
to secure a given level of wages.

How far the possible further consequences of
raising wages are likely to influence a union in making
claims—how far it is likely to abstain from demanding
an advance because of a fear that in consequence of its
being granted a proportion of its members would become unemployed—is not a question that we can easily
discuss at present. Some influence of this kind there
undoubtedly sometimes is; but experience seems to
indicate that it is a good deal less than a superficial
examination of the economics of the situation would
suggest. This is one of the things we shall have to try
to explain.

We may now turn to examine the employer's concession curve. The wage an employer will pay rather
than submit to a strike of given length will depend on
the relative costs of concession and resistance; anything which raises the cost of a strike to him will raise
the wage he is prepared to pay, anything which raises
the cost of paying a given wage will lower the wage
obtainable. Once the duration is given, the most important conditions which determine the cost of a strike
are: (1) the degree to which the union can make the
strike effective in causing a stoppage of the employer's

business; (2) the direct costs of the stoppage—the profits unearned and the fixed charges uncovered; (3) the indirect losses through breaking of contracts and disappointment of customers. Anything which increases these things increases the wage which Trade Union action can secure. The most important factors which govern the cost of concession are: (1) the length of time the settlement is expected to last; (2) the extent to which a given rise in wages will diminish profits. Anything which increases these will diminish the wage the employer is prepared to offer.

One of the best ways of illustrating the significance of these factors in Trade Union strength is to adopt an historical method, and to follow out their working at different stages in the development of collective bargaining. This we shall endeavour to do in the next chapter. But before passing on to that, there are certain general deductions from these points which may conveniently be made here.

First, the power of Trade Unions to raise or retain wages above the competitive level is much greater in times of good trade than it is when trade is bad. Not only is the direct strength of the union likely to be greater—it is nearly always easier to get members when trade is good, for the men can afford union subscriptions more easily. The funds of the union are likely to be higher for this reason, and also, if it pays unemployment benefit, because there is likely to be less drain from that source. But more important than either of these is the fact that when trade is good, the cost of a strike to the employer will be immensely enhanced. Once an employer is making large profits, and expects those profits to continue in the near future, he is an easy mark for union demands. He will nearly always be prepared to make some concession in order to avoid a strike. On the other hand, when trade is bad, the loss imposed upon him by a strike of moderate length may be very small indeed (he may have been considering a temporary closing-down of his works in any case) so that the union will have to be abnormally strong, which it is very unlikely to be, in order to be able to bring to bear any significant pressure at all.[1]

Next, some special attention must be paid to the last of the five conditions on which we found the form of the employer's concession curve to depend: the extent to which a given rise in wages will curtail profits. This is perhaps the most important of all the conditions, and yet it is frequently overlooked.

Trade Union gains, like taxes, do not necessarily stick where they are put, but can be passed on.[2] If an employer pays higher wages to a particular class of workmen, he does not necessarily content himself with allowing everything else to go on as before, so that his profits are reduced by exactly the amount paid in the higher wages. The fact that this kind of labour can only be engaged at a higher wage than before sets in motion all those adjustments which were discussed in an earlier part of this book (Chapter I). Since costs have arisen, he will, if he can, raise selling prices. But since any increase in selling prices will probably mean a contraction in output, this will only be profitable to a limited extent, depending on the elasticity of demand

[1] It is true that in times of bad trade the efforts of the Union may be powerfully seconded by an independent reluctance to cut wages on the part of employers (see above, p. 55).

[2] For the classical statement of this argument, see Marshall, *Economics of Industry* (1879), p. 206. At present we are only concerned with these further effects of Trade Union action as far as they affect the willingness of employers to concede Trade Union claims. They will be elaborated much more fully in Chapters IX. and X.

for his product.[1] Yet in so far as a reduction in output takes place, it may have further favourable consequences for him, to set off the direct fall in profits which was occasioned by the rise in wages. For his demand for other factors of production, other kinds of labour, raw materials, transport, and so on, will be reduced, and under favourable circumstances, the reduced demand may mean a considerably lower cost. To some extent, then, a rise in the wages of a particular class of labour can sometimes be shifted by the employers of that labour on to the shoulders of other sections of the community, both those to whom they sell and those from whom they buy. To the extent to which they expect to be able to shift their losses in this way, their resistance to union pressure will be reduced.

Another effect of raising the wages of a particular class of labour is to make that class expensive relatively to others. It therefore supplies an incentive to employers to use less of the labour in question and more of other factors of production. In so far as such substitution is possible without great loss, the employers will give way more readily.

But though easy substitution diminishes employers' resistance to wage-advances, at the same time there can be no doubt that this is a case where union policy is considerably influenced by apprehension of the consequences on employment which would be likely to follow from success. Although any increase in wages must mean fewer jobs than would otherwise have been available—whether by this route of substitution, or by the direct effect of higher costs in

---

[1] If he has direct competitors not subject to the same Union pressure, then the extent to which he can pass on his losses is nearly negligible. Competition is extremely elastic demand.

M

checking output—there can be no question that the effect is much more obvious along this route than along the other. As we shall afterwards see, the effect through increased costs is usually deferred, and thus less easy to recognise; but, at any rate, in an industry whose methods are very flexible, where technical change is very frequent (and it is only in such an industry that the possibility of technical change will generally affect the issue of disputes) the workman always feels his job to be insecure because of the progress of invention. It is not difficult for him to get some rudimentary idea that he is more likely to be displaced if he becomes more expensive; and apart from this, he naturally directs most of his attention to using his union to safeguard his job, rather than his wage. In the engineering trades, which are perhaps more exposed than any other British industry to the impact of technical change, the policy of the unions has been more anxiously concerned with putting restrictions on the introduction of automatic machines than with the control of wages; it is a very natural tendency in the circumstances.

CHAPTER VIII

THE GROWTH OF TRADE UNION POWER

SINCE the publication of Mr. and Mrs. Webb's great history in 1894, much has been written on the development of the English Trade Unions. But it is the social and political aspects of this evolution which have been most thoroughly examined; the economic aspects have been much less adequately treated. The economist, seeking an answer to the most fundamental economic problems of Union development, can get little help from the historical literature, and is largely left to his own devices. To him the most important question is not any of those which have been so exhaustively studied, but rather the determination of the extent to which, at different periods, the Trade Unions have been able to affect wages. And to this economic historians, with their eyes fixed on the qualitative rather than quantitative differences between competitive and collective wage-fixing, have rarely attempted to give an answer.

In order to be able to answer this question at all, some theoretical apparatus of the kind developed in the preceding chapter is absolutely necessary. Without some such apparatus it is impossible even to ask the right questions, to get on the right road towards a solution of the problem. With it we can at least hope to do that; and although a fully adequate answer must await more intensive historical research than it has been possible to devote to the following pages, even a smattering of historical knowledge, rightly used, may at least throw some light upon the economic side of Trade Union history.

When our analysis is applied to the main facts of that development, it becomes clear that the various stages through which Collective Bargaining has passed in this country form a natural sequence, the deficiencies of each stage offering an economic stimulus for the closer organisation of the next. We must beware of any hasty conclusion that the economic stimulus was the only one operating, and still more that it was the dominating cause of closer organisation. But there can be little doubt that the economic analysis does throw a good deal of light on the causation of the process.

I

Like other things, Trade Unionism began on a small scale—small clubs among the employees of a single business, or of a small group of businesses in a single town or village. Now it is clear that the power of such embryonic unions must have been very limited—for two reasons. One was the presence of available sources of labour supply outside the combination, and the consequent difficulty of making a strike effective. If on the declaration of a strike, considerable numbers of men, working for the employers affected, refused to obey the orders of the Union, and remained at work, the costs laid upon the employers were reduced (in all probability more than proportionately to the numbers of those who remained) and hardly anything could be won from the employers as the result of so mild a threat. Very naturally, pressure (and not always peaceful pressure) was brought to bear upon non-unionists. But the law and public opinion frowned very severely upon the more violent methods; and "peaceful persuasion," although in the end fairly effective, took a considerable time to reach its goal.

Even when organisation reached the point of making strikes fairly effective in this sense—in that nearly all the men actually at work for the firms concerned would withdraw—another danger of the same kind remained. When the area covered by the Union was small, employers could generally carry on (at somewhat increased cost, it is true) by importing labour from outside the area. It is not surprising that for both these reasons, the "blackleg" trouble was one of the dominating features of the situation in these early days. It was a natural consequence of the weakness of organisation and the limitation of membership.

Even apart from blacklegs, it is improbable that at this stage the Unions could have made very appreciable gains, owing to the impossibility of employers passing on the concessions which might be extorted from them to other parties.[1] So long as each employer was faced with competition from other firms whose men were not unionised, or at least not organised in the same Union, the possibility of raising selling-prices, or lowering the buying-prices of other factors, was small, and the resistance of employers was therefore intensified by the fact that the whole burden of concession must fall on profits. It is true that, now and again,

---

[1] This statement requires some modification with respect to those trades where interlocal competition was still very imperfect; since in these cases a considerable rise in selling price may have been possible without too serious a reduction in demand. But as time went on, the extent of these opportunities must have been diminished; and it is very possible that this was one of the reasons for the extension of the area of Trade Union organisation.

when an employer was caught with a contract which he must fulfil to avoid heavy loss, strikers might catch him at a disadvantage, and score a temporary success. But such gains would inevitably be fleeting, since he could not afford to carry on for any length of time with costs higher than his competitors'. As soon as opportunity arose, he would defy the Union, and beat it.

Now although this second limit was certainly one of the penalties of small-scale organisation, and although in all probability it was largely responsible for the weakness of early Unions, it is most unlikely that at this period unionists had sufficient insight into the motives of employers for it to have had much influence in stimulating the extension of their organisations. Sometimes, it is true, we do find in Trade Union history traces of a suspicion that the ill-success of unionism in one district is a factor limiting the possibilities of success elsewhere; but these are generally vague, and mostly belong to a time when the movement as a whole was past this initial stage. Blacklegs, on the other hand, were an obvious nuisance; the danger of direct undercutting by non-local labour must have been the main economic consideration encouraging the extension of unionism from small districts to large, and even to the whole of an industry within the national frontier. Doubtless there were less specifically economic causes at work as well—feelings of working-class solidarity, and the fact that capable organisers would be easily flattered by size. And once it had been discovered that financial organisation, the accumulation of funds and the payment of benefits, were the easiest way to hold a large Union together, more members meant more subscriptions, and a financial motive for extension gathered considerable force.

II

This second phase of Union history appears to correspond, in the case of England, to the middle part of the nineteenth century. It was only after the repeal of the Combination Laws that open canvassing, without which it would have been nearly impossible to form large Unions, became really feasible; but for a long while the sheer difficulty of organising large masses of men presented insuperable obstacles. The organisation of 1,000 men was a problem different in kind from the organisation of 100, and a new technique had to be invented. From 1825 to 1850 the story is therefore a monotonous record of failures, and it is only after 1850 that any real success in the formation of large unions is achieved.

Once this organisation had been accomplished, the strength of the Unions was greatly increased. Although Union members were still in most cases not a very large proportion of the total number of men working in each trade, the blackleg trouble must have become appreciably less serious, and at the same time the accumulation of funds greatly increased the Unions' staying power. A local strike could be supported by the aid of funds raised in other districts, and so by careful husbandry the funds at the disposal of a local branch might sometimes be made so large that an employer could be confronted with the possibility of his men staying out almost indefinitely. In such circumstances it is conceivable that Union gains might be large; though since the burden of concession must still fall almost entirely upon profits (competition with other firms making it impossible to pass it on) the resistance of employers would generally be strenuous.

Some things of considerable consequence the Unions, in this second phase, could, and generally did, achieve. It will be remembered that in our discussion of the mechanism of wage-reductions in a free market, we found that the process is generally initiated by the action of some "bad" or pessimistic employers; and that these subsequently, if the conditions of trade remain unfavourable, force the others into line. Now if a strong Trade Union were to concentrate its attack upon these "bad" employers, it could very effectively postpone reductions, since any single employer who desired to cut wages would find the whole force of the Union against him. (If the decline in trade was not too protracted, this policy might prevent reductions altogether.) The most convenient means of achieving this end was to set in the forefront of Trade Union objectives the maintenance of a "common rule"—definite minimum wages or recognised piece-lists throughout a district, enforced by the concentration of Union strength upon any employer who sought to reduce these standards.

Nearly all Unions in this second period had some success in the establishment of standards, although naturally the area through which the standard could be enforced varied immensely. In localised industries, like Cotton and Coal, strongly organised and well-led Unions might extend standards over large and busy districts; while, on the other hand, in less concentrated trades the standard might apply to no more than two or three firms in a small town. But the relation between the standards established in two districts must inevitably have been loose, even if the men working in both were organised in the same National Union; for costs of movement had allowed large local differences in wages to persist in the competitive market, and the achievement of a common standard, even for places twenty miles apart, usually remained for a long while beyond the Unions' strength.

Thus although this is the period of the first decided successes of the Unions, their power was still very limited. Save in exceptional cases, their membership was not as yet very large, and although the weight of their funds was beginning to tell, the competition of employers in the selling markets made great successes difficult. The average level of wages over a period of years could not be much affected; the most that could usually be done was to moderate or delay the adjustment of wages to conditions of bad trade by the enforcement of standard rates.

Under these circumstances, it was natural that many Unions should turn to indirect ways of reaching their end. One of the most important of these was the limitation of entry to the trade. When a trade is in a flourishing condition, it draws immigrants to it, and the presence of these immigrants retards the rise in wages. This in itself the established workers may feel to be a grievance; but in general the source of their resentment is probably different. The good times are unlikely to last for ever, and when the tide turns, the newcomers, although the first to be dislodged, will be a supply of potential blacklegs whose presence will make it appreciably harder to resist reductions. Thus, in addition to its direct and immediate effect in forcing up wages, the limitation of entry to men with certain defined qualifications strengthened the future position of the Union. And once organisation had reached a moderate stage of effectiveness, it was a tolerably easy regulation to enforce. For the times at which it became most irksome to employers would be times of extremely good trade, when the Union found it easiest to enlist members, when funds were at their highest, and when the cost of a stoppage to employers (owing to the high profits sacrificed) would be most alarming. But though all these things made limitation of entry an attractive method of control, it could never be a satisfactory alternative to direct regulation of wages. For one thing, it was far harder to make it appear respectable (a man ignorant of economics nearly always feels the regulation of prices to be more justifiable than the limitation of supply—although they come to the same thing); and for another, the use of limitation of entry, by itself, would have meant that wages, instead of being steadied through periods of good and bad trade, fluctuated more violently. The result of this has been that while Trade Unions have continued to use limitation of entry as one weapon in their armoury, it has generally had a secondary importance, in comparison with the direct control of wage-rates.

III

The transition to the third phase of Trade Union history is marked by the rise of Employers' Associations.[1] It is far more difficult to secure information about these bodies than it is to get similar information about Trade Unions; they are more secretive, and do not present the same social interest as a lure to in-

---

[1] To be distinguished, of course, from those other associations of firms, formed to operate in the selling market—cartels and rings.

vestigators, however great their economic importance
may be. But it seems unlikely that we shall get a
radically wrong impression if we date the most active
period of their formation as the last quarter of the nineteenth century. Local understandings of a loose kind
had probably existed before that time; there is even
the great authority of Adam Smith for holding that
they were of some importance in the eighteenth
century.[1] But it is not unlikely that Adam Smith's remarks relate essentially to the pre-industrial or very
early industrial epoch, when the reluctance of employers to change ancient customary rates might well
induce a species of combination; with the progress of
the Industrial Revolution they became more accustomed to the idea that wages do change, and (so at
least the evidence seems to suggest) employers' combination became decidedly uncommon.[2]

But as the Unions grew in power, the situation inevitably changed. Where district minima were successfully achieved, the incentive to combination among
employers as the only possible means of enforcing
necessary wage-reductions became very strong. At the
beginning of a period of bad trade, the "good" employers might not have been ill-satisfied to see their
weaker competitors restrained from cutting rates; but
as time went on, and opinion in favour of reduction
made headway among the employers concerned, the
idea of combination must always have arisen. No one
would care to expose himself single-handed to the
attacks of the union—and allow his competitors to
steal trade from him while he was fighting their battles;
but all (or nearly all) would desire to profit from the

[1] *Wealth of Nations*, bk. i., ch. viii.
[2] See Hutt, *The Theory of Collective Bargaining*, pp. 25-30.

reduction. Sooner or later some employer must have taken the initiative, and asked his rivals to join him in threatening a lock-out; and circumstances inevitably arose in which such an invitation would be warmly accepted.

Over districts through which standards had been established, employers' combination inevitably followed; but it was only in exceptional cases that the unions' policy had been sufficiently successful for these districts to be very large. Nevertheless, once employers' combination had begun, it spread fairly quickly; even against a union which had failed to make its standards uniform over wide districts, employers tended to associate themselves on a larger scale. For the standard rates were only one aspect of the piece-meal policy; even when the rates in two districts had not been standardised to the same level, the employers had still to fear separate attacks—the whole force of the union's funds being used as a powerful threat to win concessions from one small group of employers after another. Combined action could force the union to spread its power thinly over a wide area, so that no individual employer had to face a very serious threat. The most famous example of this process is the Engineering Lock-out of 1897, when the Amalgamated Society of Engineers declared a strike in London (to win a reduction of hours there) and then found itself countered by the newly formed Engineering Employers Federation with the declaration of a National Lock-out.

This general organisation of the employers marks the third phase, which reached its most perfect development (though of course there were exceptions and differences between particular industries) in the early days of the twentieth century before the Great

War. Wages were negotiated between unions and
employers in districts, large or small; it was only in
small localised industries that such agreements usually
covered anything like a whole trade. Central Feder-
ations of employers generally existed, but for the most
part they functioned purely as reserves; they took no
part in the direct negotiation of wages, but simply
prevented the unions from bringing excessive pressure
to bear on any local group. National Agreements between the central organisations did indeed exist in
several important cases; but the more we examine
these documents, the more we are struck by their
paucity of content. A few particular questions (hours
for example) did tend to be negotiated centrally; but
the National Agreements consisted, mainly, of "Provisions for Avoiding Disputes", arrangements that intractable local disputes should be referred to the
central bodies. The presence of these clauses was
really a symbol of the employers' dominance; the
limit of Trade Union gains was no longer marked by
what the whole force of union funds could win from a
small group of employers, but by the point at which
such a group of employers could effectively summon
the central organisation to their assistance.

In itself, the organisation of employers was a
factor diminishing union strength; though historically
this was doubtless offset to a large extent by increasing union membership. The rigidity of wages in
face of bad trade was greater than under competition,
since the marginal "bad" employers were restrained
from making reductions; the sentiment in favour of
reduction had to spread some way before reduction
could take place. But the initiative for a change still
came from the districts; and if any district was badly

hit, the other employers in the association could not
very well restrain it from cutting wages, for fear that
the same trick would be played on them on a future
occasion. Their best course was to play for a compromise. Similarly, the other employers would generally give a certain amount of support to a group from
whom an advance had been demanded, because one
set of advances would give a strong precedent for
others. And although any employer whose men received advances late in the series would secure a temporary gain, no one could tell easily whether he would
be an unfortunate early victim, or a fortunate late one.
As a result, we must still regard the influence of Trade
Unionism on wages, even in the immediate pre-War
period, as partial and limited—confined to anticipating
a little the gains which would have accrued under
competition in times of good trade, and delaying a
little the losses which would have resulted in any
circumstances from periods of depression. In those
industries where the force of trade fluctuations is not
generally very great, this was indeed a very significant
gain to the workers; for it meant that the temporary
wage-reductions which would probably have occurred
occasionally in competitive conditions were largely
ruled out. But neither in the case of these industries,
nor with those normally subject to greater disturbances,
was the average level of wages, even over a short period
of years, probably affected to any great extent.

IV

But this has not been the final phase of industrial evolution. In one or two industries before the War, and in most industries soon after the War, wage-fixing passed beyond the phase of local initiative under central supervision to that of central initiative. The main cause of this change appears to have been the total disorganisation of relative wage-rates in 1919-21. Under the abnormal pressure of war demand, wages in some industries and some localities had arisen relatively to others in a way which was obviously untenable in the altered conditions of peacetime. Yet no one knew where the new equilibrium would be, and no one imagined that it would be anything like that which had existed in 1914. So strange a situation, in which sharp and revolutionary changes in the wage structure had to be made, although no one really knew what changes were appropriate, gave a long wished for opportunity to those who held theories of how the wage structure should be planned. Following the example of the Trade Boards, and using the new machinery of consultation which was to hand in the Whitley Councils and other newly established conciliation bodies, several industries set to work to reshape their wage structure on new "rational" systems, while even those which found it impossible to go so far nevertheless introduced sweeping changes.

In these new systems, it was inevitable that the actual rates for each locality should be negotiated directly between representatives of the central unions and central employers' associations. There was no time for any other method but this, the most expeditious. Sometimes time was saved further by leaving the pre-War local rates unchanged as base rates, and adding to them a nationally-negotiated bonus. But in either case, direct control over the effective wage-level was handed over to the central bodies, who became responsible for it. When it became necessary to bring about any change in wages, it was to these bodies that men naturally appealed.

It is true that these systems have generally possessed a certain amount of elasticity—rather more than that possessed by Trade Board rates, for example. But their installation has meant that no considerable change in wages in the industries concerned could take place without positive action by one massive organisation or another, and without the threat of a stoppage throughout the industry.

From the standpoint of the national economy this change has been most serious; undoubtedly it has been one of the main factors responsible for the scale of the industrial strife which has marred the history of post-war England. But from the point of view of wage-regulation, it has a different significance. For the first time, it has become possible for the resistance of employers to union pressure to be largely influenced by the possibility of shifting a considerable portion of the burden of high wages on to the shoulders of other people, who are not in any direct way parties to the dispute. As long as rival employers were not subjected to simultaneous pressure, the extent to which this could be done was very limited; once the same pressure was felt by all, any firm could pass on a considerable part of the cost of concession to its customers or to the providers of other factors, confident that no one could outbid it.

But although this possibility, on a considerable

scale, was a new and vitally important factor in the situation, it was not equally present in all industries. The extent to which costs can be passed on to the consumer, for example, depends on the elasticity of demand for the product; and although our knowledge of elasticities of demand is very vague, there is no doubt that they do vary immensely from one commodity to another. It is theoretically possible for men who work at the production of a commodity of highly inelastic demand to force up their wages almost indefinitely— so long as the demand continues inelastic, and so long as no alternative method of production, or alternative source of labour, is available. Their employers (if attacked simultaneously) have hardly any incentive to resist them. The more inelastic the demand is, the easier it will be to establish a high level of wages by Trade Union pressure; but with commodities of elastic demand, the possibility of shifting is very slight, and the resistance of employers proportionately increased.

Even when wage-regulation proceeds on an industrial scale, there are some unions which are bound to encounter a highly elastic demand. These are the unions in industries with foreign competitors, whose workmen, at least in the present stage of organisation, are not organised in the same unions and do not exert simultaneous pressure. They may be "protectable" industries, whose foreign rivals compete with them in the home market, or export industries, whose foreign rivals compete with them in foreign markets. But in either case, the elasticity of demand for the home product is likely to be very high, since it has so convenient a substitute in the foreign product. Naturally, therefore, once organisation has reached our fourth phase,

N

in which some industries can effectively pass on the costs of high wages, a very considerable divergence is likely to develop between the fortunes of different unions. "Sheltered" wages must rise relatively to "unsheltered".[1]

V

This change in relative wages has been very evident since the war; but it has been much more significant in the second half of the decade than it was earlier. The new national agreements came into force in 1920-22; but it seems unlikely that they had any very pronounced effect in impeding the adjustment of wages to the catastrophically changed price-level of the latter year. Employers and men alike were quickly convinced that the circumstances of 1920 were abnormal; while the state of trade was such that the Unions could make little resistance to a determined

[1] It is not denied that some effect of this sort was probably present before the war; in those trades which transport costs, or other obstacles, made quasi-monopolistic, and in those small trades which were aided by local concentration to reach my fourth phase at an early date, some amount of shifting was possible. But there can be no question that it has become a phenomenon of altogether different magnitude in the last decade.

There is an interesting passage in Marshall's account of Trade Unionism (*Economics of Industry*, 1907, pp. 383-384) where he suggests that the "bracing influence of foreign competition," by preventing the unions in export trades from making great gains by aggressive action, and aggravating the losses caused to the industry by strikes, leads them to develop a conciliatory policy. "Those union officials who most fully realise the fundamental solidarity between employers and employed, and who oppose all demands which would needlessly hamper production or inflict loss on the employers are those whose advice is found to bear the test of experience best; their influence increases, and their character spreads itself over the union." Post-war experience moderates this optimism; but even with respect to earlier history, it may be questioned whether Marshall was not unduly impressed by the very remarkable cases of Cotton and Iron and Steel, which must surely have been in his mind when he wrote these words. Coal is also an export industry, and the history of Industrial Relations there is very different. Personally I doubt if, in the pre-war situation, the difference between sheltered and unsheltered trades was as significant as Marshall thought.

attack on wages. By the end of 1923 wages had found their new level. There was already apparent at this date a considerable divergence between sheltered and unsheltered wages, but it was not much larger than could be explained easily enough by two causes only remotely connected with Trade Union action. For one thing, the unsheltered trades were largely war trades, which had been abnormally expanded for the provision of munitions, and which were in consequence now saddled with an abnormal surplus of labour. And for another, they were largely heavy trades, in which wages had always been particularly influenced by the Trade Cycle. In Shipbuilding, Engineering, and Coalmining, wages in 1923 were relatively low by pre-war standards; but then 1923 was a year of trade depression. When trade recovered, it was reasonable to expect that wages in these trades would recover too, while sheltered wages would share in the advance to a much more limited extent.

These expectations were not fulfilled. In 1924 there was indeed an appreciable recovery in trade, and with it the expected recovery in export trade wages. The coal-miners exacted that short-lived and fatal agreement whereby the minimum percentage was raised from 20 to $33\frac{1}{3}$. Wages in engineering and shipbuilding also rose. But the recovery was not confined to the export trades. The workers in sheltered trades also had not been satisfied with the wages they had been forced to accept in the slump. In a considerable number of cases they succeeded in getting their wages revised. With improved trade, Trade Union strength was increased, and that strength was used to exact a rise in wages at a very early stage of recovery.

But the recovery did not persist. In April 1925,

England returned to the Gold Standard, at a par of exchange which cannot now be denied to have been too high to be consistent with the then existing level of wages. But the downward pull on wages which thenceforward existed was not catastrophic like the slump of 1921; it was much milder, and could to a large extent be resisted by the Trade Unions with their new-found strength. Not all the Unions, indeed, could resist it effectively; for here the divergence in position between sheltered and unsheltered trades began to show itself in its true significance. The sheltered trades stood up to the pressure, for they felt it very little, or hardly at all. But it was very different with the export trades. Even with these, of course, the pressure was not simultaneous; particular influences crossed with the general monetary deflation. But, one after another, Coal, Wool, Cotton, became storm-centres. The resistance of the Unions was prolonged and powerful, though this only sometimes showed itself in a lengthy stoppage like the 1926 Coal Strike. More often the employers did not like the prospect of a strike, and bore their losses for a long while.

The rigidity of wages, or successful resistance of wages to downward pressure, which was a dominating factor in Britain's economic position between 1925 and 1931, was further reinforced by an indirect consequence of the national agreements. The threatened wage-changes could not take place gradually and on a small scale; they thrust themselves into the front pages of the newspapers, and became events of which politicians had to take notice. It was impossible for Governments to avoid interfering in the disputes; and once they did interfere, they acquired a certain amount of responsibility for the outcome. For obvious electoral reasons, no democratic Government cares to be associated with wage-reductions; and thus the influence of the State was nearly always directed against those adjustments which it had made necessary by its own policy.[1]

Further, throughout the post-war period, all Governments have undoubtedly been strengthening the hands of the Unions, by the system of Unemployment Insurance. If it had not been for Unemployment Insurance, there can be little doubt that many of the national agreements would long ago have broken down, or been rendered much more flexible. It is not so much that the Unions, if they had had to look after their own unemployed, would have been financially weakened, and thus less able to resist wage-cuts, although this may be of some importance. The significance lies rather in that clause, which has run through all the multitude of Insurance Acts, decreeing that employment "at a rate of wages lower, or on conditions less favourable, than those generally observed in that district by agreement between associations of employers and employees" shall not be regarded as suitable employment, refusal of which disqualifies for benefit. If it had not been for this clause, it is impossible to believe that it would have been possible to enforce agreements in the face of large and persistent percentages of unemployed in regular trades. New firms would have started up, absorbing the unemployed at low wages; many of those firms which have actually closed down would have remained open with "blackleg" labour. And in face of competition from these

---

[1] The Coal Mines Eight Hours Act of 1926 is not really an except on to this rule. An increase in hours seemed to be the only alternative to still heavier reductions in wages than those which came about. The Government was faced, from its own point of view, with a choice between two evils.

sources, the national agreements must have given way.

This is not a pretty alternative; but on the question whether the choice we have made is better the following chapters may perhaps throw some light.

CHAPTER IX

I

IT is now time to return from this historical digression to the general issues of theory with which we are more directly concerned. We have examined the conditions which make it possible for Trade Unions to secure at any time the payment of wages higher than would have been paid in a competitive market. We may now assume that such wages are being paid, whether as the result of Trade Union pressure or because they have simply been imposed by the State; and we may proceed to enquire what the consequences of such a situation are likely to be.

Very simple and familiar economic reasoning suggests at once the main answer—unemployment. A raising of wages above the competitive level will contract the demand for labour, and make it impossible to absorb some of the men available. As the employment of labour contracts, the marginal product of the men still employed will rise; when the marginal product has risen to a level corresponding to the new wage, the increase in unemployment will stop.

There is nothing in the arguments put forward in this book to suggest that this analysis is not substantially right. But it is obviously a simplified picture of what goes on, couched in terms which remove it further from reality than is necessary; so that it is hardly surprising if those engaged in industry have not found it easy to recognise as their own experience. Some further discussion even of this simple direct reaction seems to be desirable if we are to have clear ideas on the matter.

First of all, we must distinguish between the cases of a partial control of wages—in some firms or industries only—and a general control of wages extending throughout a whole community. If the control is limited to particular employments, then certainly the demand for labour in those employments will contract below the level which it would otherwise have reached. Some men who would have got employment there cannot now do so; they must go off and seek employment elsewhere. This may indeed cause temporary unemployment, if men have to be shifted from one trade, or one district, to another; but it is essentially the same kind of thing as results from an ordinary change in the demand for labour, common enough in a perfectly free market. In this case, it is not the unemployment which is, economically speaking, the most significant effect of regulation (in an extreme case, where the affected firms are abnormally prosperous, and the rise in wages is only just sufficient to prevent them expanding employment or to diminish their expansion, there may be no net unemployment due to the regulation); the important effect is the redistribution of labour— the fact that some men are prevented from securing employment in a trade where they would be better off than they are otherwise condemned to be.

When the control of wages is general, the situation is different. If there are not sufficient uncontrolled industries to absorb the men who cannot get employment in the controlled industries—or absorb them at a real wage above starvation level—then the unemployment which results is not temporary in the above sense. It must go on, until the long-run economic forces which determine competitive wage-levels—invention, the accumulation of capital, and, in an open community, the direction of foreign trade—produce such a change in the wages which would have been paid in the competitive market as to enable the unemployed to be absorbed. That is to say, the unemployment must go on until the artificial wages are relaxed, or until competitive wages have risen to the artificial level.

It will be one of the principal tasks of the next chapter to determine to what extent it is possible to hold out a hope of this taking place. But for the present it is worth our while to concentrate on the more immediate reactions, on the unemployment-manufacture which results directly from Trade Union action and the policy of wage-boards. We can leave until later the question of how far secular changes in economic resources may cause this unemployment to disappear.

II

It should be clear from our analysis of the Marginal Productivity theory in Chapter I that the effects on employment of artificially high wages may easily be slow in making their appearance. Take first the case of a single firm, carrying on in a condition of moderate prosperity, which is compelled to raise wages. Apart from the possible reactions of the change in wages on the efficiency of labour (on which we shall have something to say later) this means a reduction in profits. But although some reduction in profits is inevitable, the employer will obviously do all he can to make it as small as possible; and the ways which lie most directly open to him all involve a reduction in his demand for labour.

First, there will probably be some men who are doing work of relatively small importance to the conduct of the business, and who can consequently be dispensed with. So long as the wages they received were relatively low, it was estimated that their employment brought in more than they cost; but at the higher level of wages this is no longer the case. Secondly, there may be certain lines of business where the profit on turnover was small; and these again, although they just paid at the old rate of wages, may not pay at the new. If they are abandoned, that is another reason why employment should contract. But it is probable that in most cases the contraction of employment which arises in these ways would be fairly small, so that the *immediate* effect on employment of a rise in wages may not be considerable.

But the reason for this is that an entrepreneur, by investing in fixed plant, gives hostages to fortune. So long as that plant is in existence, the possibility of economising by changing the methods or the scale of production is small; but as the plant comes to be renewed, it will be to his interest to make a radical change. Either he will reinvest his capital in some form of plant which uses less of the labour whose wages have risen—if a form can be found which reduces output less than it reduces costs; or alternatively, instead of reinvesting his depreciation allowances in a new form of plant for this business, he will decline to replace his plant, and will keep his capital in the form of shares in other businesses, so long as these yield a higher rate of return than he would get by reinvestment in his own.

Naturally this is a slow process, for some reinvestment in old forms will very often be necessary in order to preserve the earning-power of the old equipment. But there wil be a continual urge to such transformation; and as it takes place, more and more of the high-wage labourers will be unemployed, and driven to seek work at lower wages elsewhere. This process will only stop when the contraction has proceeded so far as to raise the rate of profit upon that capital which is kept in the business sufficiently to remove any incentive for the employer to change methods to the disadvantage of labour, or to withdraw capital and reinvest it outside.

If, instead of considering a single firm which has been in a stationary condition, we consider an industry, or group of firms, then there is another possibility. For even if the group as a whole is stationary, in the sense that, apart from the rise in wages, its total output would have tended neither to expand nor contract, individual firms in the group may reasonably be supposed to be changing in scale and prosperity, in accordance, perhaps, with the changing ages and efficiencies of their managers. Some firms will be on the downgrade; and the rise in wages, by diminishing their already meagre profits, will hasten their decline. Ordinarily, their place would have been taken by the establishment of new firms; but since profits are now abnormally low in this industry, the incentive to capitalists and entrepreneurs to choose it as a field for investment will be seriously diminished. The number of firms in the industry will be diminished, for more will go out, and fewer will come in. Thus output and employment will fall.

This will be the process in a stationary industry. In an expanding industry, where profits were abnormally high, the artificial raising of wages may cause, not contraction, but only a retarding of expansion. For the reduction of the abnormal profits, caused by the rise in wages, diminishes the incentive to transfer capital to this industry; it therefore diminishes the incentive for the old firms to expand, or for new firms to enter; and the expansion of the whole industry is therefore less than it would otherwise have been. In a contracting industry, where profits are already abnormally low, high wages will accelerate decline.

It is now easy for us to see why Trade Unionists bother so little about the connection between their wage-policy and unemployment. The unemployment caused by their policy does not all appear at once, but only declares itself gradually. Even if the initial advance was made at a time when the state of trade was neither particularly active nor particularly depressed, there would probably still be very little unemployment to begin with. The unemployment which is actually a result of the original advance will only show itself as plant comes to be renewed, or as the marginal firms die off and there is none to replace them. Thus to the Trade Unionist wages and unemployment naturally appear to have little connection. The initial unemployment may be too small to be really noticeable; and the later additions are most easily ascribed to quite different causes. That which comes from substitution is put down to "labour-saving machinery"; that which comes from bankruptcy and closing-down is ascribed to the inefficiency of employers. That the wage-policy which has been going on so long and has seemed so successful has anything to do with present calamities seems too far-fetched to be considered.

When, as is indeed most likely, the initial discrepancy between Trade Union rates and the rates of the competitive market arises, not at a time of normal trade, but in the midst of an upward or downward swing, even the initial unemployment may easily be masked. The earliest stages of the growth of unemployment which actually results from wage-policy are completely hidden in the unemployment which comes from a depression in trade.

III

Whatever may be the case with the ordinary Trade Unionist, no one with an economic education is likely to deny what has just been established with perhaps unnecessary detail—that a raising of wages in one industry will diminish the demand for labour in that industry. But even economists sometimes find a difficulty in seeing that what is admittedly true for each industry separately is also true for all industries taken together. Once we have universal Trade Union action, the *ceteris paribus* assumptions, with which Marshallian economics is accustomed to work, break down; it is no longer fair, for example, to suppose that the demand curves for the products of the industries remain unaffected by the changes; and a way of looking at the problem which had sufficed with one industry considered alone, becomes unsatisfactory in the more complicated case.

But it is not really difficult to adjust our views to this case. It is true that we must not look at the various industries successively; we must look at them simultaneously. But we can then prove conclusively that an all-round rise in wages must cause unemployment (apart, again, from reactions on the efficiency of labour) by supposing it does not, and then proving the continuance of such a situation to be impossible.

We now suppose that the free labour market has entirely disappeared. It does not matter very much if we regard all industries as unionised, and all the Unions forcing wages above the competitive level; or whether, initially, only some Unions are doing this, and the others are resisting the fall in their wages which the rise in the first trades tends to produce. There is no serious theoretical difference here. But for simplicity's sake we shall for the present assume that we are dealing with an isolated or closed community, and also with one that is stationary, having no tendency either to economic progress or decline. We may also assume that by "wages" we mean real wages. The complexities which are introduced in practical affairs by the absence of these limitations we can examine later.

Suppose now that a rise in wages takes place and that initially no one is discharged. The rise in wages does not directly increase the spending-power (measured in terms of goods available for exchange) which is coming forward to take off the market the goods offered for sale. All that happens is a redistribution of that spending-power; more of it comes from wage-earners and less from the receivers of profit. This may, and indeed probably will, alter considerably the relative demand for different commodities; the demand for some commodities (those which wage-earners would buy if they had a little more money) will increase, while the demand for those commodities which are consumed mainly by the capitalist and employer classes will diminish. This will affect considerably the relative profits of different trades—employers in some trades may find themselves better off than before, even with the higher wages they have to pay, but employers in other trades (doubtless the great majority) will be worse off. The general rate of profit will diminish.

The disturbance in the relative rates of profit earned in different trades will lead to a good deal of shifting of industrial activity, those in which profits are now higher tending to expand, and the others to contract. But in so far as this merely reflects the changed relative demand for different products, there is nothing to suggest that it is likely to lead to permanent unemployment. For, on the whole, as many men as are thrown out from the one class of businesses are likely to be absorbed in the other. (There may of course quite well be serious temporary unemployment owing to the difficulties of transfer.)

But the shifting of demand for products is not the only reason why a transference of resources will take place. Some trades use a higher proportion of labour to capital than others; so that while, in the more capitalistic trades[1] (speaking generally, and apart from the variations in demand for products) the burden of the high wages on profits will be small, in the less capitalistic trades it will be much more considerable. Profits will therefore be higher in the first class than in the second, and there will thus be a tendency for

---

[1] By "more capitalistic" industries, I mean those industries which use a relatively large proportion of capital to labour in making a unit of product; similarly by "a more capitalistic method" I mean a method which uses a larger proportion of capital to labour.

capital to shift—from the less capitalistic to the more capitalistic trades.

But this second tendency—unlike that which arises from the change in the demand for products—is not in the long run innocuous to the employment of labour. For a given amount of capital, which enabled a large number of labourers to be employed in the less capitalistic trades, will employ far fewer men in the more capitalistic industries. Although employment expands in the latter, they cannot absorb all the labour which is thrown out elsewhere.

Now even if this kind of transference were to take place completely up to the point where it ceased to be advantageous to the capitalists—and, for all the reasons we have previously mentioned, this is bound to be a slow process—the rate of profit would still in the end be lower than it would have been in a free market. For capital is being forced into uses less advantageous than those which would then have been open to it, and its net productivity is therefore lower. And so there is still an incentive to further change. And a further change can advantageously be made—by making each industry more capitalistic than it was before. The wages of labour are higher and the rate of interest lower than they would have been in a free market; so that more capitalistic methods of production which would not have been profitable then become profitable now. But the adoption of these methods lowers still further the amount of labour which is required with a given volume of capital; and so increases unemployment.

But although this change of methods, like the shifting of resources between industries, must increase net unemployment, it will not increase unemployment at all regularly, nor necessarily increase it in every industry. Under modern conditions, the use of more capitalistic methods means, to a large extent, the increased use of machinery; and since the making and the using of machines are now generally specialised into different trades, the fate of these trades will be different. After a certain lag, maybe, the demand for the products of the machine-making trades will begin to expand—at least relatively to other industries; for it is conceivable that the reduction in employment, by reducing the demand for final products, may set off this increase. But it remains perfectly possible that employment in the heavy industries—those specialised to the production of capital goods—will be well maintained; and, as far as the things we have hitherto taken into account are concerned, it is certain that there will be relatively less unemployment in the heavy trades than elsewhere.

On the other hand, unemployment will be concentrated in those trades where relatively little capital is employed, and among the producers of consumption goods. The providers of services will also suffer severe unemployment, particularly if the services in question have been previously demanded mainly by the wealthier classes, who may be expected to suffer worst from the fall in profits. (This will be the case particularly in the early phases of the process. As the various transferences and substitutions which we have been describing are carried through, total wages will fall owing to unemployment, while total profits will rise, since more profitable investments for capital are being discovered than those which were at first available. This will of course be beneficial to the chances of employment of the class just mentioned.) Further, the dis-

o

tributive trades will contract heavily; cooks, tailors, repairers of all sorts will suffer severe unemployment, both on account of a direct decline in the demand for their services, and because their labour will be substituted by more mechanical methods, and by the mass-production of standardised goods. So great will be the unemployment in these trades (if the original rise in wages has been at all considerable) that it is most unlikely that they will be able to maintain a level of wages comparable with that enforced in the rest of industry. Their wages will therefore fall, and the pressure of unemployment will thereby be somewhat relieved.[1]

IV

This picture of the incidence of unemployment appears to follow inescapably from our reasoning; but it is extremely surprising. For in an earlier chapter we have seen good cause to suppose that the situation of Great Britain between 1925 and 1930 was essentially similar to that of the community whose economy we have just analysed; and it is well known that British unemployment was very differently distributed from this. Indeed, the position was not only different; it was almost diametrically opposite. Unemployment was concentrated in the heavy industries, while the distributive trades, which ought, on our analysis, to have been most severely hit, positively flourished. The antithesis is, however, so complete, that we need not

---

[1] Up to this point, my analysis of the effects of a general rise in wages is largely based upon the classic study of Böhm-Bawerk (*Macht oder ökonomisches Gesetz* in *Gesammelte Schriften*, vol. i.; see particularly pp. 270 ff). What follows owes a great debt to Dr. F. A. Hayek. (See his article, "Kapitalaufzehrung," *Weltwirtschaftliches Archiv*, July, 1932.)

despair, and conclude that we are on altogether wrong lines. So perfect a negative can hardly be a coincidence.

A partial explanation of this extraordinary discrepancy is obviously to be found in the fact that Britain is not a closed community, but is extremely dependent on foreign trade. Largely owing to her historical position as an international lender, a considerable proportion of her exports are capital goods. The concentration of depression on the heavy industries is partly explained, therefore, by the fact that they are export industries. Even if they had suffered relatively little by a contraction in home demand, they would still have been hit by the unprofitableness of export in competition with foreign firms not exposed to the same kind of pressure.

Another partial explanation, though even less general in its significance, is to be found in the fact, noted in the previous chapter, that the heavy industries had been expanded by the abnormal demand of wartime (when they were practically converted into consumption goods trades), and they were now due for a contraction owing to a natural shift in demand.

Neither of these explanations, however, is wholly satisfactory. For the relative prosperity of the distributive trades, and of those sheltered trades engaged in the manufacture of consumption goods, still remains quite unaccountable. Even when we allow for these supplementary considerations, we still cannot see why the distribution of unemployment should have been so perfectly opposite to that which we first deduced. A piece of the puzzle still seems to be missing.

Now one important possibility was left out in our

previous analysis. We began then by assuming that the community was in a stationary condition, tending neither to economic progress nor decline. This implied (although the implication was not stated) that the community's stock of capital remained approximately constant; for the accumulation of capital is one of the principal causes of economic progress, just as the destruction of capital is perhaps the chief cause of economic decay. By taking it for granted that the fundamental conditions of stationariness remained unchanged after the change in wages, we made the tacit assumption that the transference of capital to new uses, the principal way in which the economic system reacts to a change in wages, could take place without affecting the total supply of capital. This assumption must now be called in question.

It is most unlikely that a stationary community, in which the supply of capital was constant, would be a community in which there was no saving. For portions of the social stock of capital are continually being destroyed, through accidental losses, mismanagements, and investments that do not come up to expectation. In order to maintain the total capital supply unchanged, there must be enough new saving to make up for these losses. Part of that saving will take place within firms, reserves being built up to cover the various risks to which their capital is exposed; but since we may expect that in any given period some firms will suffer losses large enough to drive them into liquidation, some private saving will also be necessary to cover these losses.

We can now see that it is most improbable that a general artificial raising of wages can take place without there being some effect on the quantity of social capital. Changes in the quantity of available capital will occur in four ways:

1. More firms than usual will be driven into liquidation and their capital lost.

2. Firms which are not driven into liquidation, but suffer a severe decline in profits, will have a strong incentive to reduce their dividends by less than the decline in profits, in order to keep shareholders quiet in these "bad times."[1] This is particularly likely to happen if a large portion of their capital is raised by fixed-interest securities.

3. Capitalists, suffering a decline in dividends, and consequently a decline in income, are very likely to save less—whatever is the effect of a reduction in the rate of profit on their willingness to save.

4. To some extent this will be set off by an increased saving by wage-earners.

Now since the capitalist class, by reason of their being already capitalists, may fairly be assumed to have a more developed habit of saving than wage-earners will have, it is improbable that (3) will be completely set off by (4). If this is so, there can be no doubt that the total effect of the raising of wages will be to diminish the total supply of capital.

Once we admit the probability of this reaction, we are confronted with a new situation, with whose full complexity we are not yet in a position to deal. But certain preliminary conclusions may be stated, while

[1] Those firms which anticipate that the bad times will continue are perhaps unlikely, save in extreme cases, to eat into their capital in this way. But since, in the more depressed industries, the trouble may easily not be traced to its source, but may be put down merely to a decline in demand, which is not further analysed, entrepreneurs are very likely to maintain dividends, in much the same way as they would maintain wages in a free market under apparently similar circumstances. (*Cf.* above, p. 52.)

their more precise elaboration must be left over to Chapter X.

In so far as the total capital available is reduced, the extension of more capitalistic methods and the consequent activity of the heavy industries will be damped down. For every reduction in the supply of capital will tend to raise the rate of interest higher than it would have been on the basis of our previous assumptions, and so diminish the incentive to substitute labour by machinery.[1]

On the other hand, the fact that the capitalist class as a whole has declined to contract its consumption *pari passu* with the fall in profits, means that one very important stage in our argument—the conclusion that the demand for consumption goods would not be stimulated on balance by the rise in wages—is no longer valid. There will be a net increase, at any rate to begin with, in the demand for consumption goods, because a portion of those funds which would otherwise have been devoted to the replacement of productive equipment is now spent on them. This is clearly a factor making for less unemployment in the consumption goods trades, although it will be directly set off by more unemployment in the heavy industries.

Although we are not yet in a position to comprehend properly the situation which arises in these circumstances, it is easy to see that our picture is now taking a shape much more recognisably consonant with the facts, with which, at an earlier stage of the discussion, it clashed so violently. It is true that in post-

---

[1] In so far as it makes substitution more difficult, the destruction of capital is a factor favourable to the maintenance of employment; but on the other hand, it will have obvious bad effects on employment, since less capital will be available to employ labour even on the old methods. Which of these tendencies will be dominant is a question that we cannot adequately discuss at present (see below, p. 199).

war England the control of wages was probably not imposed upon a stationary community, for it is likely that some increase in the national stock of capital was all the while going on. But this makes very little difference, so far as the distribution of unemployment is concerned. For if a community has been increasing its capital by net saving at a given rate in the past, the same circumstances which diminished the capital of a stationary community would come into force to check, in a progressive community, the rate of increase. In the stationary community the scale of the industries which produced capital goods would be adjusted merely to the replacement of the existing stock of those goods; in the progressive community net additions to this stock would also be made. And thus, even if, in the latter case, the decline in the rate of increase of capital was not sufficient to cause an absolute reduction in the supply, the heavy industries would nevertheless experience a decline in the demand for their products below the level which they had expected, except in so far as this was set off by the substitution of machinery for labour and the use of more mechanical methods in the other trades. Similarly, the reduction of net saving would operate as a relative increase in the demand for consumption goods, leading to relative activity in those trades which most directly minister to the wants of the consumer.

It must not be supposed, however, that the tendency in this direction, which has been so striking a characteristic of post-war England, is solely due to the causes already mentioned. It has been pointed out in the preceding chapter that artificial rates of wages, resulting in long-continued and extensive unemployment, can only persist if some means are taken by which the unemployed are kept alive at a standard of living with which they are not too actively dissatisfied. This could be done simply by a levy on wages, on the lines of the old Trade Union unemployment benefit. In that case, what has been said so far remains perfectly valid; for the fact that a portion of the high wages are handed over to the unemployed more or less as a present makes no significant difference to economic structure. Of course the advantages gained from wage-control, even by those who remain in employment, are heavily diminished. If on the other hand, as has been the case in the practical instance, the unemployed are sustained by funds raised through loans and by taxation (the employers' contribution to the insurance fund being a tax that raises, in the most direct manner possible, the cost of labour), then the effects which we have been describing are considerably intensified. The supply of capital to industry is still further reduced, the depression in the heavy industries is intensified, and the demand for consumption goods is maintained with even less reduction than before, or possibly even increased. We have certainly no longer any difficulty in accounting for the distribution of unemployment.

This completes our survey of the direct reactions on employment of the maintenance of artificially high wages. But it does not by any means exhaust the questions which have to be answered if we are to have a satisfactory understanding of this causal process. It shows how a community may get into a certain rather disagreeable position, a position which obviously has a good deal of relevance to much recent history (in England and elsewhere); but it does not show what are the prospects of getting out of that

position—or, generally, where the process leads. We
frequently find that writers who successfully diagnose
the presence of high-wage unemployment, conclude
that the only prospect of a cure is an improvement in
productivity. It is the conditions under which such a
cure is possible that we must now examine.[1]

In Chapter VI. we have already been concerned
with the working of those fundamental causes of
economic progress from which alone an improvement
in productivity can be sought. The analysis of
Chapter VI. thus begins to have a distinct relevance
to our present discussions. With the slight change in
method, in which we are thus involved, it seems convenient to begin another chapter.

[1] The solution will be given only in general terms, and it must not be
understood that the author would wish to apply it without qualification to
the historical instance which has been used for illustration in the above
argument. A full survey of the causes and prospects of unemployment in
modern Britain would involve the examination of many matters which fall
outside the scope of the present study. But it may be claimed that our
analysis throws light on some aspects of the problem.

CHAPTER X

How far can we expect the process of contraction described in the last chapter to lead to the establishment of a new equilibrium? This is the first question which we must endeavour to solve with the aid of our analysis of Distribution and Economic Progress. (It is true that we are now concerned with a process of decline, rather than one of progress; but, within limits, our earlier analysis was equally applicable to either case.)

I

We may begin with the case considered in the central portion of the last chapter: that which arises when, in a stationary closed community, the general level of real wages is raised, and maintained, at a height inconsistent with normal employment. We saw then that (provided there is no wastage of capital in the process) capital will be transferred to the more capitalistic industries and to more capitalistic processes within the same industries; and that this must go on so long as there is any possibility of increasing profits by such transformations. We can now see that a final position must be reached which is precisely the same as that which would have occurred if there had been a direct reduction in the number of labourers available, and a consequent rise in their marginal product on account of the increased capital per head available for

198

them. (Naturally their average productivity rises as well on account of the increased capital per head employed; while a further apparently favourable effect on productivity arises because the men excluded are likely to be on the average less efficient in themselves than the men who remain in employment. But neither of these things conflicts in the least with the fact that the total social product is reduced.)

The final position thus reached is one of equilibrium, if the existence of the unemployed is left out of account.

II

Other things being equal, an increase in the supply of capital will raise the real wages at which a given number of labourers can be employed; similarly it will raise the number who can be employed at a given level of real wages. On the other hand, a reduction in the supply of capital will reduce the number whose employment at a given wage-level is consistent with equilibrium. Thus, if capital is destroyed, through firms becoming bankrupt, and replacement funds and circulating capital being paid out in dividends and not reinvested, that is a powerful force making for the increase of unemployment. But this does not merely mean that the number of men who can be employed is lower in the final equilibrium; it means that that equilibrium itself is harder to reach. For it is the contraction of industry itself which puts businesses into a condition in which they are tempted to consume their capital; but the greater the destruction of capital, the more industry must contract; and this in its turn encourages further capital consumption, which can only be avoided if a drastic cut is made in either dividends or wages. If once the tendency to cut into capital can be removed, equilibrium is attainable; but there is clearly a possibility that this may not be the case. The contraction may prove cumulative.

There are three reasons why the equilibrating tendencies, which usually prevent the effects of an economic change continuing indefinitely in one particular direction, may possibly be absent here. First, the consumption of capital within particular firms may easily induce a considerable amount of capital-wastage outside. Those firms which are driven into bankruptcy cease to demand machines and other kinds of plant from the makers; the firms which dissipate their capital are compelled at the best to renew their equipment less frequently. The demand for the products of the constructional industries thus falls off heavily. Some counteraction to this—but most improbably a sufficient counteraction—may be found in the increased demand for constructional goods from those firms which keep their capital intact, but "rationalise"— that is to say, invest their capital in more capitalistic or roundabout forms in order to reduce costs by saving labour. However, in so far as there is a falling-off in the demand for these goods, their makers find themselves in difficulties; they have to cut dividends, or eat into their capital, and it is probable that in many cases even those firms which survive will choose the latter alternative. And this reduces the funds which will be available for capital purposes in the further stages of the adjustment, and consequently makes it necessary for the contraction to proceed further.[1]

[1] We now reach a point where the theory of Wages abuts so closely on matters which properly belong to the theory of Capital, that it becomes difficult to describe accurately the processes under consideration without

Secondly, it is improbable that any community could get into the position just described unless it possessed an extensive system of unemployment relief, since otherwise the high wages could not be maintained in the face of mounting unemployment. And unemployment relief is itself a factor making for the wastage of capital; since, when once the total amount of benefit paid out passes a certain figure, it becomes hardly possible for it to be met solely by a contraction of the expenditure on consumption of wage-earners or capitalists—the only innocuous source from which it can be paid. If it is met from the taxation of industry, it raises the costs of industry; if it is met by loans, it diminishes the supply of capital available for industry; if it is met from personal taxation, it is likely to diminish saving. Since the burden of unemployment relief, and consequently the rate of destruction of capital from this cause, is likely to increase with every increase in unemployment, the seriousness of this factor can hardly be exaggerated. If a high level of unemployment benefit is maintained, the cessation of contraction becomes nearly impossible.

Thirdly, the process of decline is greatly aggravated by the series of disappointed expectations which must almost inevitably mark its course. If it were possible for business men to foresee that at some given level of

---

an incursion into capital theory which would drive us very far afield. In particular, it is difficult to be precise, when describing a process of change which involves, as one of its most important features, the accumulation or decumulation of capital, without making use of the Böhm-Bawerkian terminology, which introduces into these matters a precision similar to that secured in other parts of economics by the use of mathematics. The full seriousness of the considerations here adduced in the text only becomes readily apparent when we think in terms of the "time-structure" of production.

For a much more extensive elaboration of the argument in the text, see Hayek, *op. cit.* The whole of this section is based on Dr. Hayek's work.

employment there would be no further incentive to contraction, and if they could get some idea of the structure of industry appropriate to that situation, then they might be able to move to that situation without more than the anticipated loss. But, in fact, there can be little doubt that they would not be pessimistic enough. In the first place they would nurse stubborn hopes of a return by some magic means to the earlier days of prosperity, and they would keep their workmen employed, and their dividends intact—regardless of the fact that the reduction in the community's supply of capital inevitably involved in this robbing of reserves must cause an immediate decline in employment elsewhere, and a much more serious future decline in employment owing to the reduced productivity of industry in general which must follow when equipment wears out which has now become irreplaceable. To some extent, employment may well be maintained in the present at the expense of greater unemployment in the future.

At a later stage in the process of contraction, the same kind of faulty anticipation would lead to considerable quantities of capital being invested in only apparently profitable enterprises—cinemas in shortly to be derelict mining villages, for instance. In the state of employment and consumers' demand at the time of their construction, these might pay handsomely; but a little later, when the disease had gone further, they would prove to be worthless. Thus more capital would be lost.

Another important aspect of the process, in which faulty anticipation may very well aggravate the wastage of capital, is the following. The constructional trades will, at the beginning of the decline, possess large quantities of fixed plant. It soon becomes clear that under the new conditions it will not pay to replace this plant; but it remains profitable to operate it so long as it gives any net proceeds at all. Consequently these trades will not contract production in proportion to the fall in demand for their products; but will continue to produce at a level of prices which is profitable in the short period, though it will not be profitable in the long period. This temporary relative cheapness of the products of the constructional trades gives an incentive to the producers of other goods to use more capitalistic methods, in apparently much the same way as would have occurred if there had been no loss of capital. At first, therefore, "rationalisation" proceeds apace; but as time goes on the fixed plant in the constructional industries wears out, the supply of equipment contracts, and the "rationalised" processes become unprofitable. A great movement of apparently fruitful activity has run to waste, and the other industries have to adjust themselves as best they can to less capitalistic, less productive, and probably more primitive methods.

III

This last aspect of the process of decline has particular relevance when we are considering one of the possible ways out—through improvements and inventions. In normal circumstances, inventions are on the whole much more likely to raise the marginal productivity of labour than to lower it; and even in the conditions we have just been considering, there can be little question that, apart from the transfer unemployment which it inevitably causes, invention is on balance a force making for the reduction of unemployment. But it must be observed that the temporary cheapness of the products of constructional trades has a definite tendency to encourage the making of "induced" labour-saving inventions, which are the kind least likely to diminish unemployment.[1] A great deal of activity is likely to go in this direction; and not only is this a factor making only to a very limited degree for a reduction of unemployment in the short run (such effect as it has may easily be cancelled out by transfer unemployment), but it is only too likely that these inventions will prove unprofitable in the long run, when the fixed plant of the constructional trades wears out, so that this activity too largely runs to waste.

For this reason it seems that very little comfort can be derived from that *Deus ex machina* who sometimes appears to still the consciences of people who perceive that high wages cause unemployment, and yet cannot abandon their hankering after a forward wage-policy: the stimulus given by high wages to the efficiency of entrepreneurs. Certainly Trade Union pressure will force entrepreneurs to look about them, to reorganise and to introduce "up to-date" methods. But at the best these activities can only slightly raise the marginal productivity of labour, and so only slightly weaken the effectiveness of the forces tending to unemployment. For reorganisation is bound to have a bias in favour of labour-saving changes; its effect on the marginal productivity of capital is bound to be much more favourable than its effect on the marginal productivity of labour.

In so far as the reorganisation is simply "rationalisation" of the kind we have discussed—the substitu-

[1] See above, p. 125.

tion of labour by machinery now only temporarily cheap—then its long-period effects are still less favourable. It is almost certain to involve wastage of capital, and so does nothing to impede the process of contraction, but rather the reverse.

Nevertheless, these considerations do not outweigh the fundamental fact that increases in technical knowledge or in the activity of entrepreneurs do generally have favourable effects on the real income of labour. Even in the midst of a process of contraction, these elements of economic progress can still exercise a beneficial effect. Just as they will generally raise the marginal productivity of labour (and consequently real wages) in a period of normal employment, so, even when employment is declining, they can do something to arrest the decline. But they work under difficulties; and their effect is less beneficent than it would be if wages were lower.

IV

In this discussion of invention, we are already moving away from the hypothesis with which we began—that the initial rise in wages takes place in a stationary economy. It is now time for us to examine the effect of a similar rise in wages in a community which is advancing in wealth by the accumulation of capital—a rather more cheerful case, and one which is more directly relevant to the recent history of England, at least up to the beginning of the World Depression.

If, under such circumstances, the transformation of production, which must still follow from the rise in wages, can take place without loss of capital, then the trouble is purely temporary. There will still be unem-

P

ployment at first, but as accumulation proceeds, the marginal product of labour will rise, and (provided there is no further rise in real wages) abnormal unemployment will gradually disappear.

But it is much more probable that there will be a loss of capital in the transformation. Now if the rate at which capital is thus dissipated is less than the rate of saving, then there will simply be a reduction in net accumulation, and therefore a slowing-up of the recuperative process. It will take longer for unemployment to disappear, but (again if wages are not raised further) the abnormal unemployment will disappear in the end, even if it is a distant end.

But if the rate of consumption of capital should come to exceed the rate of saving, then the same process of decline must set in which we have found to occur if wages are raised in a stationary community. And since capital is likely to be consumed more rapidly the greater the initial rise in wages, it seems clear that while a small raising of wages will only cause what is, on a long view, temporary unemployment, there must be some point beyond which the situation will be irretrievable, except at the expense of a drastic cutting of wages, dividends, unemployment benefits, or (most probably) all three, which must be more drastic the longer the process of decline is allowed to go on. Thus in a progressive community there is some degree of high-wage unemployment which is relatively innocuous, considered as to its effects on the general economic system; but a rise in unemployment beyond a certain critical point is infinitely more dangerous, since it puts in peril the seeds of progress themselves, and seriously diminishes the prospect of future automatic diminution of unemployment, or, indeed, of avoiding an economic decline, which can only be checked by heavy sacrifice.

This will be the situation if we start with a community where capital is increasing, but population is stationary, or increasing less rapidly than capital. If population is increasing more rapidly than capital, then the elements of declining wealth are already present, and what has been said hitherto applies with increased force. If population is diminishing, that to some extent eases the position, since declining population is a factor making for a rise in the marginal productivity of the available labour, and consequently diminishing the amount of unemployment caused by a given imposed level of wages.[1]

V

We pass on next to consider variations in the individual supply of labour—a source from which salvation has not infrequently been sought. The position here is a little more complicated. If we assume the demand for labour in general to be elastic,[2] then it follows that an increase in the supply of labour per head (the imposed rates being time-rates) must diminish labour-costs and then raise the demand for labour more than proportionately, so that the number of men employed increases. But if the imposed wages are piece-rates, this is less certain. For although an increase in the supply of labour per head will diminish costs somewhat (owing

---

[1] It is probably true, however, that a diminishing population would be accompanied by greater transfer unemployment, owing to the smaller proportion of the population who would be entering industry (the most adaptable section) in any given period. See Robbins, "Note on the Advent of a Stationary Population," *Economica*, April, 1929, pp. 76-77.

[2] See above, p. 132, and below, p. 246.

to the better utilisation of plant) it will not diminish them in proportion to the increased supply of labour per head. Consequently, unless the demand for labour is very elastic indeed, it will not increase in proportion to the increased supply. Employment will thus probably diminish.

In our discussion of Individual Supply of Labour in Chapter V., we saw that a rise in wages might generally be expected to have some favourable reaction on ability to work, and although in some circumstances this would be offset by unfavourable reactions on willingness to work, this is not necessarily the case. We may now proceed to enquire how far these reactions are likely to play a part in determining the net effects of an artificial rise in wages. It has often been maintained that the raising of wages (by Trade Boards, for example) has no deleterious effect on employment, because the high wages are matched by a rise in efficiency. How far is this possible?

First of all, there is the fact that although increased efficiency reduces labour-costs, it simultaneously increases the supply of labour per head. Thus a mere fall in labour-costs in this way is unlikely to increase considerably the number of men employed, unless the demand for labour is very elastic, and unless the increase in efficiency is large. Whatever is the elasticity of demand, an increase in efficiency in the same proportion as the initial rise in wages does no more than prevent labour-costs from rising as a result of the rise in wages[1]; so that, other things being equal, only the same quantity of labour would be demanded, and since this is being provided by fewer men, there must be a considerable amount of unemployment. If un-

_____

[1] Assuming time-rates; on piece-rates it would not even do this.

employment is to be prevented altogether by a rise in efficiency, then efficiency must rise more than proportionately to the rise in wages; though the necessary increase in efficiency is less, the more elastic is the demand for labour.[1]

Now there are several reasons why so great an increase as this in the individual supply of labour seems highly improbable save in exceptional cases. It is only among the worst-paid classes of labourers that we shall expect the higher wages to result in a marked increase in ability to work, while among them it is perhaps most likely to be counteracted by a decrease in willingness, due to the diminished pressure of poverty.[2] With other grades there are also tendencies working in both directions. To some extent, the appearance of unemployment might be expected to make people work harder, since, from their own private point of view, the harder they work, the less likely they are themselves to lose their jobs. But this is just the kind of incentive which is most likely to be countered by social pressure working the other way.

It is also important to observe that the favourable effects on efficiency must show themselves fairly rapidly if they are to come to anything. As we have seen, there is nearly always likely to be an initial

---

[1] If time-wages are raised by a fraction a of their original level, and the individual supply of labour consequently increases by a fraction b; then if the increased efficiency is to prevent unemployment, b must be not less than $(1+a)^{\frac{\eta}{\eta-1}}-1$; that is, approximately, $\frac{\eta}{\eta-1} \cdot a$. ($\eta$, the elasticity of demand, is assumed greater than 1.) If demand is inelastic, then of course increased output will diminish employment.

[2] We are told, on the one hand, that the artificial raising of wages stimulates the efficiency of labour; and, on the other hand, that the low wages in unregulated trades lead people to "spoil the market" by working excessively hard. I see no reason why both should not be true—in different circumstances; but it should be observed that each argument weakens the force, or at least the generality, of the other.

phase in which the effect of the high wages on employment will not be considerable. If, during this phase,
the individual supply of labour expands, well and good.
The unemployment will be diminished. But once unemployment has appeared to any appreciable degree,
it is itself a factor diminishing efficiency. In the case of
relatively casual trades, where the unemployment is
shared out among the main body of workmen, unemployment will diminish efficiency all round. In
relatively regular trades, it will diminish the efficiency
only of those men who suffer from it directly. But this
means that the cost of employing these men at the
imposed level of wages is raised; and so the increased
demand for labour, which may proceed from the increased efficiency of the men who stay in employment,
is largely offset by the decline in the quality of the
labour available for satisfying the increase in demand.

Although there can be little question that the demand for labour in general is elastic—when time is
allowed for re-organisation—there is equally little
doubt that we must allow for the possibility of inelastic
demand in particular trades. In a trade where the
demand for labour is inelastic, increased individual
supply of labour as the result of higher wages would
only increase unemployment. Restriction of output
would have a more favourable effect; and its occurrence is not altogether improbable. But although restriction of output would diminish unemployment in
that trade, it would increase unemployment or lower
wages outside. For the high wages must be passed on
in the end, either in higher prices to the consumer, or
in lower prices for the producers of raw materials or
capital equipment, or in both. The second alternative
will lead to a pressure on wages in the trades immedi-

ately affected; the first must force the consumers (since by hypothesis they are not economising on the products of the trades where wages have risen) to economise on something else. This must lead to a decline in demand there, and a consequent tendency to falling wages or unemployment.

Looking at the community as a whole, it is only from increased efficiency that we can look for a moderating effect on unemployment. But although it is evident that there may be some tendency in that direction, it seems unlikely that it will very considerably modify our previous conclusions.[1]

VI

The wages which throughout this discussion have been supposed fixed are real wages—that is to say, money wages corrected for movements in the price-level of consumption goods. Thus if wages were universally fixed in terms of cost-of-living scales, the preceding analysis could be applied with only minor adaptations, due to the imperfections which any actual

---

[1] To what extent the analysis of this section is really applicable to the case with reference to which arguments of the sort under consideration have most frequently been brought forward—"Sweating" and the Early Trade Boards—it is impossible to say. Probably not very much. Most of the recorded facts about that episode can be explained in much simpler terms, without reactions through the individual supply of labour having much to do with it. After a survey of some of the more readily accessible literature on the subject, I see little in the facts adduced which can possibly be regarded as inconsistent with the general analysis put forward here—though of course much in the interpretation which is generally given of them (see, for example, Sells, *The British Trade Board System*, passim). The pools of sweated labour which disfigured England at the beginning of the century have now been succeeded by pools of unemployed; the fact that the latter are not in the same places as the former will surprise no one who has understood the analysis of Chapter IX.

But it is much to be desired that some critically minded person would examine this Sweating episode properly.

cost-of-living scale must almost inevitably possess. But if it is money wages which are fixed—and this is practically the most important case—then evidently monetary disturbances may affect the situation. If the price-level rises from monetary causes, and money wages do not rise too, then the seriousness of the situation is considerably lessened, and the prospect of reducing unemployment, or at the worst retarding its increase, is considerably improved. The reverse holds if the price-level falls.

These conclusions are simple enough; but it is improbable that they exhaust the complications introduced by the monetary factor. In nearly every thinkable monetary system, the kind of process we have been examining would itself have reactions on the monetary machine; and these would have further repercussions on the "real" process. But perhaps the writer will be excused if he decides that, for the present, these repercussions lie outside the Theory of Wages. If economic science was fortunate enough to possess generally accepted principles on the broad subject which underlies this problem—the effect of monetary policy on the structure of production—then we could apply these principles to our particular problem, and round off our discussion more completely than it is now possible to do. However, the relation of Prices and Production is to-day perhaps the most hotly contested issue in all economic theory. There is thus no *via media*; either we must avoid the subject or plunge into it at considerable length. And here it is obviously necessary to take the first alternative.

VII

A little more may be said about the relation of the foregoing discussion to another branch of economic enquiry—the theory of International Trade. So far we have assumed the fixing of wages to take place within a closed community; and to that extent our discussion has been seriously removed from reality. For the only closed community which possesses any economic importance nowadays is the world; while wage-fixing has nearly always been limited by national boundaries. The prospects of international wage-fixing through international Trade Unionism (or through the International Labour Office) are dim; but it is to them that our previous analysis applies most exactly.

Nevertheless, the case we have examined is a case of very great general importance, since it is the case where the consequences of wage-fixing throughout a community are likely to be least serious. The prospects of wage-fixing within national boundaries are decidedly worse. For the situation which then arises is closely parallel to that which would emerge in the case where wages were fixed at a high level, not throughout an industry, but in some particular firms only. Clearly these firms would suffer much more seriously than they would suffer if the same wage-level was imposed throughout the industry. Their contraction would be much more severe.

If a high level of wages is imposed in one country only, the burden of these high wages falls first, and most catastrophically, upon the export industries, and upon those industries which compete with imports.

Both of these suffer extremely from foreign competition and are forced to a violent contraction. This leads to an unfavourable movement of the balance of trade. A smaller portion of the country's production goes abroad, owing to the difficulty of competing with "low-paid foreign labour". A larger portion of expenditure goes on imports, since foreign firms can charge prices in the home market with which domestic producers cannot compete. The balance of imports and exports must therefore move in an adverse direction.

Nor can anything be hoped from the non-merchandise items to correct this. If we begin with our first case of Chapter IX., in which there is no wastage of capital, then it is clear that the rate of profit on investment within the high wage country must be reduced, and this must affect the international flow of capital. If the country has been an international borrower, it will be able to borrow less; if it has been an exporter of capital, capital will flow abroad in increasing quantities. The balance of payments will thus be in even worse plight than the balance of trade.

The second case, where there is wastage of capital, is once again a little more complicated. Capital consumption is itself a factor tending to raise the marginal productivity of capital and therefore the rate of interest. To some extent wastage of capital is thus likely to counteract the previous tendency. More capital will be invested within the country, not of course in the depressed constructional trades, but in the trades making consumption goods.

However, such investment must necessarily be abnormally risky, since a further continuation of the same process which rendered it profitable may easily make it unprofitable again.[1] Thus although increased investment of this kind may very well offer temporary assistance in the task of maintaining international equilibrium, a time will probably come when there is a run of losses, and it will hardly be surprising if investors then begin to fight shy.[2]

This is one way in which wastage of capital is likely to lead in the end to a serious worsening of a country's exchange position; but there are other ways as well. It may reasonably be supposed that, during the period under consideration, foreign countries are investing capital productively, and this normal economic progress will steadily lower their relative costs of production. But although investment is taking place at home, that investment does no more than offset capital losses; the increase in the productivity of home industry, with a few probably temporary exceptions, is negligible. Thus while costs are falling abroad, domestic costs are not generally falling. Consequently the pressure of foreign competition continually grows.

Taking all these things together, we can hardly doubt that, at any rate at some stage of the process of contraction, a very serious pressure on the exchanges must arise. The banks can only resist this pressure by a rise in interest rates and consequent deflation. This, indeed, only adds to the difficulties of industry; but it is precisely the way in which the sheltered industries are forced to take their full share of the medicine. In an open economy, the effect of artificially high wages

---

[1] See above, p. 202.

[2] It is impossible not to suspect that in the recent history of Germany we have a case closely corresponding to this. *Cf.* Bresciani-Turroni, *Le Vicende del marco tedesco*, pp. 507 *ff.*

is inevitably more drastic than in a closed economy; and this is the way it takes place.[1]

This analysis has of course assumed an international currency standard—whether gold or another. And we should like to go on to enquire how far these difficulties would be removed if national currencies were independent. But this question—of obviously immense practical importance—cannot be considered here. For it involves once again those difficulties which, a few pages back, we decided to avoid. If it is real wages that are fixed, then clearly no managed currency will save the situation. It can only be a solution if we are supposing fixity of money wages; and it can only then be a complete solution if we believe in the sovereign virtues of credit expansion.

---

[1] Of course, there is the other alternative—the one which has usually resulted in practice—the collapse of the international standard. But even this is not necessarily the end of the story.

CHAPTER XI

HOURS AND CONDITIONS

THE only subject which now remains for us to discuss is one that need give us very little trouble. All the principles, on which an examination of the effects of regulation in the field of hours and conditions must be based, have already been investigated in other connections. There is no need for us to go over yet again ground which is by now sufficiently well trodden. We may confine ourselves to making directly the necessary deductions, without discussing them in detail.[1]

I

The initial situation which is created by Trade Union demands for reduced hours does not generally differ in any material respect from that which arises from a demand for increased wages. It is true that if the working day has previously been fixed at a length which is greater than the "output optimum",[2] the Union will not usually need to exert any considerable pressure in order to bring about a reduction. For the main reason why it has not paid the employer to reduce hours on his own initiative, is his unwillingness to bear the temporary costs of the period which must elapse while efficiency is being worked up; the threat of a

---

[1] For a general study of the economics of hours-regulation, see Robbins, "Hours of Labour" (*Econ. Jour.*, March, 1929).

[2] See above, p. 105.

strike will consequently be very effective. For he can now no longer avoid immediate costs if he refuses the reduction of hours; the strike costs will probably last a much shorter time than the costs of working up efficiency, but per unit of time they will be proportionately much heavier; so that he has little advantage in the short run to gain from resistance. On the other hand, in the more distant future, a reduction of hours will improve efficiency; and there is now nothing considerable to set against this. A very moderate degree of rationality on the part of employers will thus lead them to reduce hours to the output optimum as soon as Trade Unionism has to be reckoned with at all seriously.

II

But once the output optimum is passed (and it is this situation with which we shall concern ourselves in the remainder of this discussion), reductions in the working day, with unchanged weekly wages, involve permanent increases in costs; and they will thus be resisted by employers in much the same way, and to much the same extent, as demands for advances in wages. The whole situation becomes closely parallel with that we have examined previously when dealing with wages. As we shall see, reductions in hours in a single firm, or throughout a closed community, stand on exactly the same footing as wage-advances; it is only in the intermediate cases of single industries, or (less probably) single nations, that there may be some difference.

Take first the single firm. A reduction of hours below the output optimum, while weekly wages are unchanged, leaves the firm in a position where its total labour cost remains the same, but its total output is diminished. So long as the firm is no monopolist, the reduction in output can have no considerable effect on selling prices, and gross receipts consequently fall. Since labour costs are unchanged, and gross receipts reduced, profits must be diminished. There will thus set in the same process—withdrawal of capital, and contraction of employment—which we have described on earlier occasions.

If the reduction in hours is accompanied by a reduction in weekly wages, then of course the tendency to contraction is less serious. But even a reduction in wages proportional to the reduction in output will not necessarily remove all incentive to contraction. For although the share of each unit of output going to capital is no longer diminished, the total return to capital is still reduced, more or less in proportion to the reduction in output, and there is thus still an incentive for capital to be withdrawn.

Take next a whole industry. Here again there is a contraction in output, but here we can no longer neglect the effect of the reduced output on the price of the product—and the similar effect of reduced demand for raw materials on their prices. Of course, if by "industry" we mean simply those firms producing a particular type of goods within a national frontier, they may still be exposed to foreign competition in one or other of these markets. But if they are not exposed to competition in these markets, the effect of reduced output on prices may be considerable. If the demand for the product is inelastic, the reduced output may actually increase the total gross receipts of the industry—measured in money, or in command over the products of other industries—so that, even if weekly wages are unchanged, net profits will actually expand, and there will be a tendency for employment in this industry to increase, instead of diminishing. The same thing may happen even if the elasticity of demand for the product is slightly greater than unity, if the producers of the raw materials are "squeezable"—that is to say, if a falling off in demand leads to a considerable fall in price, and consequently to a very considerable fall in the total amount which has to be paid for the raw materials. Nevertheless, this is only a special case; if the demand for the product is elastic, and the supply of the raw materials is elastic, then very much the same kind of thing must happen with an industry as with a single firm.

Further, we must remember that while it is sometimes possible for a particular industry to reduce hours without causing unemployment among those who are "attached" to it, it only does so by shifting its burden on to the backs of other people. Consumers are directly damaged by the reduced supply of the product; the raw material producing industries find the demand for their products contracted, so that capital in them becomes less productive, and the wages of their labourers have to be reduced, if the withdrawal of capital is not to lead to unemployment. If consumers have an inelastic demand for the product of the first industry, so that they actually spend more money on the smaller supply than they did on the larger (and this is of course the case most favourable to the maintenance of employment in that industry), then these consumers have less money to spend upon other commodities, so that other industries are faced with a reduced demand, which must finally lead to unemployment or reduced wages. A reduction in output must be at the expense of somebody; even in those cases where the men working in the industry concerned are able to avoid bearing the burden, they only do so by shifting it on to other people.[1]

Obviously such shifting cannot come to the rescue when we pass from the case of reduced hours in one industry to the case of reduced hours throughout a whole closed community. It is still possible that some particular industries—those producing the most necessary commodities—will be able to maintain employment, in spite of the reduction in hours; but even these will generally be affected by reduced demand for their products owing to unemployment elsewhere. Further, it must be remembered that the contraction of production will generally send up prices, so that constant money wages will mean reduced real wages.

Thus in this connection the distinction between real and money wages becomes once again of outstanding importance. First of all, let us examine the case of a general reduction of hours below the output optimum, and unchanged real wages per week. Then the gross production of the community will be diminished, while in the first place the absolute share of labour remains unchanged. The share of capital is therefore diminished, and the net product (per unit)

---

[1] It is extremely unlikely that these people will only be the wealthy. For this to be possible, it is necessary that the consumers of the product should all be wealthy; and it is also practically necessary that the elasticity of their demand for the product should equal unity. For if the elasticity is greater than unity, some people will be unemployed in the trade where hours have been reduced (except in so far as the cost can be pushed off on to raw material trades, diminishing the demand for labour there); if the elasticity is less than unity, the consumers' demand for other products will fall, and this will lead to a fall in the demand for labour in other trades producing finished goods. Even if the elasticity is unity, there is still a danger of unemployment in the raw material trades, though this (the one conceivable case in which popular superstition is justified) could be prevented if they also reduced their hours.

of capital falls.[1] Capital is now cheap relatively to labour, and the same process of "rationalisation"—the same going over to more capitalistic and mechanical methods—will set in as we have observed in the case of artificially raised wages. The whole further process will work exactly as in that case. Capital in its new forms will need less labour, and unemployment will ensue.[2]

The effect of reduced hours with constant money wages depends on monetary policy. If the price-level of consumption goods is kept constant, then real wages are being kept constant, and the same results will follow as in the former case. If, on the other hand, we assume (as in Chapter VI.) a monetary policy which preserves a constant money value of the social income —and consequently raises the prices of consumption goods—then real wages are being reduced, and the effect on employment is less certain. The central analysis of Chapter VI. becomes applicable. The supply of labour is being reduced relatively to the supply of capital,[3] and the effect on the equilibrium level of money wages depends on the elasticity of substitution. If the elasticity of substitution is greater

[1] Apart from the possibility of capital consumption, as in the last two chapters.

[2] Any reduction in weekly wages will of course do something to offset this tendency to unemployment. In a closed community, a reduction in weekly wages proportional to the reduced hours is almost certain to offset it altogether. For this case can be looked at as a reduction of the supply of labour units, with the wage per unit unchanged. Although in the resulting transformation there may well be some loss of capital; yet so long as the loss is not great we shall have a situation in which there is an increased supply of capital per unit of labour, and therefore a tendency to a rise in the marginal product of a unit of labour. The demand for labour will therefore increase.

But of course this only holds for a closed community, and it cannot be predicted with any certainty for a fall in weekly wages less than proportional to the reduction in hours.

[3] Again apart from capital consumption.

than unity, equilibrium money wages will fall, and therefore a fixed minimum level of money wages will mean unemployment. In the reverse case, equilibrium money wages will actually tend to rise, although of course not to such a point as will prevent a fall in real wages.

Naturally, this only holds for the general level, and assumes mobility of labour between occupations. But although it is not directly applicable to the case where such mobility is absent, it gives us a clue to the situation which will then arise. Almost certainly there will be unemployment in some occupations; though it is very probable that in others there will be a rise in the demand for labour. If this increased demand cannot be satisfied by movement towards these occupations, money wages in them will rise; in extreme cases they may even rise to such an extent as to prevent a fall in real wages in some industries. But this only happens because these trades are shifting their burden off on to others, in some of which there will be a rise in money wages less than the rise in prices, while in the rest there will be a definite fall in the demand for labourers, so that, with constant money wages, there is unemployment. In different circumstances, the proportions of the population falling into each of these three classes will be different; but in no circumstances is the proportion of those who get a rise in real wages likely to be large. They only secure this rise in real wages by preventing entry into their occupation; if the unemployed and the men who have retained employment in less fortunate trades were allowed to enter the high-wage occupations, real wages there must fall to a level lower than that which they would have reached if there had been at the beginning no restriction of output. In so far as higher real wages may be secured in certain trades, it is only at the expense of lower real wages or unemployment in other occupations.

III

A very similar analysis to that of the preceding section is applicable to the proposal of which a good deal has been heard in recent years—the International Regulation of Hours. But before passing on to the problems raised by that proposal, it will be well to examine a simpler case of hours-regulation, which has international aspects: the case of a general reduction of hours in one country—a country engaged in international trade.

There is a good deal of similarity between the situation created by a reduction of hours in one country only, and that created by a reduction of hours in one industry only—as considered above. It is conceivable that the world demand for one country's exports might be inelastic; and in that case reduced output, leading to reduced exports, would turn the terms of trade violently in that country's favour. The reduced exports would bring in a larger quantity of imports, and the country's international trade position would therefore be improved; but it would still be uncertain whether the level of real wages within the country would be raised by its restriction of production. For hours in industries producing for home consumption would be reduced simultaneously; these industries would yield a smaller product, which might or might not be balanced by the increase in imports.

In any case, inelastic demand for a country's exports in general is very much less likely than inelastic demand for the product of a particular industry. Nearly all countries have a number of different exports, most of which compete to some extent with the products of other countries. If its competitors do not restrict production simultaneously, restriction on the part of one country can hardly be expected to raise prices sufficiently for it to be a very paying policy. It is just conceivable that the loss imposed by a general restriction of production in one country could be shifted entirely on to the shoulders of the foreigner; but if there actually are any countries which could do this, it is not easy to find them.

If the reduction in hours takes place in all countries simultaneously, then the prospect of some particular countries gaining from it is rather improved. For if its competitors reduce output simultaneously with itself, the prices of its exports are much more likely to rise considerably. It is true that its imports will simultaneously rise in price, but they need not necessarily rise to the same extent. For if its exports are largely necessities, the demand for which is not greatly reduced under the new circumstances; and its imports are less urgently wanted goods, for which other people's demand falls off very rapidly with the reduction in supply; then the wealth of this particular country may be quite definitely increased, since the reduced home production is made up by a large movement of the terms of trade in its favour. But this means simply that the sacrifice which must be laid upon someone by the reduction of output has been wholly borne by other countries.

Although this possibility is not without significance in a general view of the prospects of International Regulation of Hours, it is not suggested here that it

has much to do with the actual proposals which have
been under discussion at Geneva in recent years.
For one thing, the most obvious cases of "necessary"
exports, where a reduction of output might increase
the wealth of the exporting country, are to be found
in staple agricultural products; and an effective regulation of hours in agriculture has never been seriously
regarded as feasible. But for another thing (and this is
more important) the concrete proposals were chiefly
for a reduction of industrial working hours in all
countries to a level which had already been attained—
or practically attained—in some of the most advanced
industrial nations. The restriction of output in these
advanced countries would therefore have been relatively small; and they might have expected a considerable advantage from the much larger reduction of
output in other countries competing with them. The
prices of their exports would rise, without (in all
probability) a serious contraction in volume; in so
far as their imports were derived from agricultural
countries where the regulation of hours was imprac-
ticable, there would be no tendency to a rise in the price
of their imports; and this situation could hardly have
failed to be decidedly to their advantage. In the
relatively backward countries, however, the restriction
of hours must have led to a serious fall in real wages.
Since wages there were already relatively low, it is
most improbable that the fall in wages would be considered to be compensated by increased leisure. Thus
it is hardly surprising that the proposal for International Regulation of Hours has not met with better
success.[1]

[1] It is assumed in the above argument that all countries enforce the con-
vention equally. If the richer countries enforce it, and the poorer countries
do not, then it may conceivably be to the advantage of the poorer countries.

IV

In addition to the direct fixation of minimum wages and maximum hours of labour, collective agreements between employers and Trade Unions usually contain some provisions which are best classified as being concerned with "other conditions of labour". These provisions are extremely various, but they are capable of a rough economic classification. First, there are those which guarantee privileges of various kinds to the workmen: privileges which make work more pleasant, but which must as a general rule raise the costs of the employer—in the most general sense of diminishing the net advantage which he draws from his occupation or investment of capital. For, in general, if these privileges did not raise costs in this sense, it would not be necessary to bring pressure on the employer in order to induce him to grant them. The economic effect of the introduction of such privileges is essentially similar to the economic effect of a rise in wages—unless wages are reduced to compensate. But their quantitative importance is probably small.

Another class of provisions is designed to prevent the employment of men on particular kinds of work which may be specially disagreeable to them. This may be done by actual prohibition, or, more probably, by specially high piece-rates for such work. Economic effects here are a little more complicated. In so far as these provisions actually prevent the performance of the kind of work in question, they act as a reduction in the individual supply of labour, and consequently have similar effects to a reduction in hours. If, as is more probable, some of the work is still performed at higher

costs, then their effect is intermediate between the
effect of reduced hours and the effect of higher wages.
They reduce the individual supply of labour to some
extent, and, at the same time, they raise wages per
head to some extent. But the importance of such cases
is not very great, and the reader may be left to deduce
their working from what has gone before.

A much more important class of provisions is not
directly concerned with improving the terms upon
which the employed man performs his labour. Their
aim is rather to safeguard his job. Apprenticeship
regulations limit entry to the trade; demarcation rules
prevent particular kinds of work being transferred
from one class of workman to another class whose
wages are lower; rules about "the manning of machines" discourage the introduction of mechanical
methods. In a community where wages are relatively
plastic, the principal effect of such rules is to safeguard the privileged position of the better paid trades;
they impede the movement of labour which would
otherwise be continually at work to undermine these
privileges, and at the same time, by preventing the
employment of labour in the places where its productivity is highest, they lower the average level of real
wages. In a community where wages in general are held
rigid above the competitive level, demarcation rules
must, on balance, increase unemployment; for a given
quantity of capital will employ more men of the lower-
wage class than of the higher-wage class. The dis-
couragement of mechanical methods, on the other
hand, may do something to prevent the substitution
of capital for labour, and so far assist to maintain employment. But it is hard to believe that much can be
expected from this. The ways of substitution are often

obscure; it can hardly be prevented altogether without bringing the effective management of industry to a standstill. And even if it could be prevented, unemployment would still be created by the movement of capital between industries, and (in an open community) by the export of capital. The less the possibility of substitution, the greater the possibility of evading high wages in other ways.

V

In the last analysis, it is by this difficulty—the final impossibility of preventing evasion—that Trade Unions and Wage Boards, like almost all systems of economic regulation since the dawn of history, are defeated. Capitalist enterprise is the child of evasion; and on the long road from ancient smuggler to modern industrialist, the entrepreneur has learned more tricks than are easily reckoned with. In this field as in others, regulation is not possible at all until the more obvious and speedy methods of evasion have been stopped: Trade Unions must be able to prevent blacklegging, Wage Boards must be able to see that their decisions are not evaded by connivance between employers and employed. But although the stoppage of these most direct means of escape secures to the regulating authority a temporary success, so that it enjoys a short and happy period of self-gratulation, it appears later that the task is not finished. The entrepreneur falls back on his second line of defence: the changing of methods to the advantage of capital and the disadvantage of labour. On this line it is still possible for Trade Unions to make some impression, for they can oppose, more or less effectively, the introduction of

automatic machines. (It is much more difficult for
public authorities, such as Wage Boards, to take
effective action here; for they can hardly oppose
changes which seem obviously directed to increasing
productivity—even if it is only productivity per head
of the men still employed. And Trade Union action
against this line of evasion is much more liable to public
disapproval than are its earlier efforts at regulation.)

Even if this line of defence can be blocked—and
this is a very large assumption indeed—the defences
of the entrepreneur are not yet at an end. He can
withdraw his capital from the industry—and how is a
Trade Union to prevent that? Or he can consume his
capital in maintaining his own consumption—and how
is that to be prevented?

When the fundamental problem of regulation is
stated in this way, we seem almost driven to the conclusion that the only way.out is a supersession of the
entrepreneur by some kind of Socialism. But—to prevent misunderstanding—the writer must be allowed to
express his personal belief that this, too, is a delusion.
For, excepting in a completely static community,
where the fundamental determinants of economic
activity are always fixed and constant—and such a
community is a pure theoretical figment—adjustments of economic life to changes in natural environment and human ability must continuously be made.
And for these adjustments some institution with the
same function as the entrepreneur must always be
necessary. It is certainly conceivable that this function might be carried out by some authority which paid
more attention to justice and less to efficiency than the
entrepreneur does; but this must involve a sacrifice
in efficiency, and consequently a sacrifice—probably a

large sacrifice—of social wealth. The adjustments made by the entrepreneur in his escape from labour regulation are precisely the same kind of adjustments as he makes in order to minimise the effects of natural scarcity—bad harvests or the working out of mines. In his actions the two are inextricably bound up together; and a system in which the first adjustment was prevented would be seriously handicapped in its endeavours to make the other.[1]

Our study of the working of the labour market under industrial capitalism results in making clear a dilemma. Free competition is liable to prove intolerable, not because it fails to raise the real income of labour—decidedly it does not so fail—but because it raises expectations of security which it cannot fulfil. It must be remembered, however, that it is not the insecurity which is the product of industrialism; it is the expectation of security. In more primitive societies changes in natural environment and in his own human equipment react directly upon the economic well-being of the individual. He experiences changes from prosperity to misery far more violent than those to which nearly all members of a capitalist community are subject, but their origin is obvious, and he is under no temptation to blame them upon any other origin than that from which they actually come. With the division of labour there proceeds a concentration of risk-bearing on to a small class; by receiving a fixed contractual payment for their services other people acquire a degree of security which would have been impossible at an earlier stage of development. But the

[1] For an examination of the working of a socialist economy, which is highly relevant to this matter, see Mises, *Die Gemeinwirtschaft*, esp. pp. 201 *ff*.

capacity of any man to bear risks is limited, and therefore the insulation of the wage-earner can never be complete. Yet he easily comes to think it complete, and then, when realities jar against him, he feels himself to have been abused.[1]

So he endeavours to protect himself, through Trade Unionism and the democratic State. But our examination of the effects of regulation has shown that this protection can rarely be adequate. Carried through to the end, it can only result in a great destruction of economic wealth. But of course in fact it is not carried through to the end. Sooner or later, in one form or another, a crack comes; if it comes soon, there is not much damage done; but if it comes late, the illusion is shattered most disastrously.

The Theory of Wages, as elaborated in this book, has not proved a cheerful subject; but perhaps that may be accounted to it for realism. If there had been a panacea for labour troubles, men might have been expected to show more signs of discovering it. Just as the problem of individual economy arises from the limitation of resources, so do the economic problems of society arise from the hard necessity of cutting a coat according to the cloth.

[1] *Cf.* Clay, "Irresponsibility in Economic Life," *Political Quarterly*, January, 1931.

APPENDIX

THE principal object of this appendix is the construction of a mathematical proof of the conclusions about absolute and relative shares in the Social Dividend put forward in Chapter VI; but since the chief value of such a mathematical proof must lie in the disclosure of the exact assumptions and the precise limitations under which the propositions are true, it is convenient to begin with a consideration of certain problems whose connection with these propositions may appear at first sight a little remote.

(i.) THE CO-ORDINATION OF THE LAWS OF DISTRIBUTION

Ever since the early days of the marginal productivity theory in the eighteen-nineties, the mathematical application of the theory has been greatly hampered by the difficulty which was raised by P. H. Wicksteed, in his essay, "The Co-ordination of the Laws of Distribution" (1894). If each factor is paid according to its marginal product, is the total product exhausted, or is there a surplus or deficit? Clearly it is most consonant with the conditions of equilibrium that each factor should be remunerated according to its marginal product, including the factor which "employs" the others, and takes the surplus for its share. But will there be enough residue to pay the employing factor its marginal product?

The solution which Wicksteed himself offered to his own problem is unsatisfactory, as, indeed, he admitted on subsequent occasions.[1] But it is not true, as most English and American economists seem still to imagine, that the problem remained unsolved. Within a few months of the publication of

---

[1] *Common Sense of Political Economy*, p. 373. The argument in the text of the *Common Sense*, while perfectly valid, does not meet the mathematical difficulty. See also Robbins, "The Economic Works of Philip Wicksteed" (*Economica*, November, 1930).

Wicksteed's Essay, Léon Walras put forward a solution which is altogether free from the objections to which Wicksteed's own solution is liable.[1] But, unfortunately, Walras expressed himself in so crabbed and obscure a manner that it is doubtful if he conveyed his point to anyone who did not possess some further assistance. Anyone who knows the answer can see that Walras has got it; but anyone who does not must find it almost impossible to get it from Walras.

A perfectly intelligible solution did, however, appear a few years later in the *Vorlesungen* of Knut Wicksell.[2] With Wicksell's aid it is not difficult to clear up this matter; after which we shall be in a position to proceed with our principal enquiry.

The first thing on which we have to be clear, if we want to see our way towards a solution of this question, is that we are concerned solely with the internal coherence of the conditions of economic equilibrium. Our problem is purely one of the conditions of equilibrium, and therefore it is extremely unwise to complicate our discussions with the consideration of phenomena which only arise in the real world because the economic system is not in equilibrium; and among these fall the greater part of the activities of enterprise and management. If we persist in thinking of the factor which receives the residue as the "entrepreneur", we shall get into endless difficulties; but fortunately, without any serious departure from reality, we can think of our typical firm as a Joint Stock Company, and suppose the residue to fall to the capitalist as capitalist, management (so far as management is required) being hired like labour of other grades. Or, alternatively, we can follow Wicksell's example, and suppose the landlord or the labourer to take the residue, hiring other factors.

Once we adopt this assumption, the most ordinary non-mathematical analysis shows that every factor must get its marginal product. For every *hired* factor must get its marginal

---

[1] "Note sur la réfutation de la Théorie anglaise du fermage de M. Wicksteed." This was republished as an appendix to the third edition of Walras' *Eléments* (1896). It is omitted in subsequent editions.

[2] Vol. i., pp. 186-191.

product, since otherwise the demand for it would expand or contract; and every *unhired* factor (which is "acting as entrepreneur") must get its marginal product, since if it got less, its owners would prefer to hire it out; and if it got more, some would be transferred from the hired to the unhired class.

This is a perfectly satisfactory line of argument, and it is evidently reasoning of this kind which has generally persuaded non-mathematical economists (for example, J. B. Clark and his followers) that the "adding-up" difficulty is a delusion. And we shall see that they are right.

The trouble is that the alternative mathematical line of approach did not appear to lead to the same conclusion.

Let $x=$ the amount of product, and a, b, c. . . . the quantities of factors required to make that product x. In order that the marginal productivity law should be fulfilled, the share of the product which goes to the factor a must be $a\,\frac{\partial x}{\partial a}$, and similarly for the other factors. If the product is to be exactly divided among the factors, leaving no residue, positive or negative, then

$$x=a\,\frac{\partial x}{\partial a} + b\,\frac{\partial x}{\partial b} + \ . \ . \ . \ .$$

Wicksteed's explanation was based upon the well-known mathematical proposition, due to Euler, that if x is a homogeneous function of the first degree in a, b, c . . . so that it can be written

$$a f\left(\frac{b}{a},\ \frac{c}{a},\ .\ .\ .\right)$$

this relation

$$x=a\,\frac{\partial x}{\partial a} + b\,\frac{\partial x}{\partial b} + \ . \ . \ . \ .$$

will always be satisfied.

It was this that drew the scathing remark of Edgeworth: "There is a magnificence in this generalisation which recalls the youth of philosophy. Justice is a perfect cube, said the ancient sage; and rational conduct is a homogeneous function, adds the modern savant."[1]

---

[1] "Theory of Distribution," in *Papers*, vol. i., p. 31.

But when it is expressed in economic language, the Wicksteed-Euler proposition appears much less ridiculous than it seems to have appeared to Edgeworth. It means simply that there will be no residue, positive or negative, if the commodity in question is produced under conditions of "constant returns" —using that ill-treated expression in yet another unfamiliar, but nevertheless highly convenient, sense. The production function will have the requisite form if a proportional increase in *all* the quantities of factors employed will increase the quantity of product in the same proportion in which the factors were increased; that is to say, if the amounts of factors required per unit of product (the "coefficients of production") are independent of the amount of product.

Put in this way, the condition appears much less startling; yet it is doubtful if it can be considered to be generally satisfied. So long as all the factors are increased in the same proportion, the general condition of diminishing returns—the disproportionate increase of some factors—is absent. But the condition of increasing returns—economies of specialisation and co-operation due to size—may be present. It does seem possible that "increasing returns" (used here in a special sense, but one that has many of the implications of the ordinary meaning) may come in to upset the marginal productivity theory, as they are inclined to upset, unless we are very careful, so many economic generalisations.

We may now turn to the solution of Walras and Wicksell.

We are concerned here solely with one part of the general equilibrium system, the conditions that a particular firm should be in equilibrium. We assume perfect competition, both in the market where the firm sells its products, and in the market where it buys its factors. Thus, so far as the action of this particular firm is concerned, we can assume all the prices with which it deals to be given; for the influence of its individual action on prices, whether of product or of factors, will be negligible. In order that the firm should be in equilibrium, two conditions have to be satisfied: (1) the unit cost of production of its product must be a minimum; (2) that unit cost must equal the selling price of the product. The first condition must be fulfilled, since otherwise the owners of that factor which is "acting as entrepreneur" could increase their profits by a change in methods. The second condition must be fulfilled, since otherwise the owners of that factor would be receiving a return either higher or lower than was being earned by similar services elsewhere in the market, and someone would therefore have an incentive to act differently. In order to minimise its costs of production, the firm can vary indefinitely the quantities of factors which it uses, and therefore, of course, the quantity of product it turns out. The production function (the relation between the quantities of factors and the quantity of product) is naturally given by technical considerations.[1] The coefficients of production do not only have to be chosen so that the unit cost of production for a given output is a minimum; the output has also to be chosen so that the unit cost of production is a minimum.

We have then

$$x = f(a, b, c. \ldots) \quad \text{(production function)}.$$

Total cost of production $= ap_a + bp_b + \ldots$

where p_a, p_b are the prices of the factors.

Cost of production per unit $= \pi_x = \dfrac{1}{x}(ap_a + bp_b + \ldots) \text{——(1)}$

$\pi_x = p_x$, i.e. cost of production = selling price.

In order that π_x should be a minimum

$$\frac{\partial \pi_x}{\partial a}, \frac{\partial \pi_x}{\partial b}, \ldots \text{ must all} = 0.$$

Now $\quad \dfrac{\partial \pi_x}{\partial a} = \dfrac{\partial}{\partial a}\left\{\dfrac{1}{x}(ap_a + bp_b + \ldots)\right\}$

$$= \frac{1}{x}p_a - \frac{1}{x^2}\frac{\partial x}{\partial a}(ap_a + bp_b + \ldots)$$

---

[1] Once we grant the universality of substitution, as we have seen cause to do, as a result of the discussions of Chapter I., the existence of a production function follows necessarily.

R

$$= \frac{1}{x}\, p_a - \frac{1}{x^2}\, \frac{\partial x}{\partial a} \cdot x\pi_x$$

$$= \frac{1}{x}\left(p_a - \pi_x\, \frac{\partial x}{\partial a}\right).$$

Then, since $\dfrac{\partial \pi_x}{\partial a} = 0$, $p_a = \pi_x\, \dfrac{\partial x}{\partial a} = p_x\, \dfrac{\partial x}{\partial a}$, and similarly for the other factors.

This is the marginal productivity law, and by substituting in (1) we have

$$x = a\, \frac{\partial x}{\partial a} + b\, \frac{\partial x}{\partial b} + \cdot\ \cdot\ \cdot\ \cdot$$

proved independently of any assumption about "constant returns".

The explanation which lies behind this proof lies in the essential hypothesis that each firm is producing at that scale of output which makes its unit cost a minimum. If, as before, we assume that the prices of the factors are constant, and if we assume further that the proportions in which the factors are employed remain unchanged as output varies, we can construct a (very specialised) cost curve for the firm, giving the cost per unit of producing various outputs. Wicksteed thought he had proved that it was a necessary condition for the truth of the marginal productivity theory that this curve should be a horizontal straight line. Walras and Wicksell showed that it was only necessary that the curve should have a minimum point, and that in equilibrium output must be at that point.

Now it is clear that in the neighbourhood of the minimum point, where the tangent to the curve must be horizontal, the curve will approximate very closely to the straight line. It is not surprising that, at this point, Wicksteed's condition should be satisfied. Where Wicksteed went wrong was in his assumption that he could argue from the shape of the curve at one particular point to the general shape of the curve.

Wicksteed's difficulty can therefore be overcome by substituting for his untenable condition of "constant returns" the condition of "minimum cost" which appears, on the surface at least, more in keeping with the fundamental assumptions on which it is reasonable to base an equilibrium theory. But, as Mr. Sraffa has pointed out,[1] the condition of minimum cost is not without its difficulties. We are excluded from the assumption of diminishing returns in the usual sense; but if we assume no tendency to diminishing returns—that a simultaneous increase in all the factors in the same proportion will never increase the product less than proportionately—then either competitive equilibrium is impossible (which will be the case if increasing returns go on indefinitely) or alternatively the distribution output among the different firms in an industry will be altogether indeterminate (if increasing returns give way to constant returns). Neither of these conclusions is welcome; but if we are to avoid them, we are driven to assume that "technical diseconomies" will, after a certain point, induce diminishing returns. There can be little question that in fact there is generally a limit to the extent to which any firm can grow under given conditions, independently of the limitation of the market. But a doubt must remain how far the limitations which we do find in experience have not been assumed away on the level of abstraction on which we are now working.

Further consideration of this point would lead us too far into the more arid regions of higher general theory; its relevance to the theory of distribution is remote.

(ii.) INCREASING RETURNS

The marginal product which measures the actual return which a factor of production must get in a state of equilibrium, is the addition which is made to the product of a firm when a small unit is added to the supply of the factor available to that firm, when the organisation of the firm is adjusted to the new supply (so that it is used in the most economical way), but when the rest of the organisation of industry, including the general system of prices, remains unchanged. Now there is no

[1] "The Laws of Returns under Competitive Conditions" (*Econ. Jour.*, 1926).

reason why this increment should be the same as the increment of production which would accrue if the additional unit were made available to the whole of industry, and the whole organisation of industry, including the general price-system, were adjusted to the new supply.

If all the firms were operating in accordance with Wicksteed's law, under conditions of "constant cost"; and if we leave out of account the fact that the allocation of the increase in resources to one firm only would mean an uneconomic distribution of production; then there can be no question that these two "marginal products" would be equal. But in fact an increase in the supply of one factor generally involves a complicated redistribution of production between firms and between industries, and in consequence of these changes it is quite likely that the marginal product of a factor in the second sense will be greater than the marginal product in the first sense. The division of labour progresses as the supply of the factors increases, and the advantages of the division of labour are gained as much, or more, through an increase in specialisation between firms and between industries, as through an increase in the size of firms.[1]

Thus we have to distinguish between the "private" marginal product, which does, in equilibrium, equal the wage of labour; and the "social" marginal product, which results from an increase in the supply of labour, when we suppose that increase to have worked out its full effect. And in general it is safe to assume that the latter will exceed the former.

This divergence has awkward consequences for the application of the general marginal productivity theory. If we can assume "constant returns" and a consequent equality of "social" and "private" marginal products, it is possible to deduce certain not uninteresting results about the effect of increases in the factors on the distribution of the product. But in so far as we have to allow for increasing returns, these re-

---

[1] *Cf.* Allyn Young, "Increasing Returns and Economic Progress" (*Econ. Jour.*, 1928); Shove, "Varying Costs and Marginal Net Products" (*Econ. Jour.*, 1928).

sults are surrounded by a margin of doubt. Yet it does not seem probable that the divergence would be very great.

Nevertheless, the reader is asked to bear in mind that the exact conclusions of the following pages depend for their strict validity upon the assumption of "constant returns" in the Wicksteed-Wicksell sense; and thus upon the identity of "private" and "social" marginal products.[1]

(iii.) THE ELASTICITY OF DERIVED DEMAND

In examining the effects on Distribution of changes in the supply of the factors of production, it is convenient to begin with the special case of a change in the supply of a factor which is specialised to some particular purpose, and can only be used in one industry. The problem which is then raised within that industry is then simply a problem of the elasticity of derived demand—the problem which was studied by Marshall in his well-known example of plasterers' wages. Marshall gave four rules for the things on which the elasticity of derived demand depends; and in their discussions of this matter, economists have generally been content to use Marshall's rules, without making them the subject of any further investigation. These rules are an excellent example of the convenience of the elasticity concept, in enabling essentially mathematical notions to be used in formally non-mathematical arguments. But such procedure, although convenient, is dangerous; it will enable us to proceed more securely, if, instead of merely accepting Marshall's conclusions, we examine their mathematical foundation.

Marshall himself no doubt derived his rules from mathematics; Note XV. in the mathematical appendix to the *Prin-*

---

[1] Of the two rules about absolute and relative shares in the Dividend put forward in Chapter VI. and to whose consideration this discussion is ultimately leading, it seems extremely improbable that the rule about absolute shares could possibly be affected by increasing returns. The rule about relative shares, on the other hand, almost certainly must be affected to some extent, although it is unlikely that the difference would be very serious unless it could be shown that an increase in one particular factor would be much more likely to call forth a strong development of those tendencies making for increasing returns than an increase in the other.

ciples is enough to assure us of that. But he does not there give the full mathematical derivation; he confines himself to a simplified case, that in which the proportions of factors employed (the "coefficients of production") remain constant. A more extended enquiry, he assures us, would lead to "substantially the same results." But we may as well see for ourselves.

The four rules (in Professor Pigou's more convenient formulation) are:

I. "The demand for anything is likely to be more elastic, the more readily substitutes for that thing can be obtained."

II. "The demand for anything is likely to be less elastic, the less important is the part played by the cost of that thing in the total cost of some other thing, in the production of which it is employed."

III. "The demand for anything is likely to be more elastic, the more elastic is the supply of co-operant agents of production."

IV. "The demand for anything is likely to be more elastic, the more elastic is the demand for any further thing which it contributes to produce."[1]

We may now proceed to our mathematical enquiry.

A product is being made by the co-operation of two factors, a and b, which are remunerated according to the value of their marginal products. Let x be the quantity of product (x is thus a function of a and b), p_x its price; p_a and p_b the prices of the factors a and b respectively. If η is the elasticity of demand for the product, and e the elasticity of supply of b, how is λ, the elasticity of demand for a, determined?

We have $p_a = p_x \dfrac{\partial x}{\partial a}$, $p_b = p_x \dfrac{\partial x}{\partial b}$ (marginal products).

Also $\qquad \eta = -\dfrac{p_x}{x \dfrac{dp_x}{dx}}$, $\quad e = \dfrac{p_b}{b \dfrac{dp_b}{db}}$, $\quad \lambda = -\dfrac{p_a}{a \dfrac{dp_a}{da}}$.

[1] Marshall, *Principles*, bk. v., ch. vi.; Pigou, *Economics of Welfare*, bk. iv., ch. v.

Since the total expenditure of the firm equals total receipts,

$$p_x x = p_a a + p_b b.$$

This can also be written

$$x = a\frac{\partial x}{\partial a} + b\frac{\partial x}{\partial b}.$$

Since we are assuming "constant returns" we can treat this last equation as an identity, and differentiate it partially with respect to b,

$$\frac{\partial x}{\partial b} = a\,\frac{\partial^2 x}{\partial a \partial b} + b\frac{\partial^2 x}{\partial b^2} + \frac{\partial x}{\partial b}.$$

$$\therefore\quad b\frac{\partial x^2}{\partial b^2} = -a\,\frac{\partial^2 x}{\partial a \partial b}\quad . \quad . \quad . \quad . \quad (1).$$

Further, the total differential of x,

$$dx = \frac{\partial x}{\partial a}\,da + \frac{\partial x}{\partial b}\,db$$

$$\therefore\quad p_x dx = p_a da + p_b db\quad . \quad . \quad . \quad . \quad (2).$$

Since the condition of equality of receipts and expenditure must still be satisfied after we have made our small change in a,

$$p_x dx + x dp_x = p_a da + a dp_a + p_b db + b dp_b.$$

But from (2) this becomes

$$x dp_x = a dp_a + b dp_b.$$

And by the elasticity formulæ,

$$\frac{p_x dx}{\eta} = \frac{p_a da}{\lambda} - \frac{p_b db}{e}\quad . \quad . \quad . \quad . \quad (3).$$

Now the change in b, which results from the change in a as independent variable,

$$= db = \frac{be}{p_b}\,dp_b = \frac{be}{p_b}\,d\left(p_x\frac{\partial x}{\partial b}\right).$$

By expansion and application of (1), this becomes

$$db = \frac{be}{p_b}\left\{ -\frac{p_b dx}{x\eta} + p_x\frac{\partial^2 x}{\partial a \partial b}\left(da - \frac{a}{b}\,db\right)\right\}.$$

Now write $\sigma = \dfrac{p_a p_b}{p_x{}^2 x \dfrac{\partial^2 x}{\partial a \partial b}}$ and $\kappa = \dfrac{p_a a}{p_x x}$, and simplify.

Then $\qquad \dfrac{p_x dx}{\eta} = \dfrac{p_a da}{\sigma} - \dfrac{p_b db}{1 - \kappa}\left(\dfrac{1}{e} + \dfrac{\kappa}{\sigma}\right)$ . . . . (4).

Eliminating dx, da, db between (2), (3) and (4), we get

$$\frac{\lambda - \sigma}{\eta - \lambda} = \frac{\kappa}{1 - \kappa} \cdot \frac{e + \sigma}{e + \eta}$$

or $\qquad\qquad \lambda = \dfrac{\sigma(\eta + e) + \kappa e(\eta - \sigma)}{\eta + e - \kappa(\eta - \sigma)}.$

This gives us a value for the elasticity of demand for a, in terms of η, e, κ, and σ.[1]

These are in fact the four Marshallian variables. κ, e, η correspond to the rules (II), (III), and (IV) quoted above. σ is a suitable measure for (I); it is the "elasticity of substitution". Its principal component, $\dfrac{\partial^2 x}{\partial a \partial b}$, gives the rate of change of the marginal product of one factor for a change in the other factor. If $\dfrac{{}^2 x}{\partial a \partial b}$ is infinite, $\sigma = o$, and there is no substitution possible at all; the coefficients of production are strictly proportional. If $\dfrac{{}^2 x}{\partial a \partial b} = o$, σ is infinite, the factors are perfectly rival or their use is indifferent. If we had a third factor, or more, then $\dfrac{{}^2 x}{\partial a \partial b}$ might be negative, and the factors would be rival in the more ordinary sense of the term; an increase in one would diminish the marginal product of the other. But with only two factors, and under the assumption that there can be no "diminishing returns" to all the factors together, this is impossible.

But although $\dfrac{\partial^2 x}{\partial a \partial b}$ is thus to some extent a test of the amount of substitution possible, it is not a suitable measure of

[1] When $\sigma = 0$, this reduces to Marshall's formula (*Principles*, Mathematical Appendix, Note XV.).

the "elasticity of substitution". For its magnitude depends on the units in which x, a, and b are measured. Just as we have to multiply $\frac{dx}{dp}$ by $\frac{p}{x}$ in order to get the *elasticity* of demand, so we must multiply $\frac{\partial^2 x}{\partial a \partial b}$ by a further factor in order to get the elasticity of substitution. $\frac{p_x^2 x}{p_a p_b}$ is a suitable multiplier. But I have taken the reciprocal of this expression, in order to have a measure increasing with the facility of substitution.

Since $\dfrac{p_a p_b}{p_x^2 x \dfrac{\partial^2 x}{\partial a \partial b}} = \dfrac{\dfrac{\partial x}{\partial a} \dfrac{\partial x}{\partial b}}{x \dfrac{\partial^2 x}{\partial a \partial b}}$, σ could also have been written in this latter form.

So far we have only shown that the elasticity of derived demand depends upon Marshall's four variables. We have still to examine how it moves with the four variables—*i.e.*, to test the rules.

Taking the formula for λ, and differentiating it partially by each in turn of the four variables on which it depends, we get:

(1) $\dfrac{\partial \lambda}{\partial \sigma} = (1 - \kappa) \times$ a square.

(2) $\dfrac{\partial \lambda}{\partial \kappa} = (\eta - \sigma)(\eta + e)(e + \sigma) \times$ a square.

(3) $\dfrac{\partial \lambda}{\partial e} = \kappa(1 - \kappa) \times$ a square.

(4) $\dfrac{\partial \lambda}{\partial \eta} = \kappa \times$ a square.

The first, third, and fourth of these expressions are always positive. The first, third, and fourth rules are universally true. But the second rule is not universally true. Even if we concern ourselves only with cases where e is positive (η and σ must be positive) the second rule is only true so long as $\eta > \sigma$; so long as the elasticity of demand for the final product is greater than the elasticity of substitution. Of course, in the usual cases taken for illustration of this rule, the condition for its validity is fulfilled. It is supposed that the demand for the product is fairly elastic, while substitution is difficult. But if technical change is easy, while the product has an inelastic demand, the rule works the other way. For example, a factor may find it easier to benefit itself by a restriction in supply if it plays a large part in the process of production than if it plays a small part. *It is "important to be unimportant" only when the consumer can substitute more easily than the entrepreneur.* Further even if $\eta > \sigma$, but if the difference is small, the importance of this second rule will be negligible.

(iv.) THE DISTRIBUTION OF THE NATIONAL DIVIDEND

The last part of our enquiry—the application of these re-sults to the wider problem discussed in Chapter VI.—now presents little difficulty. We are now concerned no longer with the money demand for a factor of production engaged in the making of a particular product, but with the real demand for a general group of factors of the traditional kind "labour" or "capital". To this we can still apply our formula, but in a con-siderably simplified form. Since the total product of a closed community does not need to be sold outside that community, we can write $p_x = 1$, and $\eta =$ infinity. The elasticity of de-mand for one of these groups of factors is therefore given by the following formula, derived from the formula of the last section:

$$\lambda = \frac{\sigma + \kappa e}{1 - \kappa}.$$

From this formula[1] the second and third of the rules given above in Chapter VI. can be directly derived.

[1] It may be interesting to illustrate the significance of this formula by an arithmetical example. If we suppose $\sigma = 1$, the elasticity of supply of the factors to be zero, and the dividend to be divided between labour and capital in the proportions of 75 per cent. to 25 per cent., then the elasticity of demand for labour (measured in terms of real goods) will be 4; and the elasticity of demand for capital $1\frac{1}{3}$.

For

$$\frac{d}{da}(bp_b) = \frac{p_a(1 + e)}{\lambda}$$

$$a\frac{d}{da}\left(\frac{ap_a}{x}\right) = \frac{\kappa(\sigma - 1)}{\lambda}.$$

The rules are therefore valid so long as λ is positive; that is to say, in practically every conceivable case. (It was shown above on p. 98, footnote, that e may always be taken to be greater than -1).

It only remains for us now to make a few remarks on the reason which led Dr. Dalton[1] to arrive at a conclusion so different from that which is evidently to be derived from the last of the above formulæ. Dr. Dalton constructed a formula giving a test for the conditions under which an increase in a would increase its relative share. In our notation, his formula is $\lambda > \dfrac{1}{1 - \kappa}$. It is evident that this formula is correct, so long as e can be neglected. He then proceeded to apply to this formula estimates for the elasticities of demand for labour and capital—estimates derived from Marshall's rules, but not from any formula. He thus naturally overlooked the precise way in which λ increases with κ. The larger κ is, the higher is the obstacle that has to be jumped before a factor can increase its relative share; but since the jumper increases in strength at exactly the same rate, the obstacle is irrelevant. The condition for increased relative share depends on σ, and on σ alone.

[1] See above, p. 119.

DOCUMENTS

1

REVIEW OF "THE THEORY OF WAGES"
BY G. F. SHOVE (1933)

"THE task which is attempted in this book," the preface tells us, "is a restatement of the theory of wages in a form which shall be reasonably abreast of modern economic knowledge." It cannot be said that the task is accomplished. A theory of wages must surely formulate a definite set of principles which determines the whole system of wage-rates (*i.e.* the various rates ruling in the various industries, occupations and localities) either in actual circumstances or, at least, in the hypothetical conditions selected for treatment. Mr. Hicks does not do this, nor, so far as I can see, does he attempt it. His discussion of the principles governing the distribution of the total labour supply between trades (and grades) is, for example, very cursory and inexact. It is easy to criticise the "Marshallian" view that the numbers employed in any trade result from a balance between demand and supply: that each industry or occupation absorbs first (in logical order) those workers who are most "suitable" to it in the sense that their productivity there is highest in relation to their "supply-price" (defined as the lowest wage which would suffice to secure or retain their services for that trade): that this supply-price differs as between different workers according to their earning-capacity elsewhere, their preferences for various kinds of work, their opportunities for acquiring any special skill required in this and other trades, their parents' wealth, their access to information about the prospects in various occupations, their parents' occupations, their social connections, their place of residence, their means of subsistence if unemployed, and so on—so that there is a sort of "supply schedule" of labourers for any trade: that each trade absorbs less and less "suitable" workers until the productivity of the last man taken on (who may be the most efficient if he has also the highest supply-price) is equal to his supply-price to the trade—so that, given each worker's system of preferences between trades, his aptitudes, opportunities, etc., and given also the conditions of demand, the distribution of labour between trades becomes determinate: and that the efficiency-rate established at this "margin of transference" governs the rate throughout a trade in so far as competition and mobility are effective within it—so that the more "suitable" men get a rent or surplus above their supply-price corresponding to their greater degree of "suitability" for their occupation. All this, I say, offers a wide target for criticism. But at least it has the merit of recognising that the wage-rates at which various numbers of workers are available at any point (the conditions governing their supply) are no less important, as a determinant of the numbers employed and the rate paid there, than the rates at which they can be absorbed (the conditions governing the demand for them) and need equally prominent and equally detailed treatment, and it does lead to a definite statement of the conditions of equilibrium. Mr. Hicks puts nothing in its place. He is content to argue (pp. 76-80) that

"wages throughout a nation are subject to the equalising force of movement in search of betterment" and
that, although "the equalisation is not completely
effective" even within a trade and is "much less
effective" between trades (owing to differences in
ability, costs of training which few people can afford,
and so on), yet "there is in a free market some considerable degree of mobility between trades," with the
result that a fairly stable system of relations between
the rates in various occupations becomes established.
He does not expound the principles which determine
how far the movement goes—at what points it stops—
and accordingly what distribution of labour and what
system of rates become established. And in consequence
he puts forward no criterion by which it would be
possible to judge whether the number employed, and
the rates ruling, in any particular trade or occupation
or firm or locality are in equilibrium or likely to change.
Similarly, he excludes from the theory of wages the
reaction of earnings upon the total number of workers
available. This may, no doubt, be defended on the
ground that within the range of wage-changes encountered in practice, the reaction is too small to be
taken into account; but, in view of possible migration
when we are considering a single country and of the
large numbers still living near the subsistence level
when we are looking at the world as a whole it needs
more defence than the mere statement that "most
modern economists" are content to regard the question
of numbers as "belonging to the theory of population"
(p. 2). Moreover, the reaction of wage-rates upon the
supply of capital, though it is rightly given great
prominence, is not worked out at all fully, so that even
on the demand side the influences governing the general

level of wages are not described with any approach to exactness. In short, it is impossible to extract from Mr. Hicks's pages any precise and comprehensive formulation of the forces determining either the level of wages generally or the relation between the rates ruling in different industries, occupations and places. He has given us a series of more or less connected comments upon certain parts of, and problems in, the theory of wages—not a statement or restatement of the theory as a whole.

This is not, of course, a criticism. It means merely that his book is less comprehensive and less ambitious than its title and its preface might seem to imply.

It is divided into two parts. Of these the first (Chs. I.-VI., pp. 1-147), which occupies rather more than half the space, is, in the main, a commentary on one element in the demand side of Marshall's theory of wages—the theorem, namely, that in a competitive *régime* "the wages of every class of labour tend to be equal to the net product due to the additional labour of the marginal labourer of that class" (*Principles of Economics*, VI. i. 8, p. 518). Save for the last chapter, its value is mainly pedagogic. It meets a number of the difficulties and objections which the Marshallian analysis is apt to arouse in the mind of a beginner. Mr. Hicks writes simple and lucid English un-encumbered by diagrammatic apparatus and, in these first five chapters, reduces his use of symbols to a minimum. Selections from this part of his work should, therefore, prove a serviceable adjunct to the ordinary textbooks.

One could wish, however, that the author had carried out more completely his expressed intention "to bring into clear relief the extremely abstract assumptions on which alone it is rigorously true to say that wages equal the marginal product of labour" (p. 9). His statement of the doctrine as he interprets it does indeed expose several of these assumptions (though they are nowhere brought together); but it introduces one at least which is not necessary to the doctrine as it is ordinarily understood and gives too little prominence to another which is of fundamental importance.

To begin with the first and less vital point. Mr. Hicks takes the doctrine to mean that wages tend to equal the marginal product of the total quantity of labour *"available"* (*i.e.* on offer) and accordingly makes it depend on the assumption that all the labourers must be employed. "Wages, say the text-books, [we are not told which and where] tend to that level where demand and supply are equal. If supply exceeds demand, some men will be unemployed, and in their efforts to regain employment, they will reduce the wages they ask to that level which makes it just worth while to take them on" (p. 4). There may, perhaps, be writers who argue thus, but I have not been able to discover that Marshall, to whom this version of the theory seems to be attributed (p. 5), is among them. His view surely is that, in competitive conditions, the marginal net product of a given number of labourers measures *the demand price for that number* (*i.e.* the highest wage at which that number can find employment), and that accordingly what the wage tends to equal is the marginal net product of the number *employed*. Whether this is the same as the number seeking employment depends on the conditions of supply. There is no reason why the number willing to work at the ruling wage, let alone a higher one, should not be greater than the number who can find work at

s

it, provided that none of those who fail to get jobs are willing to work for less. Permanent unemployment is in no way inconsistent with the "marginal productivity theory" as expounded in Marshall's *Principles*—or indeed in most other "textbooks". Mr. Hicks is, however, justified in saying that the textbook discussions of wages pay much too little attention to the influence of unemployment, and that this whole subject urgently calls for further investigation.

Turning now to the second and more important point, Mr. Hicks does not, as it seems to me, give enough prominence to the dependence of the marginal productivity theory, as he states it, on the assumption of simple competition in a perfect market (or certain other highly abstract assumptions). He defines the value of the marginal net product which the wage tends to equal as the value of "the difference between the total physical product which is actually secured [by the employer] and that which would have been secured from the same quantity of other resources if the number of labourers had been increased or diminished by one" (p. 8). This is, in effect, the same as Professor Pigou's definition (*The Economics of Welfare*, p. 135) and differs, though Mr. Hicks does not point this out, from Marshall's, which is the increase (or decrease) in the total value of the employer's output consequent upon his employing (or dispensing with) a small increment of labour (*Principles*, VI. i. 8, p. 521, and Mathematical Appendix, note xiv, p. 849).[1] The difference, of course, is that Professor Pigou's definition does not, while Marshall's does allow for the reduction in the selling

[1] Marshall commonly speaks of the "net" increase "after allowing for incidental expenses", but that practice is not in point here.

value of the rest of the employer's output consequent
upon his putting a little more on the market:[1] it is
only when this element is negligibly small as compared
with the value of the additional product[2] that the
value of the marginal net product on the two definitions
is the same: and it is not negligibly small unless either
(a) the employer can discriminate in the price he
charges for different units of his output so perfectly
that a small addition to his sales can be made without
causing him to reduce appreciably the total charge for
the rest of his output; or (b) the elasticity of the
demand for his output is very large,[3] which it may be
either (i) if the elasticity of the demand for the total
output of the commodity he produces is very large,[4]
or (ii) if he supplies only a small fraction of the total
output of the commodity, competes freely with the
other suppliers and sells in a market which is perfect
in the sense that custom will be transferred to him
(or from him) wholesale if his price differs from that
charged by others to any the smallest extent. There is
no tendency for the wages of a given type of labour to
equal its marginal net product in the sense defined by
Mr. Hicks unless one or other of these conditions is
fulfilled (the third is the only one to which approxima-
tions are likely to be found at all frequently in practice
and the only one with which Marshall concerns

---

[1] If x is the employer's output, p its price per unit, δx the (small) increase
in his output obtained by employing a small additional increment of labour,
and δp, a negative quantity, the change in price per unit caused by putting
this on the market, $p.\delta x$ is the value of the marginal net product on Professor
Pigou's definition, $p.\delta x + x.\delta p$ on Marshall's. In some circumstances, δp may
be positive, but this possibility may be ignored here.

[2] $(p.\delta x.)$

[3] For where all units of his output are sold at the same price, the elasticity
of the demand for his output is $-p.dx/x.dp$; i.e. the reciprocal of the ratio of
the change in the selling value of the rest of his output to the value of the
increment of output, with the sign changed.

[4] When the market is imperfect, the conception of elasticity of demand
for the total output presents notorious difficulties, which cannot be considered

himself).[1] For the *general* condition for maximum profit is, of course, that what Marshall called the employer's "marginal outlay" on that type of labour (*i.e.* the addition to his total outlay incurred by employing a small additional quantity of it) should be equal to the increase in his total receipts which he obtains by employing it—which we may perhaps, using a phrase adopted by Professor Viner[2] and others in a rather different sense, call his "marginal revenue" from it. And if we are to say that the labour's *wage* (as distinct from the marginal outlay upon it) is to be equal to the value of its marginal net product, similar conditions are required on the supply side. For the additional outlay required to secure an increment of labour (or any other agent) includes not only the wage or price which the employer pays for it, but the change in what he has to pay for the rest of his supply.[3]

---

here. For the present purpose it must suffice to say that in this case the phrase should be taken to refer to the part of the market which is served by the employer in question.

[1] Marshall indeed, while clearly bringing out the distinction between the addition which an increment of any factor makes to the value of its employer's output and the value of the addition which it makes to his output, and declaring, it to be a "dominant fact in the theory of monopolies" and "in the case of any producer who has a limited trade connection which he cannot quickly enlarge" (*op. cit.* p. 517 and p. 849), held that "when we are studying the action of an individual undertaker with a view of illustrating the normal action of the causes which govern the general demand for the several agents of production", we should "avoid cases of this kind" and "take our normal illustration from a case in which the individual is only one of many who have efficient, if indirect, access to the market": so that "for the purpose of illustrating a part of the general action of the laws of distribution we are justified in speaking of the value of the net product of the marginal work of any agent of production as the amount of that net product at the normal selling value of the product", *i.e.* as $p.\delta x$ (pp. 849-850). His practice of speaking thus is liable to mislead, has indeed misled, careless readers into supposing that he *defines* the marginal net product of an agent by the expression just quoted. This he most emphatically and explicitly does not: he merely treats this expression as equivalent to his definition in the particular and, as he would say, "normal", case which he selected as his standard illustration of the general law.

[2] *Zeitschrift für Nationalökonomie*, Band III, Heft 1, September 1931.

[3] This will be a positive or negative quantity according as an increase in demand raises or lowers the price or wage per unit at which it can be obtained, but for our present purpose the latter possibility may be ignored.

This second element will only be negligible if either
(c) an addition to the total quantity of the labour
available[1] can be obtained without raising the wage
offered for it or (d) our employer employs only a small
fraction of the total supply, competes freely with the
other employers for its hire and hires it in a perfect
market,[2] or (e) the labour already in his service will
remain without any considerable increase in wage
and he can discriminate so perfectly in the wage he
pays for different units of the labour that a small
addition to the quantity he employs does not
appreciably affect what he pays for the rest.[3] For
practical purposes[4] we may say that the circumstances
in which the general condition for equilibrium, "an
employer's marginal outlay on an agent equals his
marginal revenue from it", reduces to "the price of an
agent equals the value of its marginal net product, as
defined by Professor Pigou and Mr. Hicks", are that
the agent should be hired and its product sold under
conditions of simple competition in a perfect market,
i.e. that the conditions indicated above under (b) (ii)
and (e) should hold.[5] Though Mr. Hicks quite explicitly
confines the doctrine to "competitive equilibrium" in

[1] For reasons analogous to those given above, this must, in the case of
market imperfection, be taken to mean available in the market which serves
our employer.

[2] We may say, if we like, that in cases (c) and (d) the "elasticity of supply"
of the labour to our employer is very large.

[3] This condition does not secure that all the units of the labour are paid a
wage equal to the value of the marginal net product, but only that the marginal
unit—that with the highest supply price in relation to its efficiency—is.

[4] But not in a theoretical discussion where generality is aimed at: for then
account must be taken of the other combinations of circumstances alluded to.

[5] If the "marginal net product" be interpreted in Marshall's sense, only the
first of these two conditions is required—the agent must be hired under conditions of simple competition in a perfect market: there may be any degree of
monopoly or market imperfection in the sale of the product. It should perhaps
be said that the whole argument is based on the assumption that the quantities
of the agents and of the product are capable of small variations and that all
the relevant functions are continuous,

a "free market", he nowhere defines these terms nor
therefore brings out fully the character and significance
of the limitation. He could have made the "extremely
abstract assumptions", on which alone the doctrine
is rigorously true, clearer if he had started, as Marshall
does, by enunciating the *general* condition for maximum profit (marginal outlay equals marginal revenue)
and then proceeded to show what artificial conditions
have to be introduced in order to reduce this to the
familiar "marginal productivity" doctrine. Peda-
gogically this approach is helpful, and it would surely
have led to a more thorough and satisfactory discussion
of the tendency towards "exploitation".

The notion of "exploitation" is central in the
modern defence of wage regulation. Mr. Hicks regards
the phenomenon as being on the whole unimportant.
He may well be right. But his argument (pp. 82-86)
would have been more convincing had it been based
on a clear analysis of the reasoning advanced on the
other side. It is *certain*, for example, that a monopolist
(unless the demand for his product is infinitely elastic
or he can discriminate in his charges with a very high
degree of nicety) will to some extent exploit his labour
(and every other hired factor) in the sense of paying it
less than the value of its marginal net product as
defined by Mr. Hicks:[1] for his "marginal revenue"
from it (which constitutes his demand price for it and
to which he equates his marginal outlay upon it) must
be less than the value of the last increment which it
contributes to his output, since in his case a small
variation in his output has an appreciable effect on the
price at which he sells, and the second element in

---

[1] The fact that some resources are employed to increase the value rather
than the volume of output is ignored here and throughout.

"marginal revenue" is not negligible. And this holds
not only in the case of monopoly but whenever there
is an imperfect market or the employer supplies a
substantial proportion of the total output. But,
although there is "exploitation" in these cases, *it does
not follow that the wage can be raised without causing
a contraction of employment*[1]—a point, and an important
one, against the case for wage-regulation and collective
bargaining as it is often presented which Mr. Hicks
does not make, though his general attitude to those
policies is critical. For that to hold good the wage
must be less than *the employer's demand price* for the
labour (*i.e.* his "marginal revenue" from it or, in other
words, the value of its marginal net product *as defined
by Marshall*). Various circumstances may secure this
—the most noteworthy being that which is formulated
by Professor Pigou and considered by our author; viz.
that a small variation in the quantity of labour hired
by our employer (or a group with whom he acts in
concert) appreciably affects what he (or the group)
pays for the rest of his (or its) supply—as it probably
will, for example, if additional supplies of the labour in
question can only be obtained by the offer of higher
rates and he (or the group) monopolises the market for
it in the sense of employing all, or a large proportion,
of the total supply. It is the prevalence of exploitation
in *this* sense which advocates of wage-regulation have
to establish if they are to claim that "exploitation"
makes a wage-increase possible without a contraction
of employment. And its prevalence is not so easy to
establish in this as in the other sense. Their most
promising resource would probably be to rely, as

---

[1] For if the wage were formerly equal to the demand price for the employer's
labour, *i.e.* his "marginal revenue" from it, a rise would make it greater and
it would no longer be worth his while to employ so much labour,

Adam Smith did 150 years ago, on the employers' open or tacit understandings not to bid against each other for labour.

Mr. Hicks's position on the whole matter seems to be that, as a rule, a monopolist's power to control the price he charges and the wage he pays is in the long run so narrowly limited by potential competition[1] that exploitation in either sense (he does not distinguish them) is unlikely to go to any considerable lengths.[2] He is probably right in claiming that monopolies are in the long run not nearly so strong as they appear to be and that the advocates of wage-regulation are apt to over-stress the practical importance of the tendency to exploitation. But he is in danger of running to the opposite extreme. And it must be remembered in theoretical discussion that any degree of market imperfection, whether in the sale of the product or in the hiring of labour (to say nothing of open or tacit understandings such as Adam Smith envisaged), opens the door to exploitation of one type or the other in some degree.[3]

Chapter VI., on "Distribution and Economic Progress", is different in character from those which go before it. Here, and in the Appendix attached to it, Mr. Hicks breaks new ground and brings a mathematical apparatus to bear. This part of his work is therefore less suitable for the beginner but of more interest to an advanced student. In the course of it he intro-

---

[1] In other words, that potential competition makes the demand for his output and the supply of his labour highly elastic in the long run.

[2] Marshall seems to have taken a somewhat similar, though less extreme view (*op. cit.* VI. xiii. 8, p. 705).

[3] Since this notice was written Mrs. J. Robinson has published her study of *The Economics of Imperfect Competition*, in which she analyses the tendency to exploitation on lines similar to those followed here. Her treatment is more elaborate than is possible in a notice such as this, but it also presents certain differences of detail. It has therefore seemed worth while to let the above paragraphs stand.

duces and defines mathematically a concept which is, I think, new and may well prove fruitful—the "elasticity of substitution" of a factor of production. This is a measure of the ease with which the factor in question can be substituted for the others, and is used ingeniously for combining into a formula and, in one respect, modifying the four rules laid down by Marshall as determining the elasticity of a derived demand. Even here more precision might perhaps have been expected, but the treatment is neat and further elaboration will doubtless follow. The author is to be congratulated on a very pretty contribution to pure theory.

Pure theory, however, it is, and the attempt made in the rest of the chapter to use it for interpreting and forecasting the results of economic progress in the actual world raises certain misgivings. The rigid assumptions which are made in order to simplify the analysis (*e.g.* that there are no economies arising from an increase in the quantity of resources in general at the disposal of the community) deprive the theoretical conclusions of generality; and there is no good reason for thinking that the special cases to which they apply are those most often found or most closely approached in practice—rather the contrary. Simplification of this kind is, of course, perfectly legitimate in a purely theoretical treatment and as a first approximation; but before the results are applied to the real world something more should be offered than a mere assurance that "it does not seem probable" that removal of the simplifying assumptions would cause a "very great" "divergence" from them (p. 241)—something in the nature of a proof is surely wanted. If economics is to be taken seriously as a science, its exponents must not shrink from the difficulty of constructing an

apparatus capable of dealing with the material
presented to them. As regards the particular case
before us, confidence in the practical conclusions
reached is not enhanced by the statement on p. 121,
"under the assumption of competition, it inevitably
follows that an invention can only be profitably
adopted if its ultimate effect is to increase the National
Dividend". A more fundamental doubt is raised by the
"grave weakness" frankly recognised on p. 113: if we
use the apparatus here employed in our analysis of the
effects of progress, "although we are really dealing with
a community in constant change, and comparing two
stages of that change, we are obliged to assume that in
each case the system is in equilibrium". And here the
assurance that "the error from this source will generally
be quite small if we are comparing two fairly long
periods separated by a considerable span of time" is
peculiarly unconvincing: *prima facie*, many of the
errors would seem to be cumulative through time. The
technique employed in the old equilibrium economics
of the nineteenth and early twentieth centuries is, no
doubt, admirably suited to display the conditions
which a position of equilibrium (long-period or short-
period) must fulfil. It is not well adapted to describe
and predict the process of growth and change. For that
purpose a new technique is urgently needed.

The second part of the book, in which the author puts
forward his most far-reaching conclusions and those
which bear most directly on practical problems, begins
(Ch. VII., pp. 136-158) with some theoretical discussion
of industrial disputes which does not carry us much
beyond, if indeed so far as, Professor Pigou's treatment
in *Principles and Methods of Industrial Peace* and the
chapter on the same subject (Part III., Ch. VI.) in

The Economics of Welfare, and is not so refined and illuminating as Dr. F. Zeuthen's recent contribution to the subject (*Problems of Monopoly*, Ch. IV.). The interpretation of the "employers' concession curve" and "the trade unions' resistance curve" is hazy and it seems impossible to extract from them the conclusions which are based upon them (while the employers' power of resistance and the unions' belief about it are somehow left out of the picture).

Next follows a short sketch (Ch. VIII.) of the growth of trade union power, remarkable for the claim that before the war, "even in the immediate pre-war period", neither in steady industries nor in those where the demand for labour fluctuated greatly "was the average level of wages, even over a short period of years, probably affected to any great extent" by trade union action (p. 170). It is the next two chapters, on "Wage Regulation and Unemployment" and "Further Consequences of Wage Regulation", which contain the kernel of this Part and in a sense of the book as a whole. They paint an extremely gloomy picture of the consequences which follow from an attempt, whether by trade unions or state regulation, to fix wages "higher than would have been paid in a competitive market" (p. 178). [Whether this means "higher than would have been paid in the absence of regulation" is not quite clear, since it has been conceded earlier (Chapter IV.) that the working of competition is slow and not absolutely perfect and that full competitive equilibrium is never attained in practice (p. 86)—but apparently it does.] The unrelieved sombreness of these chapters and their wide sweep make a certain æsthetic appeal; but the reasoning is too vague, incomplete and inexact to have any considerable value scientifically.

So difficult is it, for one reader at any rate, to arrive at any interpretation of the argument which is at all precise, that detailed criticism would be fruitless. It must suffice to indicate what seem to be the main sources of obscurity.

The central thesis is this; that if wage-rates generally are forced above "the competitive level" (whatever exactly that may be), unemployment will be caused in two ways: (i) by the "tendency for capital to shift from the less capitalistic to the more capitalistic trades" (and methods) (pp. 187-188), *i.e.* to "those which use a relatively large proportion of capital to labour in making a unit of product" (p. 187), from those which use a relatively small proportion; (ii) because "the total supply of capital" will be diminished (p. 193), since capital will be "lost" (p. 193), "eaten into" (p. 193), "consumed" (p. 199), "destroyed" (p. 199), "cut into" (p. 200), "dissipated" (p. 206) or "decumulated", and "savings" therefore checked (p. 193). Unfortunately "capital" is not defined and we are not told how quantities of it (or indeed of labour) are to be measured, and similarly of "saving". Presumably, these are "matters which properly belong to the theory of capital" (p. 200). But until they are cleared up it is impossible to follow Mr. Hicks's reasoning; and surely a theory of wages may not unreasonably be expected to include a precise and intelligible explanation of the processes through which wage-rates influence employment. For instance, it is not immediately apparent why employment should be diminished in the first of the two ways above distinguished. If capital means concrete capital goods, these are themselves the product of labour, so that, it would seem, the rise in wages must cause a proportionate rise in their cost of production[1] and consequently (if there is no change in the rate of interest) in the annual charge incurred by employing them. Similarly, if "capital" be identified with "waiting", the rise in wages causes a proportionate rise in the amount of waiting involved in the creation and use of a given instrument; or again, if we take it to be in essence the employment of labour in "roundabout methods of production", the cost of roundabout methods is raised in the same proportion as the cost of direct methods, so that, given the same "time-preference" or agio on present goods as before, the relative advantages of the two would appear to be unaffected. On all the ordinary interpretations of capital there would seem to be no change in the relative advantages of more capitalistic and less capitalistic methods unless and until the rate of interest falls. And though Mr. Hicks allows for the effect of a fall in the rate of interest as a secondary influence, it is as a secondary influence only, there being, according to him, a shift over to more capitalistic methods quite independently of this. It may indeed be argued that the *immediate* effect of a rise in wages upon employment is likely (not certain) to be less unfavourable in the more capitalistic trades than in the less capitalistic, since the supply of durable capital is fixed for the time being and the charges in respect of it are "overheads" which do not enter into short-period supply-price. But on this reasoning there would be a fall in the value of durable capital goods (due to their decreased earning-power) at the same time as the cost of producing them rose, with the result that the incidence of unemployment in capital-producing trades

[1] In the long run, of course, and subject to the necessary correction where factors which are neither labour nor capital enter into their production,

would be particularly heavy—which is the exact opposite of the result which Mr. Hicks's theory leads him to expect from the shift to more capitalistic methods. And it seems clear, in any case, that his argument does not refer to immediate reactions of this kind, but to long-range effects.[1] The whole matter would surely have been much illuminated if Mr. Hicks had not been so determined to avoid the "incursion into capital-theory" which, as he himself admits (pp. 200-201), is necessary for an accurate description of the processes under consideration.

Again, Mr. Hicks excludes from consideration the monetary reactions of wage-policy. He recognises that "the kind of process we have been examining would itself have reactions on the monetary machine; and these would have further repercussions on the 'real' process" (p. 212). "But", he continues, "perhaps the writer will be excused if he decides that, for the present, these repercussions lie outside the Theory of Wages" on the ground that there is no general agreement among economists about the character of the reactions. But it is not possible to separate "the real process" from "its monetary reactions" in this way when we are dealing with *all-round* changes in wage-rates—even if it be possible when we are concerned with changes in a single occupation playing a small part in the total activity of the community. For in a monetary economy it is through the monetary mechanism that the effects of such a change are brought about, and their nature cannot be discovered or understood without a clear analysis of that mechanism: the

[1] Substitution, during this transitional period, of instruments produced by highly capitalistic for those produced by less capitalistic industries may, of course, have a permanent effect on the methods employed; but this again does not seem to be the kind of influence which Mr. Hicks has in mind.

monetary reactions, in fact, are not simply "repercussions of" the process set up by the change, they *are*
the process and must occupy a central position in any
analysis of it. The only way to get rid of them is to
postulate a barter-economy; and this Mr. Hicks does
not do—his discussion hovers between what would
happen in a barter-economy and what does happen in
a money-economy. He seems, for example, to suppose
that monetary disturbances may be neglected if the
wages fixed are supposed to be "real wages" in the
sense of "money wages corrected for movements in
the price-level of consumption goods" by means of
"cost of living sliding-scales" (pp. 211-212)—which is
manifestly untrue.

Thus, the obscurity and lack of precision which
mar these chapters spring, I believe, from the attempt
to narrow down the theory of wages by excluding
from it any discussion, first, of the nature of capital
and the processes governing its supply, and, secondly,
of the monetary reactions set up by changes, or
disequilibria, in wage-rates.

WAGES AND INTEREST: THE DYNAMIC PROBLEM
(1935)

I

VERY much the most difficult and awkward part of the theory of wages is that which abuts on the theory of capital and interest. It is impossible to have an adequate theory of the determination of wages—at least in the short period—without having an adequate theory of capital and interest; and up to the present that has not been generally available.

Most modern theories of capital fall into one or two classes. On the one hand, there is the "timeless" type of theory, which treats capital as a factor of production like any other. Such a theory is that of J. B. Clark. In practice, it assimilates capital to land, treating it as the inexhaustible provider of a regular stream of resources. On the other hand, there is the "period of production" theory of Böhm-Bawerk and Wicksell. This treats capital as "stored-up labour"—labour stored up *in the past*.[1]

In spite of the controversies which have gone on between the adherents of these two theories, they both fall under the same condemnation. They are both "stationary" theories, built upon the hypothesis of a stationary state, quite satisfactory under that hypo-

---

[1] In my book, *The Theory of Wages*, I employed an unhealthy amalgam of these two theories; and for this, at least, I was very properly rebuked by Mr. Shove [pp. 264-7 above].

The present paper, which seeks to explore a better path, owes something to Fisher's *Theory of Interest*; and more to those few works of Professors Lindahl and Myrdal which are accessible to one who does not read Swedish (Lindahl, "The Concept of Income", in the Cassel Essays; Myrdal, "Der Gleichgewichtsbegriff", in *Beiträge zur Geldtheorie*). I have also had the advantage of reading some unpublished writings by Mr. A. G. Hart, of Chicago, and Mr. V. Edelberg, of London, which bear closely upon my subject.

thesis, but incapable of extension to meet other hypotheses, and consequently incapable of application. In a stationary state they are both correct. The "timeless" theory is correct, because capital, in stationary conditions, must always be renewed in exactly the same form as that in which it wore out; even if it is technically exhausted, it is economically inexhaustible. Böhm-Bawerk's theory is correct, because the amount of labour employed in producing new capital instruments must always be exactly the same as that which had been employed in the past in producing a similar quantity of those instruments which are now in use. But once we leave stationary conditions, these convenient equalities disappear, and theories based upon them cease to be applicable.

To found a theory upon an assumed equality, which is not a real equality, is a most dangerous thing to do; for the more complex the theory becomes, the more specialised it becomes. The blinkers grow, until they shut out nearly all the landscape. One distinction blurred over breeds another, until we have in the end only a special case of a special case of a special case.

If we must simplify (and of course we must—to take into account all the complexities at one bound would be ridiculous), it seems much better to simplify in another way. I propose in this paper to employ all the ordinary simplifications of economic theory—those simplifications which we can employ comfortably, because we have some idea of how to remove them—but not to employ the dangerous simplification of a stationary state.

The first advantage of leaving stationary conditions is that it imposes upon us a new responsibility about time. In a stationary state, one moment of time

T

is much like another, and it is possible to be very careless about time without going far wrong. But in dynamic conditions, the events of one moment are ordinarily different from the events of another, so that we are warned to mark them off clearly if we want to avoid confusion.

One consequence of this seems to be that in dynamic analysis the assumption of continuity, which is so convenient in statics, becomes highly inconvenient. We are accustomed to thinking of economic magnitudes as continuous "flows", but the convenience of this is limited to the static case, when the flows are constant through time. A flow which varies through time is very difficult to handle. Consequently it seems best to cut up the varying flows into short sections, each of which can be treated as constant. We can do this by supposing changes to take place, not continuously, but at intervals.[1]

Bearing these things in mind, let us draw up a set of simplifying assumptions.

(1) We shall assume a community which is wholly engaged in the production of a single homogeneous good, which we shall call Bread.

(2) Bread is made by the co-operation of labour (assumed homogeneous) with capital goods (not homogeneous) which we shall call Equipment. Equipment may include land, buildings, machinery, raw materials, and half-finished goods.

(3) Since every part of time has characteristics of its own, we cannot manage the analysis of more than a finite period of time. In particular, the period of time under consideration must have a beginning.

---

[1] It seems quite as legitimate to treat the continuous variable time as if it were discontinuous, as it is to treat the discontinuous demand schedule as if it were continuous.

Everything which takes place before that beginning is a datum.

(4) At the beginning there exists a certain amount of Equipment, and a certain stock of finished Bread. The Bread and the Equipment are owned by entrepreneurs; but against these assets, the entrepreneurs have Debts, owed either to the labourers or to rentiers. The amounts of initial Bread, initial Equipment, and initial Debts are the necessary result of what has gone before, and are therefore all data.

(5) In order to avoid monetary complications, we shall provisionally assume that all prices (including Debts) are reckoned in terms of Bread. The rate of interest is a "bread" rate of interest; it arises out of a contract to supply so much bread in the future in return for so much bread now.

(6) Transactions take place discontinuously. Let us say that the market is only open on one day in the week (Monday); on that day labour is hired, labour is paid, and on that day loans are made. (Equipment, on the other hand, is not exchangeable.) We shall also assume here that all loans are made for the week, and can be repaid if either party desires on the following Monday. This is a more dangerous assumption than most, since it implies that all loans are short. It is not, however, the sort of assumption which is very difficult to remove.

(7) Lastly, I assume perfect competition in the market for labour, in the market for loans, and consequently in the market for bread.

II

In our simplified economy there are thus two prices: a rate of wages and a rate of interest. On each market day these two prices have to be determined, the rate of wages at that level which will equate the demand and the supply for labour on that day, the rate of interest at that level which will equate the demand and the supply for loans. Now these demands and supplies are simply the resultants of the actions of individual entrepreneurs, labourers and rentiers; so that in order to discover the principles governing them, we have to examine the position of a representative entrepreneur, a representative labourer, and a representative rentier respectively.

The representative rentier finds himself on the first Monday with certain debts due to him (debts which include accrued interest, that being also a "bygone"). He has to decide how much of this sum to consume, and how much to reinvest. His decision will depend, in the general case, upon his relative preferences for present consumption, and for consumption at various future dates; upon the current rate of interest and upon the rate of interest which he expects to rule in future weeks. These are the things, that is, which he may take into account; it makes no difference to our analysis if he is, in fact, much less circumspect, and bases his decision (say) only upon the current rate of interest, and his desires to possess certain capital values at the end of the first week.

If we could assume that the labourer cannot vary the amount of labour which he is willing to perform in any particular week, then the position of the labourer would be substantially similar to that of the rentier. He receives a certain claim to bread on the first Monday (either in respect of past services or as an advance on future), and he has to decide how much to consume now and how much (if any) to invest. The only difference would be that his decision may be affected by his anticipations of future rates of wages.

If we must assume that the labourer can vary the amount of labour he performs, so that he has to choose how much labour to perform now, a rather more difficult problem emerges. But although it could be dealt with by the general methods of this paper, it seems unnecessary to consider it here.

The representative entrepreneur has to consider how much labour to employ now, and how far he will increase (or diminish) his debts. This last will depend partly upon his relative preferences for present and future consumption (in which matter he behaves just like a rentier), but partly also upon his estimates of the profitability of production. His demand for labour will depend wholly upon his estimates of the profitability of production—that is to say, upon the particular production plan he chooses to adopt.

A production plan can be regarded, on the basis of our simplifying assumptions, as a series of outputs of bread in successive weeks, together with the series of inputs of labour necessary to obtain those outputs.[1] For the entrepreneur has actually to determine, not only how much labour he will employ in the first week, but how he will employ that labour, whether in the production of bread for the next market day, or in the production of bread for the more distant future (activity which, a week after, will only have resulted in the production of equipment). He has a choice between a wide variety of production plans, but not an unlimited variety, since his choice is conditioned by the amount of equipment which is in his possession at

---

[1] Each output to be reckoned at the date when it is sold, each input at the date when it is paid.

the beginning. The fact that his initial equipment is given imposes *one* relation on the stream of outputs and inputs. Thus, if all the inputs are given, and all outputs but one, we can tell what is the maximum output which can be obtained on that remaining date; if all the outputs are given, and all inputs but one, we can tell what is the minimum input necessary on the remaining date. This relation may be called, by analogy with static theory, the *production function*.

Since he works under this limitation, the entrepreneur will only be able to increase his output at any specified date in the future, if he either diminishes his output at some other date, or increases his employment of labour at some date or other. He cannot increase the output of any period without either diminishing some other output or increasing some input.

Of the various possible plans, that one will be chosen which maximises the present value of the entrepreneur's net assets.[1] His estimation of this value depends partly upon the current rates of wages and interest, partly upon the wages and interest rates which he expects to rule at relevant dates in the future.[2] These latter rates are pure estimates, but on these estimates both the present value of his assets and the production plan adopted will depend.

Present value will be maximised when it is impossible to increase it by any variation in the production plan. Three kinds of variation are technically possible: (1) output of one date may be substituted for

---

[1] This depends upon the assumption that he can borrow or lend freely at fixed rates of interest (perfect competition). The entrepreneur's preferences about consumption at different dates do not affect the choice of a production plan. For any increase in the present value of his assets will always make it possible for him to reach a preferred consumption plan by suitable borrowing or lending.

[2] More strictly, the *probable* rates. Cf. Marshall, *Principles*, 8th edition, p. 858—the last sentence in the book.

output of another date; (2) input of one date may be substituted for input of another date; (3) one output and one input may be simultaneously increased or diminished. Examination of the third type of change gives us a set of marginal productivity conditions; and it will appear that when these conditions are satisfied, changes of the first two types cannot be profitable either.

Change of the third type will be unprofitable if the cost of any unit of future labour (discounted back to the present) or current labour (undiscounted) equals the discounted value of every alternative output that could be got from it. That is to say, the anticipated rate of wages in any period must equal the marginal product of that labour in any subsequent period (discounted back to that period), or to the marginal product of that labour in any previous period (accumulated on to that period).[1] Once these conditions are satisfied, it follows that a small change of the third type must leave present value unchanged. But a small change of the first or second type can always be reduced to two changes of the third type; if these leave present value unchanged, their sum must do so as well. The marginal productivity conditions are therefore enough to determine the production plan.

But although these marginal productivity conditions are sufficient to determine the production plan, there is no need to put the conditions into this form if it is not convenient. We can, if we like, derive con-

---

[1] It should be observed that in general the labour of any period has as many marginal products as there are periods under consideration, for it will be possible, by employing extra labour at any particular date, to increase output at any other period we choose. Future labour even has a marginal product in the periods before it is actually applied; for the output of bread in the near future might be increased at the expense of the deterioration of equipment—which could be made good at a later date. (I owe this last point to Mr. Edelberg.)

ditions from the first type of change—the substitution of one output for another. This would give us conditions analogous to Wicksell's equation—the rate of interest equals the relative marginal productivity of "time".[1] Unlike Wicksell, however, we have to take into account the possibility that the expected rate of interest may be different at different future dates.[2]

III

Like the marginal productivity conditions of static theory, our present marginal productivity conditions are only a means to an end. What we want to discover from them is the way in which the firm's production plan (and in particular its demand for current labour) will be affected by changes in the prices and price-anticipations which govern it. This we may now proceed to examine; but it is very important to be clear first of all that the changes with which we are concerned are purely hypothetical changes. We are still on our first Monday; we are examining the differences between the production plan actually adopted and that which would have been adopted if prices or price-anticipations had been different.

---

[1] *Lectures on Political Economy*, Vol. I, pp. 172-184.

[2] Like the ordinary static marginal productivity theory, the above analysis assumes that the production function is continuous. This assumption has caused trouble even in static theory (witness the disputes about "constant coefficients" or "fixed proportions") and it is much more dubious here. For there can be no doubt that a good many output-input pairs will be quite *unrelated*, in the sense that a small increase in input at date t_2 could not facilitate any increase in output at date t_2, while a small diminution in input at t_2 could not leave all other outputs unchanged, even if output at date t_2 were abandoned altogether.

The difficulty could be overcome by replacing our "marginal products" by "marginal net products" in the manner of Marshall, but it seems hardly worth while to work that out here. For the reader will observe that in the following section we never need to assume that *any* input-output pair is capable of variation; we shall only use the marginal productivity conditions to give us the laws of adjustment for those pairs which are capable of being adjusted.

The only current prices which enter into the problem are the current rate of wages and the current rate of interest; the only anticipated prices the rates of wages and rates of interest which the entrepreneur expects to rule in subsequent weeks. How will changes in these rates affect the current demand for labour?

A fall in the current rate of wages (unaccompanied by any fall in expected rates of wages, or by any change in interest) will ordinarily increase the demand for labour in two ways. On the one hand, it will cause current labour to be substituted for future labour; on the other hand, it will reduce the marginal cost of output at various dates in the future. Consequently, it will be profitable to plan an expansion of future output, in whose production more current labour, at any rate, is likely to be used.

A fall in the current rate of interest (unaccompanied by any fall in expected interest rates, or by any change in wages) will have exactly similar effects. It will raise the discounted values of all future receipts and future outpayments relatively to that of current labour; and this comes to the same thing, in its effects on the production plan, as a cheapening of current labour.

A fall in the rate of wages which is expected to rule at some future date (current rates, and all other expected rates, remaining the same) is less certain in its effects. It is natural to suppose that the labour of this future period would tend to be substituted for current labour, and therefore the demand for current labour would be diminished. But this is not certain; for it is conceivable that the labour of the two periods may be technically complementary, so that the new production plan, although it is adopted because it uses more labour at the future date (when labour is expected to be cheap), may also demand the employment of more current labour as well.

A fall in the rate of interest expected to rule during some future period (once more, other rates being equal) is most likely to increase the demand for current labour. For it raises the discounted values of all the outputs subsequent to the future period in question, and also raises the discounted cost of all subsequent inputs. It thus becomes more profitable to produce certain outputs, and this will normally increase the demand for labour of any period; but at the same time late applications of labour have become more expensive, so that the increased demand is likely to fall mainly upon the labour of earlier periods. Among these is current labour, and the demand for current labour is therefore likely to rise.[1]

These four cases give us the elements of our present problem; for all possible changes in wages and interest can be reduced to combinations of these four cases. Some particular combinations, however, are so important that it may be useful if we work them out in detail.

We have to recognise that the expectations of the future course of wages (and interest) are largely based on current rates; consequently a change in current rates is very unlikely to 'leave expected rates unchanged. When this is taken into account, we evidently

---

[1] Against this must be set the empirical fact (on which Marshall based his analysis of the "short period") that initial equipment is likely to be fairly specific. This implies that the technically possible production plans are likely to vary more widely in the opportunities they offer for the employment of future labour (particularly labour of the more distant future) than in the opportunities they offer for current labour. In the present application, therefore, it would seem that the increased demand for labour is more likely to exert itself upon future labour (though labour of an earlier date than that at which the fall in interest is due) than upon current labour itself.

ought to inquire what is the effect of a change in current wages (or interest) which induces a proportionate change in expected wages (or interest) in the same direction.

A general fall in wages (current and expected) will diminish th marginal cost of output at all dates, and must therefore lead to an expansion of output. This expansion may be general (at all dates), but it is not inevitable that it should be so. (Technical conditions may concentrate the increased output upon particular periods.) In order to produce the increased output, more labour will be needed; but how this increased demand for labour will be divided between current labour and future labour cannot be determined *a priori*. It is conceivable, though not perhaps very probable, that there might be no increased demand for current labour at all.[1] Since future labour is unchanged in cost relatively to current labour, there will be no direct substitution of one for the other.[2]

A general fall in interest (current and expected) will lead to a more complicated change. It is now not merely a matter of future labour becoming dearer relatively to present; future labour of every period becomes dearer relatively to all earlier labour (current and future), cheaper relatively to all future labour of a later date. There will therefore be a slight incentive to substitute current labour for labour of the near future, and at the same time a much stronger incentive to substitute it for labour of the distant future. Taking these together, it looks as if there would be a

[1] Compare the note preceding.

[2] Since the amount of labour employed will tend to increase relatively to the initial equipment, we may say, if we like, that there is *substitution* of current labour for past labour. But this is rather misleading, as the amount of past labour is embodied in the initial equipment, and is a *datum*. The use of such expressions in Chapter IX. of my *Theory of Wages* misled many readers, and to some extent the author himself.

very definite increase in the demand for current labour.[1]

But this is not all. The discounted values of all future outputs would be raised by an amount which would increase as the output date receded into the future. This would be a further factor tending to increase the demand for labour, which would exert itself upon labour of all periods; but particularly upon those applications of labour which are appropriate for the production of increased output in the more distant future. There can be little doubt that this would be a further factor tending to increase the demand for current labour.

Six cases are, perhaps, enough. They seem to show that any fall in wages or interest is likely to increase the current demand for labour, excepting a fall in the expected future rates of wages, unaccompanied by a fall in current rates. This is, on the whole, what we should expect; so far then our analysis has done no more than uncover a few (doubtless improbable) exceptions to a common-sense conclusion.

---

[1] Even this might conceivably be offset by queer forms of complementarity· Take the following special case. A fall in the rate of interest for all periods raises slightly the discounted cost of labour to be performed in three weeks' time, and raises much more the discounted cost of labour to be performed in 20 weeks' time. The important substitution will therefore be against labour performed in 20 weeks' time—in favour of current labour, and labour performed in three weeks' time. Now it is possible that labour performed in three weeks' time may be much more easily substituted for the distant future labour; so that this substitution would be effective, while the substitution of current labour for the distant future labour (on account of technical conditions) would be relatively ineffective. Further, if this was so, it would be possible for current labour to be complementary with the distant future labour; so that the marginal product of current labour might be diminished, by the diminution in the planned employment of labour in 20 weeks' time, more than enough to offset its own increased relative cheapness. Whence the demand for current labour might be diminished.

This is perhaps improbable, but it is not inconceivable. It is given here as an example of the things not dreamed of in the philosophy of Böhm-Bawerk and Wicksell.

IV

These things, then, determine the firm's demand for labour on the first Monday; what determines its demand for loans? Strictly, what we want is the extent to which it will desire to increase or diminish its debts; and this increase or diminution is the difference between its expenditure (on input and entrepreneurs' private consumption) and its receipts from output. The demand for loans thus depends very largely upon the demand for labour, and this dependence can be a source of great confusion if it is not treated very carefully.

There is, however, a way by which this difficulty can be avoided. The market for loans will be in equilibrium on the first Monday (demand will equal supply) if the extent to which entrepreneurs desire to increase (or diminish) the debts owed by them is exactly matched by the extent to which labourers and rentiers desire to increase (or diminish) the debts owed to them. Rentiers will desire to diminish the debts owed to them by an amount equal to their present consumption;[1] labourers to increase (or diminish) the debts due to them by an amount equal to the difference between their wages and their present consumption. Therefore, if the loan market is to be in equilibrium, we must have

Wages + Entrepreneurs' consumption − Output of bread = (Wages − Consumption of labourers) − Consumption of rentiers.

∴ Entrepreneurs' consumption + Rentiers' consumption + Labourers' consumption = Output of bread.

∴ Demand for bread = Supply of bread.

[1] It will be remembered that these debts include accrued interest.

An obvious result, so it would appear! But it conveys the less obvious message, that in order to determine the rate of interest, we need not examine that elusive thing, the "capital market"; for if the market for labour is in equilibrium, and if the market for bread is in equilibrium, the market for loans must be in equilibrium too.

The reason why we can refer back to the bread market in this way is that we have taken bread as our standard of value. There are two prices to be determined—a rate of wages and a rate of interest; and three equations to determine them—equations of supply and demand for labour, loans and bread. Of these three equations (as in the system of Walras) one follows from the other two. But it is completely indifferent which of the three equations we strike out in this way; convenience seems to dictate that we should strike out the equation relating to loans.

As an example of the sort of analysis which now becomes open to us, let us take the case of Trade Union action. Suppose that on our first Monday the labourers form a Trade Union, and insist (successfully) upon a higher wage than they would otherwise have got. What will be the effect on employment? That is to say, what will be the difference between the number of labourers employed under these conditions and the number who would have been employed at the same date if there had been no combination?

The analysis of the last section enables us to answer this question, so long as we can assume that the rate of interest is unaffected. It will depend to some extent upon the length of time for which the rise in wages above the competitive level is expected to last; but in any case the demand for labour on the first

Monday will probably fall—though, in view of the specificity of equipment, not much.

Is it necessary to make any correction of this result for a change in the rate of interest? We can investigate this by inquiring whether the higher rate of wages will affect the supply or the demand for bread. The supply of bread is (mostly) a datum, due to decisions which have been made in the past; so it is only the demand for bread which may be seriously affected. Now, since the receipts of the labourers will have been increased, and they are not likely to desire to save all their gains, their demand for bread will probably rise. There is no reason why the demands of the rentiers should be affected. The only hope of preventing a rise in the total demand for bread, therefore, comes from the entrepreneurs.

As a result of the rise in wages, the total value of the entrepreneurs' assets (measured in terms of bread) must have been reduced. Consequently, on the basis of their present expectations, they will have to plan a reduction in consumption either now or in the future. If they are quick to adjust their consumption habits, they may choose to consume less now; in which case the total demand for bread may be unaffected. But if they are not quick, the total demand for bread will rise, and the rate of interest will rise.

The effects of a rise in the rate of interest can be worked out on the same lines as before. It generally gives a secondary fall in the demand for labour in addition to the primary fall.[1]

[1] The distinction, made in Chapter IX. of my *Theory of Wages*, between unemployment due to the direct effects of a rise in wages, and unemployment due to indirect effects through "capital consumption", was therefore valid; but the analysis of both effects was very faulty.

The whole of the chapter ought to be withdrawn. Böhm-Bawerk was no substitute for mathematics!

V

This analysis of the effects of Trade Union action is, I believe, formally correct: that is, it is correct on its own assumptions. But it is not an analysis which can be applied to the real world in a rough-and-ready fashion—though it is capable of being extended in such a way as to make it applicable.

For the world we have been analysing is a world in which wages are paid in bread, and the rate of interest is a "bread" rate of interest; in the real world wages are paid in money, and the rate of interest is a money rate. This affects our analysis in two ways.

On the one hand, since the enterprise does its calculations in money, and the price of its product in terms of money is not fixed, we have to take into account, when analysing the production plan, not only current and expected rates of wages and interest, but also the current price of the product, and the expected movement of that price. This means that when we are analysing the effects of a rise in money wages, we have another set of indirect influences to take into account—indirect influences through the prices of products.

On the other hand, since money is now taken as the standard of value, it is the equation of demand and supply for money which is available to determine the rate of interest. The "consumption-good" equation which we used before is now no longer available; for it is fully occupied in determining the prices of consumption goods. This means that the reactions through interest are monetary reactions, and will depend in practice on the monetary system.

Thus, in order to analyse the effects of a rise in money wages, we ought (1) to examine the effect on the production plans, assuming unchanged (current and expected) interest rates and prices of products; (2) to allow for the effect on product prices of any expenditure of the increased wages;[1] (3) to examine the secondary effect on employment by this route, still assuming interest rates unchanged; (4) to examine the effect on the demand for money of these previous adjustments (interest still unchanged); (5) if we decide that the demand for money will be increased, to inquire whether that increased demand can be satisfied without a rise in the rate of interest. To answer these last questions will be a matter for monetary theory— but they do not look unanswerable.

Finally, it should be observed that in all our investigations we have never got beyond our first Monday. There is no reason why theory should be becalmed at that point; and it is clear that in order to give a complete answer to the problems we have raised, we ought to go on to see what happens on Monday week. However, time must go in its own order; and Monday week will have to be another story.

---

[1] It is possible that very little of the increased wages may be spent before Monday week. If this is so, then (at this stage) the capital value of the entrepreneurs' assets will be reduced, unless they expect an increased demand from the labourers later. And such a reduction might induce them to economise.

U

DISTRIBUTION AND ECONOMIC PROGRESS

A REVISED VERSION (1936)

THE prolonged controversy about the elasticity of substitution, which has occupied the pages of the *Review of Economic Studies*, has laid, I feel, a certain responsibility upon the first inventor of the concept. When I reread the chapter on "Distribution and Economic Progress" in my *Theory of Wages* I am conscious that it has become seriously out of date, even though it is not, I think, much misleading. But I do feel it incumbent upon me to produce a revised version, which shall take account of the latter contributions. That is the object of this article.[1] In it I shall draw particularly freely upon the work of those writers who have taught us simpler ways of establishing the fundamental propositions. Thus, so far as the main argument is concerned, I shall be able to do without the mathematical apparatus which so encumbered my original treatment.

I

1. The distribution of the social income between factors of production has striking points of similarity

---

[1] There has been only one earlier attempt at synthesis, that of Dr. Machlup (*Review of Economic Studies*, June 1935), but as appeared at once from the controversy which followed it (*Review of Economic Studies*, February 1936), Dr. Machlup's presentation cannot be regarded as finally acceptable.

Other relevant writings include, besides my chapter cited above, and Mrs. Robinson's *Economics of Imperfect Competition*, the following: Notes by P. M. Sweezy, A. P. Lerner, R. F. Kahn (*Review of Economic Studies*, October 1933); Notes by L. Tarshis, A. P. Lerner, J. E. Meade (*Review of Economic Studies*, February 1934); "The Elasticity of Substitution", by A. C. Pigou (*Economic Journal*, June 1934); Notes by R. F. Kahn and D. G. Champernowne (*Economic Journal*, June 1935); "A Reconsideration of the Theory of Value", by J. R. Hicks and R. G. D. Allen (*Economica*, February-May 1934).

I shall say nothing here on the subject of inventions, for I have nothing to add at present to what I have already written on that topic.

to the parallel problem for a single firm. The firm puts together factors A, B, . . . to make a product X; the community puts together a greater multiplicity of factors to produce a complex "product", which is really a collection of products. If we can discover the laws according to which the firm's product is divided between (or imputed to) its factors of production, we may hope to have a basis for generalising, so as to be able to solve the wider problem.

This was the method of my chapter. It involves a jump, and the jump was not taken quite carefully enough to avoid misapprehension.

Further, the "firm" problem was simplified in several ways. I assumed: (1) only two factors, and (2) perfect competition in all markets. (3) I neglected complications due to increasing returns, and (4) I neglected complications about the maintenance of capital. All these points need consideration here; and on the way from the "firm" problem to that of the community, we ought also to consider at least (5) complications due to the existence of different sorts of products. and (6) complications due to international trade.

Here I propose to deal with these complications systematically; but before I come to that, I shall restate the central argument in the simple way it is now possible to restate it. All these complications are thus, for the present, omitted. We are concerned with the division of the physical product of a single firm among the factors engaged in making that product. We assume only two factors, perfect competition, "constant returns to scale", and that we are somehow absolved from worrying our heads about the difficulties of maintaining capital intact.

2. Let us begin by considering exactly what is

meant by that hypothesis of "constant returns to scale", with which we exclude the complications of increasing returns. We define "constant returns to scale" as that technical condition in which an increase in all factors in the same proportion will leave the marginal product of every factor unchanged.[1] Thus non-proportional returns can arise only from a change in the proportions in which the factors are employed, not from a change in the scale of production.[2]

Starting from some particular combination of factors, let us consider the variation in product which would result from varying all the factors in the same proportion. Since the proportions of factors are unchanged, the group of factors may be regarded as a single complex factor, whose composition remains unchanged, but whose quantity varies. The marginal product of the factor-group is the sum of the marginal products of the individual factors (units being appropriately chosen). Since they remain constant against changes in the quantity of the complex factor, it must remain constant too. There are thus constant marginal returns to the complex factor. But if marginal returns are constant throughout, marginal returns *equal* average returns. Thus if each factor is paid according to its marginal product, total product will be exactly exhausted.

It follows that if all factors but one are paid according to their marginal products, what is left over for the other factor is a payment which also equals its marginal product per unit. Under perfect competition, hired factors are paid according to their marginal

[1] Thus it is what we used to call a "linear and homogeneous production function". It seems desirable to do without such mathematicisms as soon as possible. The economic concept is intelligible, and the above will probably be found the most convenient definition.

[2] Cf. Knight, *Risk, Uncertainty and Profit*, pp. 97-99.

products; the hiring factor must therefore be paid in the same way, for what remains for it is just enough for this—no more and no less.

Under perfect competition and constant returns to scale each factor is thus paid according to its marginal product. But the marginal products depend only upon the ratios in which the factors are used. The relative values of the factors therefore depend only upon the ratios in which the factors are used.

In the case where there are only two factors, we can thus draw a curve,[1] measuring along one axis the ratio of the quantities of factors used (A/B), along the other the ratio of the values per unit of the factors (p_a/p_b). Under the conditions assumed, this curve is perfectly determinate, and it is a necessary condition for the stability of equilibrium that it should be downward sloping.[2] The elasticity of this curve we call the *elasticity of substitution*.[3]

If the elasticity of substitution is greater than unity, an increase in the employment of A relatively to that of B will increase the area under the curve. But this area measures

$$\frac{p_a}{p_b} \times \frac{A}{B} = \frac{p_a A}{p_b B}$$

which is the ratio in which the total product is divided between the factors. A's relative share will thus be increased by a relative increase in its employment if the elasticity of substitution is greater than unity.

That the elasticity of substitution of B for A is the

---

[1] First suggested by Mr. Lerner (*Review of Economic Studies*, Vol. I, p. 71).

[2] The proof of this is substantially the same as that given for the constant sign of the elasticity of substitution between commodities in "A Reconsideration of the Theory of Value" (*Economica*, 1934, pp. 57-59).

[3] This is the definition given in Mrs. Robinson's *Economics of Imperfect Competition*, p. 256.

same as the elasticity of substitution of A for B may
be sufficiently indicated by remarking that a relative
increase in A is the same thing as a relative decrease
in B. The condition for a relative increase in A increasing A's relative share is the same as the condition
for a relative decrease in B decreasing B's relative
share, and the critical point is the same for both
factors. And, so long as the curve is continuous,[1] an
increase in B will increase B's relative share in all
cases when a decrease in B will diminish it.

3. If the amount used of factor B is kept constant,
while that of A increases, the marginal product of A
will fall. (This is the ordinary law of diminishing
returns.) It follows directly from this that, if A is paid
according to its marginal product, the total share in
the product imputed to factor B must rise when the
employment of A rises.

Further, under conditions of constant returns to
scale, an increase in factor A must raise the marginal
product of factor B. For we know that an increase in
B alone must lower the marginal product of B, while
a proportional increase in both factors will leave that
marginal product unchanged. The increase in A must
therefore offset the effect of the increase in B. An
increase in A alone will, therefore, raise the marginal
product of B.

We may now pass over to the case where there are
a number of competitive and similar firms, producing
the same product by the combination of factors
A and B. The factors are paid according to their
marginal products, and the rules just enunciated will

---

[1] This is the general condition for most *a priori* propositions in economics.
Of course, the curve may not be continuous at all points; but the chance of
one's so hitting a point of discontinuity that the proposition becomes seriously
untrue is very small.

give us the effect of a change in the supply of A on the remuneration of B—so long as the supply of B can be taken as fixed.

But even if the supply of B cannot be taken as fixed, we have still a rise in the demand curve for B; and this must ordinarily result in an increase in B's aggregate remuneration.[1]

4. We have seen that a relative increase in the employment of A will increase A's relative share if the elasticity of substitution is greater than 1. This may obviously be read as the condition for an increase in A's relative share if its relative supply increases, when we are considering a group of competitive firms.

The question remains: when the supply of B is not fixed, so that we have to allow for repercussions on the supply of B, can we assume that an absolute rise in the supply of A will always result in a rise in A's relative abundance? Three cases may be distinguished:

(1) If the supply curve of B is negatively inclined, in such a way that a rise in its remuneration per unit diminishes its supply, an increase in the supply of A diminishes that of B, and, therefore, the relative supply of A is increased *a fortiori*.

(2) If the supply curve of B is positively inclined, an increase in the supply of A will raise that of B.

---

[1] This remuneration must be taken throughout as being in terms of the product.

If we are interested in the remuneration of B in terms of something else (*e.g.* money), allowance must be made for any consequential change in the value of the product in terms of that something, that is to say, we must allow for the elasticity of the demand for the product. The problem thus arising has been solved by Mrs. Robinson (*The Economics of Imperfect Competition*, p. 258). She has shown that an increase in the supply of A will raise the demand for B (in terms of money), if the elasticity of demand for the product is greater than the elasticity of substitution. This is an extremely significant and valuable formula. It is entirely consistent with our present theory. The reader may try this out for himself if he will consider the case when the elasticity of demand for the product and the elasticity of substitution are both equal to 1.

This is a more dangerous case, but not fatal. For the limit to which the supply of B can possibly increase is that in which its remuneration per unit (*i.e.* its marginal product) remains unchanged. But this (by the hypothesis of constant returns to scale) is the case where both factors increase in the same proportion. Anything less than perfect elasticity of supply of B will therefore only damp down the increase in A's relative abundance; in no case can the relative abundance of A diminish when its supply increases.

(3) A case where our rule does break down has been noted by Mr. Kahn.[1] If B is a "produced factor", itself subject to increasing returns, it is possible that its supply curve may be negatively sloping, in such a way that an increase in the demand for it diminishes its supply price. This condition seems to involve some imperfect competition somewhere in the system, and it is therefore doubtful if we should admit it here. But if we do find it convenient to admit it, it is a case where a rise in the supply of A may diminish its relative abundance, so that its relative share will rise if the elasticity of substitution is less than 1.

II

We must now pass on to discuss the limitations of the above analysis. I have listed six complications which may get us into trouble when we proceed to apply it, and with these complications we must now deal. We shall be obliged to deal with them separately, although the reader will observe that this is not really an adequate treatment. But the six knights will give us enough trouble in single combat; we could hardly hope to withstand their combined onslaught.

[1] *Review of Economic Studies*, Vol. 1, p. 76.

1. *The multiplicity of factors.* We may begin by dropping the assumption of two homogeneous factors. The mathematical complications which arise when we introduce a third factor are monstrous and horrible, as witness the endeavours of Professor Pigou and Mr. Champernowne.[1] I think it is possible to get a little further with the problem of relative shares in this more general case than Professor Pigou has done; most of the relevant argument can be set out in words.

It is clear that when we have three factors the rule about absolute shares is the first to go. An increase in factor A must increase the absolute share of factors B and C together, but it need not increase those of both B and C separately. Similarly, under conditions of constant returns to scale, an increase in A need not increase the marginal products of both B and C, though it must increase that of at least one. It thus becomes clear that we have to distinguish two senses of *substitution*. Except in cases of fixed proportions, two factors are always substitutes in the *relative* sense, which only means that a given output may be secured by various different combinations. It is this sense which suggested the term elasticity of substitution. But out of a group of more than two factors, some pairs (but not all pairs) may be substitutes in an *absolute* sense, being such that an increase in one diminishes the marginal product of the other. Such factors we may distinguish as "rival" factors, while factors related in the opposite way may be called "co-operant". Out of a group of factors, all pairs may be co-operant, but not all pairs can be rival.[2]

---

[1] *Op. cit.*

[2] *Cf. A Reconsideration of the Theory of Value* (p. 70), where it was shown that among a group of commodities, all pairs might be substitutes, but not all pairs could be complementary. The curious looking-glass relation between

On the matter of relative shares, the simple elasticity of substitution theory breaks down when we have more than two factors, excepting in the case when the other factors *BCD* . . . continue to be used in the same proportions as before, after *A* has increased —so that they can still be treated as a single (complex) factor. In all other cases, an increase in *A* will affect the make-up of the complex factor *BCD* . . . and this will affect substitutibility. It is thus no longer true that the direction of change of *A*'s relative share is independent of the elasticities of supply of the other factors.

On the other hand, it is purely changes in the proportions in which the other factors are used which are upsetting. If the elasticities of supply were such that these proportions remained unchanged (this would mean that the more co-operant factors were in more elastic supply), then the direction of change in *A*'s relative share would still depend purely upon technical considerations, and would be independent of any variations in the elasticities of supply, which might take place subject to this condition being satisfied.[1] The correction which has to be made for the elasticities of supply of the other factors is therefore solely a

that proposition and this is to be explained by the fact that the definitions of substitutibility and complementarity there used referred to a particular indifference surface, *i.e.* to a constant level of utility, while the definitions of co-operancy and rivalry used here refer to a *variable* quantity of product.

Degrees of co-operancy and rivalry can be measured by Professor Pigou's elasticities of partial productivity (*op. cit.*) or by a more symmetrical measure which I personally prefer. This would be defined as the ratio of the relative change in the marginal product of factor *B* to the relative change in the product, when factor *A* is increased, but other factors are kept constant. (It is thus the reciprocal of the *formula* for elasticity of substitution given in my *Theory of Wages*; but in this case of many factors that name should be kept as far from it as possible.) I shall not trouble to give a name to this measure, for we are in danger of suffering from a plethora of elasticities; but it enables us to speak unambiguously of the relation between two factors as being more or less co-operant, more or less rival.

[1] I am assuming that we exclude Mr. Kahn's case, mentioned above.

correction for the extent to which the actual relation between the elasticities differs from the "neutral" relation.[1]

2. *Imperfect competition.* This is even more up-setting for our method of analysis, which was wholly based upon the assumption that each factor is paid according to the value of its marginal product. If there is imperfect competition in either the factor market or the product market, this ceases to be true. We are therefore reduced to a makeshift.

We may first observe that if it is possible to assume that the remuneration of each factor is proportional to its marginal product, that is really enough for the theory of relative shares. For if the remuneration per unit of $A(p_a$ say$) = \lambda_a \times$ the marginal product of A (m_a) and $p_b = \lambda_b m_b$, it will follow that

$$\frac{p_a A}{p_b B} = \frac{\lambda_a}{\lambda_b} \times \frac{m_a A}{m_b B}$$

and anything which increases $m_a A/m_b B$ (the ratio whose properties we know) will also increase the relative share of A, so long as λ_a/λ_b can be taken as constant, or approximately constant. Now λ_a/λ_b is a very reasonable measure of the exploitation of A by B (if it is $<$ 1) or of B by A (if it is $>$ 1). It seems, therefore, that we shall not get a very wrong impression if we use our theory even under conditions of imperfect competition—provided we remember to ask the supplementary question, have any new opportunities emerged for exploitation, of or by factor A, during the period we are considering?

---

[1] [A further paragraph about multiplicity of factors, together with a mathematical note to which it refers, has been omitted. It is easy to waste time on this topic. A more promising approach, of much less mathematical character, is indicated on pp. 340 and 380-3 below.]

3. *Increasing returns*. Some part of the difficulties of increasing returns are the same as the difficulties of imperfect competition. They have, therefore, been implicitly covered in the preceding paragraph. But there are also other difficulties which arise when we abandon the hypothesis of constant returns to scale. We have not only to allow for possible changes in λ_a/λ_b; we have also to admit that m_a/m_b may not depend wholly upon the ratio of factors supplied. The curve in our diagram is thus no longer determinate.

The best way of dealing with this situation is, I think, to redefine the curve. If we take only those pairs of factor quantities which would combine to give the same quantity of product,[1] a curve can be drawn connecting marginal product ratios and factor ratios for this quantity of product. The elasticity of substitution can be defined, as before, as a property of this curve. Then, when factor A increases, the change in the marginal product ratio will depend not only upon the elasticity of substitution, but also upon the extent to which an increase in product disturbs the marginal product ratio. This will have to be allowed for as well.

If a factor is such that its increase particularly favours the development of large-scale economies, it may be that an increase in both factors in the same proportion would turn the marginal productivity ratio in favour of this factor. This means, then, that a factor which is specially capable of calling forth increasing returns by its own increase is made thereby more likely to increase its relative share by increasing.

4. *Capital*. When, as is usually the case, one of our two factors is, or includes, capital (that is to say,

---

[1] Quantities which would be represented by an "equal product curve".

a stock of non-permanent and economically repro-
ducible goods) special difficulties arise on that account.
A part of the gross output must be set aside to cover
depreciation in capital, and the size of this depreciation allowance, which is, of course, debited against
capital's share, will affect appreciably the relative
shares of the factors. In practice the depreciation
allowance is highly arbitrary, for capital is not always
replaced (and is not always expected to be replaced)
in the same physical forms. And since the depreciation
allowance is expressed in money, it may be considerably affected by monetary disturbances.

Closely related to this point is the fact that the
dividends paid by firms may not correspond at all
accurately, in the short period, to their earnings. It is,
therefore, important not to take dividends as represent-
ing the "true" earnings of capital, at least, not without
reflection. Very little can be done about all this, but
one must remember that the income of capital is a
tricky concept.

5. *The multiplicity of products.* When we proceed
from a single firm to a whole community, the most
evident complication introduced is that we have to
deal with a variety of different products. This means,
of course, immediately, that a discussion of absolute
shares ceases to have any precise meaning. When
factor A increases, factor B will take out its real
reward in a collection of products which differs in
composition from that which it consumed previously;
and it is an "index-number problem" to say which is
the "larger". Nevertheless, the rules about absolute
shares, which we derived in the simple case, remain
suggestive.

The complications introduced by multiplicity of

products into the problem of relative shares have been emphasised by Dr. Machlup.[1] So long as we have only two factors to deal with, they do not create much difficulty.

A fall in the price of one factor A relatively to that of the other B will cause a relative decline in the prices of those goods in whose production A is relatively important. This change in prices will lead consumers to substitute these goods for others, and the more they substitute in this way, the more will the demand for A rise relatively to that for B. The change in A's relative share, which follows from an increase in its supply, depends therefore not only upon the technical elasticity of substitution within industries, but also upon the degree to which consumers are willing to substitute the products of these industries for one another in their consumption. A measure for this commodity substitution can be found, which is related to those already devised for use in the theory of value.[2] The combined elasticity of substitution between the factors is then the arithmetical sum of the elasticity of commodity substitution and our old elasticity of technical substitution.

In order for A's relative share to increase when its

---

[1] *Review of Economic Studies*, June 1935, p. 209.

[2] If S_{xy} is the partial elasticity of substitution between two goods X and Y in consumers' budgets (this is the same as what we called, in *A Reconsideration of the Theory of Value*, the elasticity of complementarity, save that I have changed its name *and sign*); if H_x and H_y are the proportions of the social income spent on X and Y; if k_{ax} and k_{ay} are the proportions of the cost of production of X and Y respectively spent on factor A; if H_a, H_b are the proportions of the social income going to factors A and B respectively; then the commodity elasticity of substitution between the factors is

$$\sum \frac{(k_{ax} - k_{ay})^2 H_a H_y \, S_{xy}}{H_a H_b}$$

where the summation is taken over all pairs of goods XY.

This commodity elasticity of substitution is almost, but not quite, necessarily positive. In practice, one would, I think, expect it to be positive and quite as important as the elasticity of technical substitution.

[For further discussion of this formula, see below, pp. 383-6.]

supply increases, it is only necessary that the combined elasticity of substitution should be greater than unity.

A qualification to this conclusion is, however, necessary.[1] The changes in the relative demands for products may not be only due to the changes in relative price of the products. They may also be affected by any change in the size or distribution of the aggregate income which follows from the change in factor supply. If, in the new situation, consumers of relatively labour-using products have become richer relatively to consumers who spend most of their money on products which need a great deal of capital, this is going to increase the relative share of capital. But this is not an effect about which much can be said.[2]

6. *International trade.* When, as is usually the case, we are concerned with the distribution of a nation's income, and the nation is not a closed economic system, two additional qualifications need to be made. One is obvious enough, that the theory will apply only to home-produced income. The other is an extension of the argument set out under our last heading.

A change in the supply of factor A within a country will generally affect somewhat that country's scale of comparative advantage in the production of different commodities. A part of the redistribution of production between commodities will, therefore, take place through foreign trade. If the increase in A increases the country's comparative advantage in those goods for which its comparative advantage was already greatest, the export industries will be expanded, and the extent of this expansion will affect

---

[1] *Cf.* Machlup, *Review of Economic Studies*, February 1936, p. 152.

[2] *Cf.* the expenditure effect in *A Reconsideration of the Theory of Value.*

the change in A's relative share. Now (apart from
reactions through foreign lending) the contributions
of the export industries to the national income consist
in those imports whose entry they make possible. The
extent to which the export industries can expand
therefore depends partly upon the willingness of the
consumer to substitute imports for domestic goods,
and this is simply one aspect of the commodity substitution discussed in the last section; but it also
depends partly upon the elasticity of the real demand
for exports on the part of foreigners (in Marshall's
sense).

Similarly, if the increase in A increases comparative
advantage in those goods for which the country's
comparative advantage had been least, the consumer
will tend to substitute domestic for foreign products.
But the effect upon A's relative share will still depend
in the same way upon the elasticity of this commodity
substitution, and upon the elasticity of the foreign
real supply of imports (which is the same thing as
the foreign demand for exports). Once again, the
greater this foreign elasticity, the greater will be the
growth of the more-A-using (this time the domestic)
industries.

In an open community, therefore, an increase in
factor A is more likely to increase A's relative share,
the more elastic is the real demand curve for the
community's exports.[1]

III

I may conclude with some general remarks about
the whole theory of relative shares. What sense, if any,

---

[1] While the above argument is, I have no doubt, broadly correct, it is, I
believe, liable to some queer exceptions due to cross-currents between industries. These are probably of little importance.

is left in our standard proposition—that an increase in the supply of a factor will increase that factor's share in the social dividend if the elasticity of substitution between it and the other resources employed is greater than unity?

First of all, it is evident that, if the standard proposition is to have any sense at all, substitution must be interpreted as including commodity substitution as well as technical substitution.[1] For an open area, it must also be interpreted as including substitution through foreign trade. But the elasticity of substitution can be interpreted in this manner, and the proposition is not seriously upset by such reinterpretation. Thus the reinterpreted elasticity of substitution is still symmetrical. We can allow for commodity substitution and foreign trade substitution, and still maintain that when conditions are such that an increase in labour will increase labour's relative share, an increase in capital will increase the relative share of capital.

The multiplicity (or, what comes to the same thing, the non-homogeneity of factors) is a great deal more upsetting, for here elasticities of supply of the factors begin to be relevant, and symmetry disappears. But, for the purpose of the theory of relative shares, this means only that we ought to take into account possible changes in the make-up of A and not-A, "labour" and "capital". Each of these factors will be in fact not a collection of homogeneous units, but a very mixed pickle, so that changes in them cannot be reduced wholly to terms of quantity. However, the problem

---

[1] In my *Theory of Wages* I was very careless about this, because I was working with a mathematical model which only took account of technical substitution. Sometimes, however, my economics unconsciously got the better of my mathematics.

x

of allowing for qualitative changes is very evidently unmanageable, and the prospects of a large proportion of these changes cancelling out in one way or another are fairly good; so that, in practice, we are probably justified in neglecting the whole difficulty, and are taking no more than ordinary statistical licence in so doing. However, cases may arise in which we want to make some allowance for this complication, as when some particular section of "not-A" is closely related to A. The tendencies which then come into operation have been indicated.

There remain two complications—increasing returns and imperfect competition—which may definitely upset the simple elasticity of substitution theory, and impart an asymmetrical twist to the result. If any facts were discovered which made it plausible to argue that an increase in *either* "labour" *or* "capital" would increase (say) "capital's" relative share, it would be along these lines that an explanation would have to be found. However, pending the discovery of such facts, these complications are perhaps better kept in cold storage, available as a second line of hypotheses, in case the first line gets us into difficulties. But the first line is the theory that can still be thrown into the old form, at least if we say that an increase in A will increase A's relative share if the combined elasticity of substitution of A for not-A is greater than unity.

Which of our various complications we do take into account must, after all, be a matter of judgment; the problem, it has been shown, is very intricate, and any simple theory is only a simplification. Personally, I feel that the combined elasticity of substitution gives us the elements with which it would be reasonable to begin any attempt at interpreting facts; but it must be the combined elasticity—concentration upon technical substitution alone would certainly be misleading.[1]

[1] Professor P. H. Douglas' *Theory of Wages* (a work which any commentator on the applied theory of distribution cannot fail to have in his mind) seems to me to suffer by too great an emphasis upon technical substitution.

COMMENTARY

INTRODUCTORY

I HAD better begin by telling the story of this book, as it appeared to the author. Since my thinking on these subjects has passed through several stages, which will leave their mark on what follows, my Commentary will be more readily understood if I explain something of what lies behind it.

First of all, there are some things that are rather obvious. 1932 was not a lucky date for the appearance of a book like this. It was the blackest year of the Great Depression; there has been no date in this century to which the theory that I was putting out could have been more inappropriate. That would not have mattered so much (for I had no pretensions to be writing a tract for the times) if it had not been that economic theory was at that very time undergoing a revolution—a revolution of which, at the time when I was writing, I was completely unconscious. Already, in the next year, came Mrs. Robinson's *Economics of Imperfect Competition*; three years later, Keynes's *General Theory*. So, soon after its birth, *The Theory of Wages* began to look like the last gasp of an *ancien régime*.

These, however, are (from my point of view) external events. Seen from within, the story was rather different.

When I wrote *The Theory of Wages* I was very young, young in years, young as an economist, and as an economic theorist younger still. I only took up economics at all seriously after I graduated in 1925, and at first I regarded myself as a labour economist, not a theoretical economist at all. My (Oxford) thesis was on "Skilled and Unskilled Wages in the Building and Engineering Trades". My first published articles (written while I held a junior post at the London School of Economics) were descriptive articles on industrial relations.[1] It was only in 1929, when Lionel Robbins came back to London as professor, that my interest in theoretical economics was really aroused. It is not much of an exaggeration to say that I had just three years in which to learn my economic theory, to apply it to what I knew of labour problems, and to write it up.

Inevitably there were fearful gaps. The theory which I had learned (in this short time) was much too one-sided. One of the great things that Robbins gave us, in those exciting years after 1929, was bibliography; he told us what to read, and got us to read it. In my own case, he moved me on from Cassel to Walras and Pareto, to Edgeworth[2] and Taussig,[3] to Wicksell and the Austrians—with all of whom I was much more at home at that stage than I was with Marshall and Pigou. (We were such "good Europeans" in London that it was Cambridge that seemed "foreign".) I was so out of tune with Cambridge economics that the "cost controversy" (the beginnings of the "theory of the firm") made little impression on me; I did not see what relevance it had to what I was doing. Still less did I perceive the relevance of the Cambridge work on monetary theory, though there was already so much—even the *Treatise on Money*—that was at my disposal if I had looked for it. I was entirely a victim of the

---

[1] "Wage-Fixing in the Building Industry" (*Economica*, 1928); "The Early History of Industrial Conciliation in England" (*Economica*, 1930).

[2] *Mathematical Psychics.*　　　　　　　　　[3] *Wages and Capital.*

traditional "dichotomy" between real and monetary economics; monetary economics was not my concern, for was it not organised (at the London School) in a different department from that in which I was teaching?

I was too much out of tune with Cambridge to derive much benefit, at that stage, from the criticisms which I got from Dennis Robertson, who read my book before publication. And I do not know that I got much more, at once, from Shove's review, reprinted above, which appeared in the *Economic Journal* in September 1933. But in fact, even before I saw what Shove had to say, my own mind had moved on. I can date my own personal "revolution" rather exactly to May or June 1933. It was like this.

It began (rather oddly, as it turned out) with Hayek. His *Prices and Production* is one of the influences that can be detected in *The Theory of Wages*; it could not have been otherwise, for 1931 was a *Prices and Production* year at the London School of Economics. (I fancy, however, that there are some implicit reservations about *Prices and Production* even in *The Theory of Wages*; I did not in fact find it all easy to fit in with my own ideas.) What started me off in 1933 was an earlier work of Hayek's, his paper on "Intertemporal Equilibrium",[1] an idea which I found easier to reduce to my preferred (Paretian or Wicksellian) pattern. There was indeed no particular difficulty about constructing a Paretian model of a dynamic economy (in which "data" are changing over time); but since the prices relevant to present decisions would be future prices as well as present prices, the dynamic model could only be made consistent if the prices expected

[1] "Das intertemporale Gleichgewichtssytem" (*Weltwirtschaftliches Archiv.*, 1928).

(to rule at time *t*) at all earlier dates were the same, and the same as those which actually equated supplies and demands at time *t*. Dynamic equilibrium was an equilibrium of perfect foresight. This was obviously unrealistic, even more obviously unrealistic than the static scheme which I had used in *The Theory of Wages*. In order to make it at all sensible, one had to introduce uncertainty; reflection upon the role of money in a model where expectations were explicitly uncertain led me straight to something which is recognisable as belonging to the same family as Liquidity Preference.

A first (still very crude) statement of my new viewpoint was published in German at the end of 1933.[1] The idea of a spectrum of assets, involving a relation between money and interest on liquidity lines, is already to be found in that paper. I had not yet grasped that there was no reason, within my new construction, why expectations of the prices of consumption goods should not be volatile; thus I still held to rather more of *The Theory of Wages* than I would have done later. But the wall had been breached. I already knew (and stated) that "even a pure *laisser-faire* system would be subject to monetary disturbances".

I had in fact got on to the Cambridge wavelength. When I showed what I had been writing to my colleagues in the "money" department (for I had clearly got to a point where I needed their advice), Barrett Whale said to me: "That sounds very like the 'excess-bearish factor' in the *Treatise on Money*." For the moment, however, I got more from Sweden than I did from Cambridge. It was Myrdal's *Monetary*

[1] "Gleichgewicht and Konjunktur" (*Zeitschrift fur Nationalökonomie*, 1933, Bd. IV).

Equilibrium[1] which showed me the power of a short-period analysis in which expectations (certain or uncertain) are treated as data; and Lindahl[2] who showed me the usefulness of translating "dynamic equilibrium" into "macro" terms. Where I got with their aid is indicated by the paper "Wages and Interest: the Dynamic Problem", which is reprinted above in Section II. (I have had some doubts about reprinting this article, since it looks forward in so many ways to *Value and Capital* (1939). But I shall want it at an important step in the following discussion, so I think it belongs here.) I would like to emphasise that when I wrote it, I knew nothing of what Keynes was to say in the *General Theory*. (But of course Keynes did, when he accepted it for the *Journal*!)

Already, then, when the *General Theory* appeared at the beginning of 1936, I had got a good many of the pieces. The review which I wrote, within three months of receiving it,[3] shows that there was little that was essential to the new doctrine which I did not find at once to be acceptable. I do not pretend that I had drawn the practical conclusions that were drawn by Keynes; but I was aware that conclusions of this kind would have to be drawn. "There is no reason", I had already stated a year previously,[4] "why policies which tend to economic welfare, statically considered, should also tend to monetary stability. Indeed the presumption is rather the other way round." I had indeed moved a long way from *The Theory of Wages*; though it was only

[1] Which I read in German, as it appeared in *Beiträge zur Geldtheorie* (ed. Hayek).
[2] Lindahl's influence was chiefly personal, as his writings were (then) mainly in Swedish, which I cannot read. But he was himself in London rather often at that time.
[3] "Mr. Keynes's Theory of Employment" (*Economic Journal*, June 1936).
[4] "A Suggestion for Simplifying the Theory of Money" (*Economica*, February 1935) p. 18.

Chapters IX. and X. of that book which I had publicly stated that I withdrew.[1]

In fact, it was on this side that I had most definitely moved away from my 1932 position. I was (I think I may say) an almost whole-hearted Keynesian; but I was by no means a whole-hearted *"Imperfect Competitionist"*.[2] I should not have written the "Marginal Productivity" chapter of *The Theory of Wages* (Chapter I.) just like that if I had had the advantage of reading Mrs. Robinson's book; but I don't think I would have thrown it overboard altogether. What I would certainly have admitted to be wrong was the place which it occupied at the very-start of the work; it was already apparent that it should have come in, if at all, at a much later stage. Enough would thus have been conceded, in this direction also, to make a profound difference to the structure of the book; the holes that had been blown in it, in the author's own view, were already very serious.

I did not attempt the reconstruction that was called for; I don't know that I could have done it. Probably I was better employed in writing *Value and Capital*. All that I did do was to write a supplement to the chapter on "Distribution and Economic Progress", a supplement which appeared in 1936 and which is reprinted in Section II. This "revised version" is, I think, fairly harmless, but it is very inconclusive. It is written in a form which maintains some continuity with the original version, but the continuity of substance is stated rather than proved.

That concludes the first part of the story, from my point of view. It is the story of a juvenile work, which

---

[1] See above, p. 283, and below, pp. 354-72.

[2] My "survey" of "Monopoly" theory (*Econometrica*, 1935) was pretty stand-offish,

(almost at once) I felt myself to have outgrown. I had reached a point when I should have been very happy if it could be forgotten.

I think that the first intimation which I received, quite a number of years later (but they were mostly war years), that this was not going to happen, was in 1946. I was visiting the United States for the first time. I found, rather to my distress, that I was often being received, not as the author of *Value and Capital* and of the articles (many of them mentioned above) of which I was (and still am) proud, but as the author of *The Theory of Wages*, of which I was not proud at all. There is one occasion which I particularly remember. I was entertained to dinner by a small group of very eminent economists (I will not name the others, but one of them was Josef Schumpeter[1]); we spent the evening, I trying to persuade them that my *Theory of Wages* was a thoroughly bad book, they trying to persuade me that it was a good one. They did not persuade me of that, but they certainly did persuade me that it was still alive.

Perhaps, however (I could not help reflecting at first), the survival which I had found was just a matter of politics. The issues which Keynes had raised were not, in England, a source of political division; in America they were. It was quite easy, in England, to be a conservative Keynesian; that, on the whole, was where I stood myself. But in America (at least in 1946) if one was conservative in one's politics, one must be anti-Keynesian in one's economics. *The Theory of Wages* could then be one of the straws at which one clutched

---

[1] Schumpeter's (too) golden opinions of *The Theory of Wages* have now been expressed in print, in several passages of his *History of Economic Analysis*. Even after what he had said in 1946, I felt surprise when I saw those passages. I had not quite believed that he meant what he was saying.

to justify that difficult (so it seemed to me) intellectual position. It was impossible not to consider that interpretation of what I found, though it looked unfair. And it was unfair; there was more to it than that.

I was in fact visiting America at a great moment (or on the eve of a great moment) in the history of American economics. In the thirties there was no economic work that was done in the rest of the world that had a fraction of the importance of what was done in England by Keynes (and those around him); but since 1945 it has been the Americans that have led the way. Now the new American economics (it is sufficient to think of the work of Samuelson and of Leontief) has not, in its most characteristic respects, been particularly Keynesian; and the rest of the Cambridge tradition has been even more foreign to it. But my Walrasian-Wicksellian approach (more fully developed in *Value and Capital*, but already represented in *The Theory of Wages*) was not foreign to it; it was on this kind of thing that the Americans themselves were building. That was one of the reasons (in Schumpeter's case it may have been the main reason) why they were still interested in my *Theory of Wages*.

There were other reasons, too. I have so far made no mention of another book with the same title as mine—Paul Douglas's *Theory of Wages* (1933)—a work which left a considerable mark upon American economics. There was more in common between our books than the title. Douglas used a model which was very similar to that of my Chapter VI., but it was in one respect a special model. He assumed that the elasticity of substitution between capital and labour was always unity (giving constant relative shares), with the result that his production function could be expressed in the simple form that has become so celebrated:

$$P = L^a\ C^{1-a}$$

where a is a constant. In this form, the production function was well suited for empirical "testing" and, Douglas made heroic efforts to test it. In the voluminous later work that has sprung from Douglas, my slightly more general formulation seems to have been found useful. But whether we have really learned anything if we manage to get a "fit" from the hypothesis (in either form) is a matter on which one may still feel some doubts.

It must next be noticed (and not with reference to America only) that there were some ways in which the tide of events after 1945 began to move in "my" favour. It was nonsense to maintain that the unemployment of 1932 was in any sense *caused* by excessively high wages; the movement of real wages, during the Great Depression, ought clearly to have been treated (as it was treated in the Keynes theory) as an effect, not as a cause. It did, however, become much more possible, in the years after 1945, to argue that the efforts of Trades Unions, to maintain (and then to increase) *real* wages, were an independent (or exogenous) influence on the working of the economy (of many nations). The effects of these efforts did not necessarily reveal themselves in unemployment, though there were cases where they seemed to do so (particularly, perhaps, in America). Monetary effects, with which the Keynes theory was perfectly competent to deal, were much more obvious. But there was also another kind of effect, which (as time went on) attracted increasing attention: the effect upon the rate of growth.

It has been surprising to discover that the essentially static analysis of my Chapters IX.-X. (for it is these, once again, which turn out to be crucial) should have been found to be relevant to growth theory. I did not have any growth theory when I wrote those chapters; all I had was the "stationary state" theory of Bohm-Bawerk and Wicksell, the only thing that was available at the time when I was writing. But it has turned out from one point of view, which has been represented in the growth theory of the fifties, that this mattered much less than might have been expected. For one of the things on which attention has been concentrated has been the study of a "growth equilibrium", the condition of an economy that is growing at a constant rate over time; and of this the stationary state (with a growth rate of zero) is evidently a special case. Quite a number of the properties which turned up in my "stationary" analysis have turned out to be valid for "growth equilibrium" generally.

It is largely because of the existence of this approach to growth theory that I finally decided that my old book had to be resurrected; but it has had to be resurrected in this particular form, because I do not much care for that approach myself. It is still, in my present view, too static. I do not want to suggest, in saying that, that there is anything necessarily wrong in the use of static analysis. There are real problems which run in terms of comparisons between the *states* of different economies, or of the same economy at different times; static problems, quite properly studied by static methods. (The growth rate of an economy, at a particular time, is still a part of the *state* of that economy.) As long as it is problems of that kind that are under consideration, the methods that I used in

1932 still seem to me, on the whole, to be defensible—
as I shall explain at length in the pages that follow.
But I should myself be careful not to claim that this
was growth theory. I have always come back to the
things which I learned, in a fairly hard way, during
the process of self-education that has been described.
I do not believe that a *process* of change can be analysed
so statically. It cannot be analysed without explicit
attention to expectations and uncertainties; or to the
lags which, for some analytical purposes, may be used
to represent them. The right place for growth theory
is not as an appendage to static theory; the right place
is that which I suggested at the end of my 1935 paper,
here reprinted. It is the theory of "Monday week".
"Monday week", as I said there, "will have to be
another story". It has been a long story, and it is not
finished yet.

A NOTE ON ARRANGEMENT

It was my original intention, when I first thought of
composing this Commentary, to go through the 1932
book, chapter by chapter, taking topics in the order
in which they there arise. This treatment would, I am
sure, have had many conveniences for the reader, and
I am sorry that I feel obliged to abandon it, if only to
a limited extent. It has, however, been brought home
to me, when I have tried to think through the consequences of the concessions and changes of view that
I have just been recording, that one of the main
things that is at fault in the first edition is the order
in which topics are taken up. If the book were re-
written, the topics could not be taken in that order,
and it is exceedingly awkward to do so, even for the
purpose of a Commentary.

The difficulty is this. I began the whole book with the statement (to which I still adhere) that:

"The need for a special theory of wages only arises because both the supply of labour, and the demand for it, and the way in which demand and supply interact on the labour market, have certain peculiar properties, which make it impossible to apply to labour the ordinary theory of commodity value without some further consideration."

There are thus three questions: (1) demand; (2) supply; (3) their interaction. The first was discussed in Chapter I., the third in Chapters II.-IV., and the second (so far as it was discussed) in Chapter V. This was not a very logical arrangement; why should the "working of the market" come in between demand and supply? I can only conclude (now) that the discussion of demand got pulled out of place by the (erroneous) impression under which I was working, that in Marginal Productivity I had a simple key which would unlock the heart of my problem. Once that impression is abandoned, it must be wrong to begin with demand in the way I did.

In fact, if one begins with the "working of the market" both demand and supply can be treated more satisfactorily. That, accordingly, is the order which I propose to follow here.

THE WORKING OF THE MARKET (CHAPTERS II.-IV.)

These chapters, which owe much to Beveridge[1] and to Clay,[2] and something to my own empirical work on

[1] *Unemployment: A Problem of Industry* (1910). One way of expressing what I was trying to do in these chapters is to say that I was trying to apply the original Beveridge classification of unemployment to the question of wage-determination.

[2] *The Problem of Industrial Relations* (1928), especially Chs. 1-4,

industrial relations, form the part of the book with which I am nowadays least dissatisfied. It was (I would still claim) of permanent value to have shown that the labour market is—by nature, and quite independently of Trade Union organisation—a very special kind of market, a market which is likely to develop "social" as well as purely economic aspects. The conditions for this to happen are: (1) that the worker should be free to change his employer, not being bound down by any form of quasi-serfdom; (2) that employment should be regular, *i.e.* non-casual, so that there is a presumption that the relation between the employer and at least a major part of his employees will be a continuing relation. When these conditions are satisfied, there is a strong presumption that the "social" characteristics will appear. For the purely economic correspondence between the wage paid to a particular worker and his value to the employer is not a sufficient condition of efficiency; it is also necessary that there should not be strong feelings of injustice about the relative treatment of different employees (since these would diminish the efficiency of the *team*), and there should be some confidence about fair treatment over time (which is necessary in order that the individual worker should give of his best). These requirements do not fit together at all easily. The capacities of different workers do in fact differ to a greater extent than the team spirit will allow to be recognised; and the short-period value of a man's work fluctuates over time to a greater extent than longer-run interest will allow to be recognised. Compromise is necessary, with the result that wage-rates are more uniform, both between workers, and over time, than they would be if the labour market worked like a commodity market. These

Y.

tendencies to uniformity are enhanced by unionisation, but even in the absence of formal unionisation they are likely to be present to some extent.

I still believe that this analysis was right, both as a matter of history and as a matter of theory. It gives a better picture of the working of the labour market than is given by the corresponding model used by Keynes—his awkward distinction between "voluntary" and "involuntary" unemployment.

At the time when I was writing, it might well have appeared that the analysis of these chapters was of chiefly historical interest. The actual labour market (of Britain at least) was already almost fully unionised; the only point of analysing a "free" labour market was to bring out the nature of the difference introduced by unionisation, a difference which could not be appreciated unless one had a clear idea of both sides of the comparison. Later experience has shown, however, that there was more to it than that. There have been important industries in the fifties in which it has been apparent that the wage-rates fixed by negotiation with Trade Unions are no more than minimum wages; the "free" market has appeared in a new guise, being responsible for the determination of the *gap* between "wages" and "earnings", or between actual wages and Trade Union rates. In these conditions, my 1932 analysis takes on a new importance. If it were really the case that a free labour market works just like a commodity market, it would be possible to control this wage-earnings gap (or wage-drift, as it has come to be called) by measures which act directly and entirely upon the demand for labour; thus, a widening of the gap would itself be a sufficient indication of the presence of demand inflation, with the policy consequences which are fairly generally accepted to follow from that diagnosis. On my principles, however, one cannot proceed so simply to that conclusion. I was maintaining (and I would still maintain) that there are important social (and expectational) elements even in the "free market" part of wage-determination. Even there, wages are not simply determined by supply and demand. The same forces as are operative in the determination of Trade Union rates are operative, to some extent, in the determination of the extras above Trade Union rates. Even at the "free" end of the market, wage inflation and demand inflation would thus appear to be rather different things.

I shall have a bit more to say on these matters later, when we should be readier to deal with them.[1] They are only referred to here as an indication that these chapters, at least, are not quite out of date.

THE SUPPLY OF LABOUR (MOSTLY CHAPTER V.)

The inadequacy of my treatment of the supply of labour was the first of the criticisms that was made against my book in Shove's review. Certainly I laid myself open to these criticisms by the foolish remark that I made (on page 3) that "the distribution of this population between occupations is a problem of the theory of wages, but it is one of the easiest problems of the whole theory". So I excused myself for saying little about it. The fact was, of course, that I could find nothing interesting to say about it; but it would have been much better if I had taken the trouble to write out a straightforward account of the matter (much

[1] See below, pp. 371-2.

in the way that Shove did, or that I myself was to do in Chapter VI. of my *Social Framework*). If I had done so, in *The Theory of Wages*, I might have seen that what I had to say in Chapter IV. of that book on the working of the labour market had a good deal of relevance to it.

What should have been said is (I think) something like this. Wage differentials are a good way of sorting out labour into occupations (and, more generally, into jobs) *in the long period*; that is to say, there will be a system of wage-differentials which will minimise discrepancies between supplies and demands if it is maintained over a long period (at least if demands do not fluctuate too much). But variations in differentials are a much less good way of securing a more exact adjustment to changes in demand. They have to be used, since the shortages of labour in particular directions which would otherwise result (even if they did not last for ever) would be intolerable while they lasted. The level of wages which is needed to attract labour quickly into an expanding trade is, however, higher than that which is required to maintain the larger labour force; but, having once risen, the differential does not fall back easily. It is therefore highly probable that actual wage-systems are full of differentials that have lost their economic function, being (as it were) the fossilised remains of historical shortages. The general justification of wage-differentials on the ground of economic efficiency is far from implying that particular actual differentials are so justified. They may very often be quite unjustified on that ground.[1]

---

[1] The argument of the above paragraph is further elaborated, and illustrated with a diagram, in a little paper which appeared in the *Economic Journal* in 1955 and which is reprinted as Supplementary Note A in my *Essays in World Economics.*

There are other matters which fall to be considered under the head of "supply of labour". Shove thought that I was wrong to exclude all discussion of population; but I still think that I was entitled to regard that as a subject which fell outside my scope. The supply of labour from the individual worker was a matter which I did discuss, fairly thoroughly, in Chapter V. There is, I think, not much that is wrong with that chapter. There is, indeed, a section in it which could have been improved if I had had at my disposal the distinction between income and substitution effects which I later used in *Value and Capital*. All I could do in 1932 was to explain the backward sloping supply curve by considering it as an expression of an inelastic "demand for income in terms of effort". Its significance becomes much clearer when we have learned that in all cases where the article supplied has a direct utility to the supplier, income effect and substitution effect go in opposite directions; and when we see that in this particular case the income effect is likely to be large.[1] One can then go on to notice that a rise in wages, which operates only (or nearly only) upon marginal units, will have a substitution effect but scarcely any income effect, so that it is much more likely to increase effort than one which affects all units equally. The advantage (to the employer) of "incentive schemes" (or whatever they are called) which have this result is made obvious; and the nature of that advantage can readily be understood.

THE DEMAND FOR LABOUR (CHAPTER I.)

I can no longer defer discussion of that terrible first chapter, entitled "Marginal Productivity and the

[1] *Value and Capital*, p. 36 (either edition).

Demand for Labour". There are several things that are wrong in that chapter; marginal productivity (used in the way I used it) is one of them, but it may not be the worst of them. There is, however, one thing that is right. This is the division of the effect of a factor-price change into an effect on the scale of output and an effect on the method of production (or on the proportions in which factors are combined). This, which appears in Chapter I. as a way of "explaining" marginal productivity, is in fact a more powerful and more general approach than marginal productivity. I suppose that I was in process of moving across to it, but the process was not complete.

I had realised (or rather I had got from Wicksell— but I fancy that it was only at rather a late stage in the writing of my book that I got even so far) that payments according to the value of the marginal products of the factors will only "add up" (or exhaust the value of the product) if the output which is being produced by the firm is that which it can produce at minimum cost.[1] What I had not realised is that minimum cost, in this sense, is not a condition of maximum profit, except in the case of a perfect market. Shove, of course, was perfectly clear on this matter, for he himself had had much to do with the formulation of the doctrine about it which is nowadays quite generally accepted. I am entirely ready to accept it myself.

We may, however, accept it and still hold that the "scale-proportions" approach is the best way of constructing a theory of the demand for labour. I will try to set down (in outline), the form which I now believe it ought to take.

[1] Pp. 233-239 in the text.

As a first step, we consider the demand for a particular kind of labour, which is only used for the making of one particular product. (This is the problem that was analysed by Marshall, with examples taken from the building industry; we can still follow his analysis, in this particular case, very closely.) If A-labour, as we may call it, is only used in the X-industry, we have simply to say (on the side of scale) that a rise in A-wages will increase the unit cost of the X-product; and that this (whether the X-industry is perfectly or imperfectly competitive) will tend, by one mechanism or another, to increase the selling price of the X-product. The effect of the rise in A-wages on the *demand* schedule for the X-product can surely, in this case, be neglected; so that the rise in the supply price of X will diminish the amount sold (if the demand for X has any elasticity). That, in turn, will diminish the demand for A-labour. This is the scale effect; but in addition to that, there is the possibility that (since the cost of A-labour has risen relatively to the cost of other inputs) there will be a change of proportions, a technological substitution of other inputs for A-labour. How far this can go depends upon the availability (or elasticity of supply) of the substitute inputs; in general, however, it is an additional reason for a fall in the demand for A-labour.

We next proceed to consider the case of a kind of labour that is employed in several industries. There will be simple instances of this which can be adequately analysed by a straightforward extension of the above Marshallian case; if the industries are unrelated, and the labour in question is not a large part of the total labour force of the economy, there will just be a "Marshall-type" effect from each industry, to be added together. The matter is much more difficult when these conditions are not satisfied. Even so, the "scale-proportions" distinction will come to our help.

Take scale first. The (unit) costs of the various products (X, Y, . . .) which use A-labour will now be raised to various extents, depending on the proportions of A-labour costs to total costs in the respective industries; selling prices will also rise to varying extents, depending partly upon these cost-proportions, partly upon degrees of competitiveness. What will be the effect of these rises in selling price upon the demands for the products? It is not possible to read it off from a Marshallian demand schedule when the demands are interrelated. We can, however, say something about it if we make another application of the "scale-proportions" technique, the distinction between income and substitution effects, which I introduced in *Value and Capital*. For this purpose, it is sufficient to define the distinction by saying that the substitution effect (on consumers' demand) is the effect of the change in *relative* prices of consumers' goods with real income constant (and the distribution of real income constant); the income effect is the effect of the change in real income.

There is a firm rule for the substitution effect on consumers' demand.[1] The sum-product of changes in consumption by changes in price

$$dp_x dq_x + dp_y dq_y + \ldots .$$

where the p's are the prices and the q's the amounts demanded of the various products, must be non-positive (negative, or, in an extreme case, zero). Now the change in unit cost of commodity X, due to

[1] I use the more modern statement of the rule, which is elaborated in my *Revision of Demand Theory* (see especially pp. 128-129).

a change in A-wages dw_a, is $a_x dw_a$, if a_x is the amount of A-labour needed to make a unit of commodity X. Thus if the rises in selling price are proportional to the rises in unit cost (and this is quite likely to be roughly true, even in conditions of imperfect competition), each dp_x will be proportional to $a_x dw_a$, and the above sum-product is proportional to

$$(a_x dq_x + a_y dq_y + \ . \ . \ . \ .) \ dw_a$$

The bracketed sum in this last expression is the change in the demand for A-labour, due to the substitution effect in consumption. Thus under perfect competition, with selling prices equal to unit costs, it is certain that this effect must tend to diminish the demand for A-labour, when the wage of A-labour rises; and even under imperfect competition, it is very probable that it will do so. So far as the substitution effect is concerned, this more complicated case (with any sort of demand interrelatedness) works exactly like the Marshallian case.

But now let us consider the income effect, which in the Marshallian case, where the change in wages only affected the cost of a single product, was (very plausibly, as we shall see) assumed to be negligible. What happens if it is not negligible? We can best isolate it by asking what would happen if there were no substitution effect in consumption (and of course no technological substitution in production either). The substitution effect on consumption can be cut out if we suppose that the ratios between the quantities of physical products consumed by each consumer are unaffected by the changes in relative prices. The remaining effect on demand is the income effect.

Suppose then that A-wages rise, and that the prices

of the products for which A-labour is used rise correspondingly; but that there is no possibility of substituting other factors for A-labour, either by technological change or by consumers' substitution. There is then no reason why there should be a reduction in the demand for A-labour. For suppose that the employment of A-labour is (temporarily) unchanged. The only reason why there should be any change in the demands for commodities (which would react back on the demand for A-labour) is the change, which will have occurred, in the distribution of income. A-workers have more spending power (the prices of the things that they buy will have risen less than their incomes have risen); but workers in other trades, whose wages have not risen, will have less (since they also have to pay the higher prices of products). As for the receivers of profits and other incomes, some may gain, others lose. Since, however, the total volume of goods produced is not altered, for every gain to one party, there must be a loss to another. Thus, in the conditions supposed, the demand for A-labour will *increase* if the net effect of this redistribution of real income is the transference of spending power from those who have a low marginal propensity to consume A-using products to those who have a higher marginal propensity to consume them; will diminish if the shift is the other way round. There is no rule on the matter. Thus it is possible that there may be an income effect which goes the same way as the substitution effect, tending therefore to diminish the demand for A-labour; but it is equally possible that the income effect may go the other way.

When A-labour is only a small part of the total labour force, the redistribution of real income, due to a change in A-wages, is unlikely to generate an income effect that is appreciable; so it can be neglected (as Marshall neglected it). In the more general case, there is no reason of principle why it can be neglected. But the direction of its working is still uncertain; for some sorts of labour it may be favourable, for some unfavourable.

We are left with the substitution effect, which (as appeared) is much more determinate in the direction of its operation; and with the possibility of technological substitution, on which a word must now be added.

When A-labour is used in several industries, there will be possibilities of technological substitution in each industry; it may well be that the effects of these have just to be added up. There is, however, the further possibility that some of the inputs which may be substituted for A-labour in the X-industry are themselves products of A-labour in some other industry. In that case their prices also are likely to have risen (though, if they use other factors than A-labour, their prices will rise proportionally less than the price, or wage, of A-labour). Consequently, though the possibility of substitution will ordinarily still be present, it will be somewhat damped down.

MONEY WAGES AND REAL WAGES

I have set out the theory of the effects of a sectional (but not too sectional) change in wages in some detail, because there is a sense in which this is the general theory; other cases that are more familiar can be treated as limiting cases of it. This is clearly true of the Marshallian case, with which we began; it is also true of the Keynesian case, of a general uniform change in money wages, to which I now come.

It has already been necessary, in the theory that has just been set out, to distinguish between money wages and real wages, in a way that was not necessary in the Marshallian case. If A-labour is only a small part of the total labour force, the effect upon prices in general of a rise in the money wages of A-labour can often be treated as negligible; the real wages of A-labour must therefore rise in practically the same proportion as their money wages rise, while the real wages of other labour remain substantially unaffected. But if A-labour is more important than that, the rise in prices may cancel out a substantial part of the rise in A-wages; the real wages of A-labour will then rise to a significantly smaller extent than their money wages have risen, while the real wages of other labour will perceptibly fall. The distinction between money wages and real wages is then a matter of extreme importance; the neglect of it in Chapter I. of the first edition is (to my present mind) a more important defect than the neglect of Imperfect Competition.

There is a related point that comes in at the same stage. The substitution effects, on which so much reliance has been placed, will generally involve increases in the demands for other sorts of labour in substitution for A-labour; but where are these other sorts of labour to be found? It is commonly argued, on strict Keynesian lines, that effective substitution (of B-labour for A-labour) requires that there should exist a supply of B-labour that can be drawn into employment; if there is no such supply (if there is all-round full employment) the substitution itself will not be possible. Competition for B-labour will drive up

B-wages also; ultimately there will be a general rise in prices, which will offset the rise in money wages (of each section). Money wages will thus have risen, but real wages will not have risen; employment (of each section) will be much the same as before, the whole system merely reproducing itself at a higher level of money wages (and money prices).

There are qualifications to this doctrine, even within the orthodox Keynesian corpus; some of them (in particular those which refer to the interest rate) I shall be, considering later. It is more to the point, for the present, to observe that there are other qualifications which follow from the account of the *working of the labour market*, given above; it was because I had these in mind that I finally decided to begin with that side of my subject. It seems to be implied, in the version of the Keynesian argument that has just been given (I think that it often is implied in discussions of Keynesian full employment), that the labour market works like a commodity market, so far as the effect of an excess of demand over supply is concerned; when the excess appears, wages just shoot up. It would seem to be unwise, in view of our discussion of the working of the labour market, to jump to that conclusion; there may be considerable differences in the directness, or immediacy, of the reaction in different circumstances. To say that there will be substitution if there is unemployment of B-labour, but no substitution if there is no unemployment, is to make too sharp a distinction. Even if "fully employed", labour may have some elasticity of supply. It must nevertheless be agreed that a widespread rise in money wages will not raise real wages to anything like the same extent; and that substitution effects are liable to be damped down by transmission of the wage-rise (by one means or another) to other sectors.

Keynes's proposition—that a uniform rise in money wages will leave real wages unaffected, and employment unaffected—applies in strictness only to a closed system. Thus it is not applicable to a national economy, excepting when devaluation, or restrictions on trade, make the national economy work like a closed system. If exchange rates are fixed, and if trade is unrestricted (or only restricted by fixed tariffs), a uniform rise in wages throughout the nation remains a *sectional* rise in the sense of our former argument. Opportunities for substitution (by consumers or by producers, at home or abroad) will remain open; employment will therefore tend to decline. The competition of foreign producers, whose costs (we suppose) have not been increased by a corresponding rise in wages, will prevent prices from rising in the same proportion as wages have risen; thus there will be a rise in real wages, but there will be a fall in the demand for labour.

That, of course, is not the way of putting the matter that has become conventional. It is commonly said that the diminished competitiveness of home industry will diminish exports and increase imports; it will thus reflect itself in an adverse movement of the balance of payments. But it is only possible for a country to have an adverse balance of payments (on current account) if its total expenditure (on consumption + investment) is in excess of its income. What is then happening is that the decline in the demand for labour, which would otherwise arise, is being masked by the excess of expenditure over income, involving a drawing-down of foreign reserves, in some form or other. It is just the same thing as may happen in a particular industry, when the fall in employment, which would otherwise result from a rise in wages, may be masked (for the time being) if employers are willing to go on making losses, using up their reserves. The end, no doubt, is different. In the case of the industry, employment must in the end contract (if there is no outside change which comes to the rescue); the nation, on the other hand, may take refuge in exchange depreciation or trade restriction, which (in effect) prevent the rise in money wages from being a rise in real wages.

THE REHABILITATION OF MARGINAL PRODUCTIVITY

The theory of the demand for labour which has just been presented in outline is essentially Keynesian;[1] even though it can maintain a certain amount of formal continuity with that which was presented in Chapter I. of the first edition, its substance is very different. That, however, is by no means the end of the story. There do remain (it has subsequently turned out) certain possibilities of salvaging some parts of the old construction, not (perhaps) as a theory of the demand for labour, but for other purposes that are scarcely less important for a theory of wages.

Let us look back at the theory of the firm—under imperfect competition. It may, I think, be granted that there are strong reasons why the market in which a firm *sells* should normally be imperfectly competitive (for some individuality in its products is one of the

---

[1] It does not incorporate by any means the whole of the Keynesian theory of the matter since it abstracts for effects on interest and hence upon investment; I shall be dealing with these on pp. 354-72 below.

bases on which a firm can maintain its own individuality). There is, however, no such reason why there should be "monopsony" on the buying side; it may occur, but its occurrence (one would think) would be relatively exceptional. (The tendency of the labour market, whether unionised or not, to work with standard rates, diminishes the importance of monopsony in the labour market.) Thus it can plausibly be maintained that our standard picture of a firm should be such that it is a price-taker on the side of inputs, but a price-maker on the side of outputs.

If this is granted, it will follow that if profit is maximised, cost (of the output that is actually produced) must be minimised; and therefore (as is—correctly—shown in Chapter I.) the prices of inputs must be *proportional* to their marginal products. At first sight, however, this would appear to apply to employed inputs only; the residue that is left (regarded as a "wage" of the capital or management which the employer himself contributes to the business) may be out of line. In the short run, that is doubtless the case; but it is hard to distinguish any sort of input which, by its nature, must be employing and can never be employed. Accordingly, if we assume that in full equilibrium, the "wage" of the same factor must be the same in all uses, it will follow that in the same full equilibrium, the "wages" of *all* factors must be proportional to their marginal products—their marginal physical products.

When the firm is producing under imperfect competition, then (even in full equilibrium) its average cost will be falling; so that if all factors were paid according to their marginal products, there would not be enough to go round. It then appears, by the preceding, that every factor will receive *less* than the value of its marginal produce: the marginal product being, as it were, written down by a certain percentage, which will be the same for all factors in the same business, but different for different businesses.

Since (even in full equilibrium) the percentage deduction is very likely to be different in different businesses, the equality of the "wages" of the same factor between different businesses will not equate the values of its marginal products in different businesses; the position that is reached cannot then be an optimum, in the sense of Welfare Economics. But let us consider an economy that is working on these principles, with given quantities of factors and given technology; it will have a "frontier" of maximum outputs, along which various optimum conditions, including that of equality of the values of marginal products, in different uses of the same factor, will have to be satisfied. Since, under imperfect competition, this condition is unlikely to be satisfied, the position that is attained (even in full equilibrium) will lie *within* the frontier so defined. There are many purposes—of Welfare Economics—for which the relation between this actual position and various positions that are on the Frontier, can be extremely important.

But if we are not concerned with Welfare Economics, but are interested in the way in which the *actual* position will change in response to changes in data, the frontier (which is so important in Welfare Economics) becomes irrelevant. What then concerns us is the relation between the actual position, and other actual positions which may arise in different circumstances. Suppose that the imperfection of the market

z

is taken for granted, and we look for a "reaction curve" which is to show the way in which the actual position will change if other data are varied, what do we get?

It is orthodox imperfect competition theory to hold that when there is an increase in demand for the "products of the industry", this will not be met (in long period equilibrium) by an expansion of existing firms along their falling cost curves, but by the entry of new firms. Thus, if the "wages" of the factors remain unchanged, the prices of the products will not fall (as they might well do if the previously existing firms had expanded); they will remain (approximately) constant. Though the firms are producing under diminishing cost, the industry produces or appears to produce, under constant cost. If we look at the marginal products of the factors *to the industry* (along its actual expansion path) they are less than the marginal products to the firm (along the path that it is unable to take). Since the industry is producing under constant cost, the marginal products (in the industry sense) *will* add up. There is no reason, if marginal products are understood in this sense, why the "wages" of the factors should not be equal to the values of their marginal products.

Along these lines, the original marginal productivity theory can be to some extent rehabilitated; but how much is the rehabilitation worth? Something: but not, in my present view, a great deal. As a theory of the demand for labour, it is much inferior to the "scale-proportions" theory which was set out in previous sections; for the assumptions on which it is based are much more restrictive. That, however, has not been the main way in which anyone, in recent

years, has wanted to use it. The way in which it has
been tempting to use it has been in the construction
of growth models, especially when the main purpose
of the growth model is to build a theory of changes
in the distribution of income over time. My own (by
modern standards very primitive) attempt at using
it in something like that way was contained in
Chapter VI. of *The Theory of Wages*, together with
the "Revised Version" which is reprinted above on
pages 286-303. Some of the ideas in these writings
seem to be still quite lively; to a consideration of
them we may now turn.

THE DISTRIBUTION OF THE SOCIAL PRODUCT

(CHAPTER VI.)

The first, and perhaps after all the most important,
of the things that need to be said about Chapter VI.
is that it is not a Growth Model, although it looks like
a Growth Model. It could not be a Growth Model; for
at the time when it was written, the problem which
the makers of growth models are trying to answer had
not really come up.

I did have an eye upon some statistics, which I was
trying to explain, or to help to explain. These were the
Bowley and Stamp calculations of the British National
Income and its Distribution, which (at the time when
I was writing) were available only for the two years,
1911 and 1924. Continuous series, relating to a number
of successive years, only began (in England) when
Colin Clark produced them, at a time when my book
had already left my hands. If we seek to explain a

continuous series, we must have a Growth Model. If, however, we are only concerned with *separate* observations—without any passage between them that requires to be explained—it is reasonable to suppose that we can make do with the kind of thing that I was offering: a Static Comparison.

When we are making a Static Comparison, we have in the one year certain quantities of the Factors of Production and a certain Product, in the other year certain other sets of quantities and a different Product. We do not have to ask how the one set of Factors was transformed into the other, for that must largely be a matter of what happened in the intervening years, that do not enter into the Comparison which we are making. It seems reasonable to maintain that the change in the "size" of the Product (so far as that can be measured) is to be explained by changes in the quantities of the factors, and by changes in technology ("inventions") which affect the relation between Factors and Product (the Production Function). It does not seem unreasonable to maintain that if a free market system is operating (or approximately operating) on both occasions, the Distribution of the Product among Factors will be determined (or approximately determined) by much the same considerations. That, in any case, is the hypothesis on which my chapter was based.

In the "Revised Version", however, I beat a retreat from it[1] (under the influence of Imperfect Competition theory)—a further retreat than now seems to me to have been necessary. I there admitted that in conditions of Imperfect Competition, the remunerations of factors would not coincide with their marginal

---

[1] See above, p. 295.

products (the values of their marginal products), or even tend to equal them; with this concession, the rest of my construction became dependent on the assumption that the ratios between factor prices and marginal products would remain fairly constant—and no reason was given (or could be given) why this should be so. The reinterpretation of Marginal Productivity that has been given in this Commentary[1] makes this concession unnecessary. We have found a sense in which the remunerations of the factors will tend to *equal* the values of their marginal products— provided that there is an effective tendency for the equalisation of factor prices between different employments of the same factor. That, under the influence of this tendency, factor prices will actually be equalised cannot indeed be assumed except in a very full equilibrium; and there is no reason to suppose that the economic systems which we are comparing will have been in such an equilibrium in the years that are being compared. Yet to suppose that the actual state of an economic system can be represented (at least approximately) by the corresponding full equilibrium position is something that we are rather well accustomed to swallow; most people seem to find it easier to swallow that, than to suppose that a ratio is constant, for no better reason than that it is convenient that it should be so. The change in interpretation may therefore be reckoned as a (slight) improvement.

It should be observed that, on this new interpretation, the Production Function (the non-optimal Production Function) must be supposed to obey the condition of constant returns to scale. Otherwise the

[1] Above, p. 331-5.

marginal products would not add up. In saying this, we do not of course deny the existence of the phenomena of Increasing Returns—scale economies that are realised by the sheer expansion of the system. All we are saying is that such economies are excluded from *our* Production Function; so that if new scale economies are realised, between the dates that are being compared, they must be treated *as if* they were changes in technology ("inventions"). This is not in fact so inconvenient, for it is often quite difficult to distinguish between scale economies and inventions; .we are simply to regard all scale economies as inventions that are *induced* by changes in scale. As explained on pages 125-126 in the text, inventions that are induced by changes in factor-prices can be regarded, if we choose to do so, as changes that are consistent with the maintenance of an unchanged Production Function; what has now to be insisted is that this cannot be done with "inventions" that are induced by changes of scale. They must always be reckoned as shifting the Production Function.

The way would now seem to be cleared (though, as we shall see later, it has by no means been wholly cleared) for an analysis of the kind which I gave in Chapter VI. and in the other parts of the "Revised Version". What I said in Chapter VI. represents no more than the first step in such analysis. The formal model which I had in mind consisted of a (static) system with only one (homogeneous) product and two (homogeneous) factors. If one permits oneself so drastic a simplification, the formal properties that are stated in my chapter follow at once. With constant returns to scale, the relative shares of the factors depend only on the ratio of the quantities of the factors. One can draw out a curve which exhibits a technological relation between the quantity-ratio of the factors, on the one hand, and their price-ratio on the other; the elasticity of this curve is the elasticity of substitution.[1] It is at once apparent that the condition for an increase in the relative supply of a factor to increase its relative share is that the elasticity of substitution should be greater than unity.[2]

It is, of course, obvious that this should have been no more than a first step. In the "Revised Version" I endeavoured to take the matter a bit further, exploring the effects of introducing a multiplicity of factors and a multiplicity of products. I did not make much of a hand at the multiplicity of factors; the main thing that should have been said about it is, however, rather simple.

There are two basic cases in which the two-factor theory continues to apply.[3] One is that in which the proportions in which the other factors are used remain constant; the other is that in which these proportions vary, but vary in such a way as to keep the relative prices of the other factors (*i.e.* the ratios of their marginal products) constant. In either of these cases the other factors (B, C. D . . .) can be treated as if they formed a single factor; so that it remains true that the condition for an increase in the relative supply of factor A to increase its relative share is that the elasticity of substitution (of factor A against

[1] This is Mrs. Robinson's definition (*The Economics of Imperfect Competition*, p. 256). My own (equivalent) definition (p. 245 above) is convenient for some mathematical purposes; but it brings out the point of the concept much less well than hers does. See below, p. 373.

[2] In order to get the effect of an autonomous increase in one factor one must consider the backwash on the supply of other factors. I have nothing to add, on that side of the matter, to what is said in the "Revised Version" (pp. 291-2).

[3] I did not get this clear in the "Revised Version", since I had only the first of these basic cases, not the second.

the complex) should be greater than unity. It has, however, to be noticed that it is not the same elasticity of substitution in the two cases. The elasticity of substitution will be greater in the second case; for the marginal product of A will fall less steeply if the make-up of the complex (B, C, D) adjusts itself to suit the increased relative supply of factor A than if it does not adjust itself.[1] Save in these special cases, the many-factor theory cannot be reduced to a two-factor theory. We can nevertheless see, from these two cases, that there is a general presumption that sub-stitutability will be easier (so that the relative share of an increasing factor is more likely to increase) the more adjustable are the relative supplies of the other factors $(B, C, D \ldots)$ in relation to the demands for them. I suspect that this is about as far as it is useful to get.

The main points that have to be made about multiplicity of products are made, fairly satisfactorily, in the "Revised Version". Here also we have already seen that differences in the shares of the costs of different products, that are imputable to factor A, will lead to changes in the relative prices of products, when factor A becomes more abundant; and that these will induce a substitution by consumers in favour of those products that have become relatively cheaper—which is in effect a substitution in favour of factor A. Even if there was no technological sub-stitution (the proportions in which the factors had to be combined in the production of each product were rigidly fixed), this consumer substitution could still operate as a factor substitution in the production of the Social Product as a whole. "The combined elasticity

---

[1] See below, pp. 378-81.

of substitution between the factors is the arithmetical sum of the elasticity of commodity substitution and our old elasticity of technical substitution. In order for A's relative share to increase when its supply increases, it is only necessary that the combined elasticity of substitution should be greater than unity."[1]

To this general principle there is, however (as was stated), a qualification. There is no reason why consumers' demand should itself obey the rule of "constant returns to scale"; there is accordingly an income effect (or expenditure effect, as I was still calling it in 1936) to be allowed for, as well as the substitution effect. It is clearly possible, in a problem of this character, that the income effect may be very important. Thus it could happen that a rise in the relative share of factor A involves a redistribution of income in favour of those who have a particular propensity to demand A-using products; in which case its relative share would rise further than would appear from a consideration of substitution effects alone. Attempts have been made to construct theories of distribution which rely very largely upon perverse income effects of this kind; but if the point is pushed at all far it seems impossible to stay within the bounds of a static theory. For if there are no substitution effects, and income effects are perverse, there can be no static equilibrium. The basic framework of the theory has got to be changed.

[1] Above, p. 298. The formula which is set out on that page for the commodity elasticity is, I think, correct; but the qualification which follows (that the commodity elasticity is "almost, but *not quite*, necessarily positive") is not correct. This is one of a class of unnecessary qualifications which persisted in the first edition of *Value and Capital*, but were removed in the second. See below, pp. 381-4.

CAPITAL

So far, so good. The "elasticity of substitution" theory stands up fairly well to the onset of most of the "six knights"[1] whose attack I confronted in 1936; indeed, it may stand up rather better than I thought that it did at that time. We have to insist that we are making a Static Comparison; and we have to interpret marginal productivity in the special sense that has been explained. Once these things are granted, the position does not seem to be too bad.

There is, however, one whom we have not yet encountered: the one called Capital. What is said about capital in the "Revised Version" is ludicrously inadequate; it is no more than an apology for not dealing with the subject. What was said about capital in *The Theory of Wages* was also most inadequate; it could hardly have been otherwise, for we were then at the very beginning of a debate about capital which has been a major preoccupation of economists for the last thirty years. What was said in *Value and Capital* is all right (I still think) so far as it goes; but it is not of much help here. It avoids the problem which here concerns us (and with which so many economists have later been concerned): how is capital to be fitted in to a static theory?

This is by no means the place to attempt a complete answer to that question—if indeed the question is answerable at all, of which I am by no means sure. I shall confine myself to making one point, to the clearing up of one ambiguity. I think, however, that it is a rather vital ambiguity; once it is cleared up the whole matter is considerably straightened out.

There are two basic ways in which economists

[1] Above, p. 292.

have regarded the capital stock of an economy—two quite distinct ways, with quite distinct properties, but which it is only too easy to confuse. According to the one, capital consists of real goods—"machines" it is conventional to call them, but there is so much of the capital stock of an actual economy that does not consist of anything like machines that this is not a particularly good name. It might be well to be more general, and just to talk about Physical Things. This is the more obvious interpretation of the Factor of Production Capital, but it is by no means the only (or even the chief) capital concept that appears in economic literature. There is an alternative concept in which capital appears as a Fund—Wages Fund, Subsistence Fund, or whatever it may be called. This Fund concept of capital is not by any means a historical curiosity; it is very much alive at the present, perhaps even more alive than the other.

Both concepts are equally *real*. But whereas the Physical concept treats capital as consisting of actual capital goods, the Fund concept reduces it to equivalent consumption goods, the consumption goods that are foregone to get it. Not that we should think (as some of the cruder statements of the Old Classical Economists almost suggest) of the whole social capital being accumulated, over any period, however long, by abstinence from consumption; it is simply at the margin that capital is valued (on the Fund approach) by consumption foregone.

The importance of the distinction can best be seen by taking a special case. Suppose that we are comparing two economies which have capital stocks that are physically identical; there is in each just the same number of every kind of "machine" (blast furnaces or cart horses) and they are all in just the same condition. Then, on the Physical concept of capital, the amounts of capital possessed by the two economies must be the same. But they need not be the same on the Fund concept. For we have then to look at the relative productivities of the production of consumption goods and of investment goods in the two economies. If these productivities are the same, or if their ratios are the same, the Fund concept will give the same result as the Physical concept. But suppose that there is little difference in the productivity of consumption goods production in the two economies, but a large difference in the productivity of capital goods production. The more productive economy will then be judged, using the Fund concept, to have a *smaller* capital stock than the other—because it can replace its capital goods, as they wear out, at a smaller sacrifice.

The reason why the Fund concept is of *practical* importance is at once apparent. We can only approximate these measures by taking a money value of the Capital stock and deflating it by an appropriate index-number. If we are using the Fund concept, we can deflate by an index-number of consumption good prices, such as is very readily available. But if we are using the Physical concept, we should deflate by an index-number of capital good prices; and a suitable index for that purpose will be very hard to construct indeed.

Nor is this the only reason why we should pay attention to the Fund concept. A continuous growth model, which *is* concerned with the development of the economy from one year to the next, may well proceed most conveniently if it uses the Fund concept, so that the increment of capital from year to year is measured in the same units as the saving that corresponds to it. (This, I think, is what Harrod did in his *Economic Dynamics*; the extensive progeny of that work has shown how fruitful it is to do it.)

All these things must be said; yet they do not add up to a case for abandoning the Physical concept altogether. There are still some purposes for which the Physical concept is the more convenient; one of them is the Static Comparison with which we are here concerned.

For it is only if one is using the Physical concept of capital that it is possible to have a Production Function which represents the state of technology in at all a straightforward manner. In order to bring this out, consider the simplest of all cases: that in which the Product is homogeneous and the capital Stock is also homogeneous (consisting, let us say, entirely of tractors). It is then completely intelligible that to given supplies of factors (given amounts of labour applied, and given numbers of *tractors* used) there should correspond (with given technology and organisation and, of course, given weather conditions and so on) given outputs of (say) corn. If, however, we represent the tractor by the amount of corn that has to be given up in order to reproduce it, we shall be multiplying the number of tractors by a corn-value that will ordinarily be different as the proportion of labour to tractors varies. Thus, if more labour were employed along with the same quantity of tractors, that same quantity of tractors would represent a different quantity of capital—in the Fund sense.[1]

It might, indeed, be possible to reconstruct a Produc-

---

[1] This is, of course, substantially the same point as was made by Mrs. Robinson in her celebrated article "The Production Function and the Theory of Capital" (*Review of Economic Studies*, 1954). She was however using a measure of capital in terms of labour (a third concept which also has a history); what I am saying is that the same difficulty arises if one takes the measure in terms of consumption foregone, which seems to me to be the more important.

tion Function, using the latter interpretation; but it would be a different Production Function, the properties of which would be by no means obvious. It seems to me to be evident that if we are using a Production Function, it will be with a Production Function based upon the Physical concept that we shall want to work.

Nevertheless, having said that, we are of course by no means at the end of our difficulties. Some difficulties can indeed be brushed aside. Heterogeneity of product and heterogeneity of capital stock can be dealt with by using our formal theory of many factors and many products; and it should be noticed that this now makes it unnecessary to insist that the economy is to be taken to be in a state of full equilibrium, in the sense that there is perfect equalisation of yields on every sort of capital good. All we need to say is that there is a presumption that more perfect equalisation of yields will increase the elasticity of substitution, making it easier for a relatively increasing factor to increase its relative share. Nor need we be troubled by the fact that in a growing economy, some part of the Social Product will be devoted to Consumption and some to Investment; for we are not concerned with what happens next year, and so far as this year is concerned Consumption and Investment are all on a par—they are simply different parts of the demand for products. The important distinction between products relates to the proportions of the factors that are required for their production—it does not matter whether the things that are produced are consumption goods or investment goods.[1]

---

[1] It thus appears that differences in the propensity to save of labourer and capitalist have nothing in themselves to do with distribution, not even through an income effect. It is the difference in the labour content of the whole expenditure (consumption plus investment) of the two sectors which is the thing that matters. But see below, p. 364.

Much nastier troubles arise when we begin to think about Depreciation. Is the Social Product, which we have been discussing, to be taken gross or net? Essentially the same reason as has led me to favour (for these purposes) a Physical concept of capital leads me to favour the interpretation of the Social Product as Gross Product. If there is a direct technological relation between Factors and Product, it is surely with Gross Product that the relation exists; the depreciation component that must be deducted for "netting" again depends upon cost of reproduction, so that it again introduces a complication, such as we previously preferred to avoid. But though one must (I think) posit such a relation if one is thinking statically, one is then drawing very near to the danger point at which a static theory begins to break down. That is to say, one is getting to the point where doubt must be cast upon the crucial static assumption, that the "year" within which the economy under consideration is observed, can be treated as self-contained. The Gross Product of an economy is not a tidy concept; it is not nice to have to rely upon it over much.

There is another (related) way in which a theory such as we are discussing may get into serious trouble. If there is to be any sense in a Production Function, it must be a relation between Product produced and factors applied—not total factors available, but factors actually used. In the case of labour, we have (or think we have) information about labour used, if we have statistics of employment; but there are no statistics of capital equipment used that are anything but fragmentary. Yet there can be no doubt that the unemployment of capital is as real a phenomenon as the unemployment of labour; and one that is equally relevant to the problem under discussion. It is *never* the case that the whole capital equipment of an economy is used to capacity. The supply of (physical) capital does not determine production; it does no more than set a limit (and a somewhat elastic limit) upon the amount that can be produced. These things are true and are important; it would be much better if we could take them into account. But no one, to my knowledge, has yet managed to take them into account so very satisfactorily; they are definitely among the things that we have to leave out if we are making a Static Comparison.

INVENTIONS

Before leaving Chapter VI., something must be said about its classification of inventions. This is possibly the point, in the whole book, which has been liveliest in recent controversy: to set the Hicks classification against the Harrod classification has been one of the most popular of theoretical exercises. I shall not express a direct opinion upon that question;[1] but there is one thing that I ought to say about my own classification[2] which may perhaps throw some light upon it.

The distinction which I have been drawing between the Physical concept of capital and the Fund concept is highly relevant to the question of inventions. What is really the main reason (though I have not mentioned

[1] I should, however, like to refer the reader to C. Kennedy, *The Character of Improvements and of Technical Progress* (Econ. Journ. Dec. 1962) which appeared after this Commentary was written.

[2] It was, of course, simply an adaptation of Pigou's (*The Economics of Welfare*, Book IV, Ch. 4) which I modified in order to meet my own interest in relative shares.

it up to the present) why I do not care to use the Fund concept when making static comparisons is that it gives such odd results when we come to deal with changes in technology. Consider the effects of an invention which affects productivity in the investment goods trades only. So long as we are using the Physical concept, this is just like any other invention; it only affects a part of the Social Product (that devoted to Investment), but from that point of view it is exactly on a par with an invention which only changes productivity in the manufacture of cheese. But if we are using the Fund concept, we have to say that the capital of the economy is reduced as a result of the invention. It still consists of the same physical goods, but it is reduced in Fund terms, because it can be replaced at a smaller sacrifice of consumption goods than before. The effect of such an invention cannot then be expressed in terms of simple reactions on the marginal products of the factors, for we have also to take into account the change in the "quantity" of one of the factors which has occurred, ipso facto, as a result of the invention. The same difficulty arises with any change in technology, whenever there is a difference between the effects of the improvement on investment and on consumption. It is only in the special case when the invention is neutral between investment and consumption that we get the same result whether we use the Physical concept or the Fund concept.[1]

I would not deny that it would be possible to work out a system of classification, on marginal product

---

[1] It has been explained to me by Lionel Mackenzie that some features of the work of Samuelson and Solow that I had previously found puzzling are to be explained by a tacit assumption that the inventions under consideration are neutral between consumption and investment. I myself see no reason why this assumption should be made.

Aa

lines, using the Fund concept; but it would have to be
a four-way classification, not merely into labour-
saving and capital-saving, but also into investment-
biased and consumption-biased. I shall not attempt to
do that here. For, as will be seen, my personal preference does not lie in that direction. If we are making
a Static Comparison, we ought, I think, to use the
Physical concept of capital—whatever the practical
(and, indeed, the theoretical)[1] difficulties that arise
in the application of it. There is then no special
difficulty about the classification of inventions. But if
we are not making static comparisons—if we are
working in the field of growth models, or of development planning—I would not myself claim that there
is much to be said for thinking in terms of marginal
products.

INDUSTRIAL RELATIONS AND DISPUTES

(CHAPTERS VII. AND VIII.)

Passing on, I come to a pair of chapters which
evidently hang together. I have nothing much to say
about Chapter VIII., my attempt at a *histoire raisonnée*
of British Trade Unionism from the beginnings to
1930. It is considerably marred towards the end by
inadequate attention to the distinction between real
wages and money wages; for already in the twenties
collective bargaining was sufficiently *general* for it to

---

[1] I have gone more deeply into the theoretical problems of the Physical
concept of capital in the paper which I gave to the Corfu conference of the
International Economic Association in 1958. (It is available in the proceedings
of that conference, published as *The Theory of Capital*, edited by F. A. Lutz
and D. C. Hague.) This would have been a better paper if I had been clearer
about the two concepts of capital, here distinguished, than I was when I
wrote it.

be impossible to tell its full story without regard to monetary reactions. Earlier on, this does not so much matter, so that there is little, except in the concluding section, which I would want to modify. As compared with such modern works as Professor Phelps Brown's *Growth of British Industrial Relations*, it is only a thumb-nail sketch; but I still think that the things which I brought out are the important things.

Chapter VII. is a different matter. Like the rest of the book, it has had a story; but it is quite a different story. There was another book, which appeared at about the same time as mine, which contained a quite different analysis of bargaining under bilateral monopoly—F. Zeuthen's *Problems of Monopoly and Economic Warfare*. When I first read Zeuthen's book, I did not get much out of it; but I came later to realise that his central idea—that the process of bargaining might be made "determinate" by explicit attention to the imperfect knowledge of the bargainers, and its gradual reduction in the course of negotiation—was decidedly valuable. (It is, of course, not far away from those ideas which have had such a fruitful application in the Theory of Games.) Direct developments of Zeuthen's theory are to be found in later writings by the Dutch economist, J. Pen, and by Professor Shackle.[1] These followers of Zeuthen have had some hard things to say about my "Theory of Industrial Disputes" While I have no desire to defend my chapter as a comprehensive treatment, and no desire to criticise their positive "Zeuthenist" theories, there are one or two things which I think I should nevertheless say in "my" defence.

[1] J. Pen, "A General Theory of Bargaining" (*American Economic Review*, March 1952); G. L. S. Shackle, "The Nature of the Bargaining Process" (*The Theory of Wage Determination*, an I.E.A. symposium edited by J. T. Dunlop).

First of all, I should like to call attention to the place which Chapter VII. occupies in the structure of my book. Though it is called "The Theory of Industrial Disputes", its main object is not to make a theoretical analysis of the bargaining process. What it does seek to do is to answer the question: to what extent can Trade Union pressure compel employers to pay higher wages (or to grant more favourable terms to their employees in other respects) than they would have done if no such pressure had been exercised? The instrument of pressure is the threat of a strike; what I was seeking to identify were the factors which determine the size of the excess wage (or equivalent in other conditions) which a strike threat can normally enforce.

I began by looking at the matter from the employer's point of view. What he has to compare is the cost of the higher wage and the cost (to him) of the strike; the amount of the latter will depend upon many things, but it is surely true that the length of time for which he expects the threatened strike to last is a factor which must always be present. To suppose, as is supposed in my diagram (p. 143), that the employer's choice can be expressed in terms of a comparison between the cost of the higher wage (to continue for such a period as a settlement is expected to last) and the cost of so many days' stoppage, is a simplification, but not an unreasonable simplification. I still think that it gives a useful picture of the employer's problem; and it does not in fact seem to have been much contested that it does.

So much for my "employer's concession curve" (I am not proud of these names, but it was hard to think of better); what of the other, which has been

criticised[1] much more severely? I still think that there
is some sense in it, even as I drew it; but the explanation which I gave of it could certainly have been
improved.

If one looks at the Union curve in the same way as
has been appropriate for the employer's curve (asking
how many days' stoppage Union members are likely
to be willing to endure rather than accept the employer's terms), the answer would seem to be that the
period which would be endurable would be *greater*,
the greater is the difference between the wage demanded by the Union and the wage which would have
had to be accepted if there were no threat of a stoppage.
Thus the period will be longer the higher the wage that
is demanded; the Union curve should be drawn
upward-sloping, not downward-sloping as I drew it.
That is Professor Shackle's point; if the question is
posed in that way, it must be acknowledged that his
answer is right.

I don't think that I was posing it in that manner,
or that it is correct to do so. My Union curve is a more
complicated (more "second degree") affair than that.
What is implied is that the Union negotiators are
looking forward to the date at which the strike will
already have lasted for so many days, and when
(having, I think it must be supposed, some sort of
idea of an employer's concession curve in their minds)
they will be telling their members that they can get
better terms by hanging out just a bit longer. It
seemed (and still seems) to me that this is the point
at which the diminishing marginal utility of income
may be important. The lower the wage that is offered,
the more likely it is that members will be willing to

[1] As by Shackle, *op. cit.*

stay out a little longer in order to avoid accepting it. Corresponding to each length of strike, there will thus be a wage (or set of terms) which will be acceptable, if it cannot be improved except by prolonging the strike. The longer the strike has lasted, the lower (it would seem to follow) this wage would be.

I do not pretend that considerations of this kind can be expressed very accurately on so simple a diagram as that which I was using. I could no doubt have made my statement more precise if I had allowed for uncertainties (in Zeuthen's manner); or if I had drawn families of curves for different degrees of sophistication of the two sides. But I rather doubt (even now) whether such complication would have been worth while. For the purpose of Chapter VII., I am still inclined to think that the old diagram was good enough.

WAGES AND INTEREST: THE SHORT PERIOD

(CHAPTERS IX–XI)

I come now to the queerest part of my task, to those final chapters (IX.-XI.) which appeared to me, when I wrote them, to be the culmination of the book; but on which I changed my mind quite early on, so that already in 1935 I was beginning to say that they "ought to be withdrawn".[1] A few years after that I was thinking even worse of them than I did in 1935; the dislike which I felt for them has been a main reason why a second edition of the book has been so long deferred. I still feel that dislike; I am still quite sure

[1] Above, p. 283.

that they are extremely misleading, if they are taken at their face value. But I have now come to recognise that there are some parts of their argument which can be detached from the rest, and which, if they are so detached, are not only valid, but are actually quite important. Thus there are some peculiar directions in which these unfortunate chapters still have something that is interesting (and even rather fresh) to say.

As Shove observed in his review,[1] there are in these chapters two sorts of troubles: troubles on the side of capital and troubles on the side of money. In spite of Shove, I still think that the monetary trouble is much the worse. It is possible, as we shall see, to put up some defence for them on the capital side; but on the monetary side I still think that no defence is possible. All that can be done is to put in a word of explanation.

I wrote my book (as I have explained[2]) in a state of monstrous ignorance about everything monetary; all that can be claimed was that it was at least conscious ignorance.[3] I supposed, however, that I could get by, in spite of this ignorance, not only because I trusted in the "dichotomy" between real and monetary theory, but because that dichotomy presented itself to me in a particular form. I supposed that I was abstaining from having a monetary theory, but in fact I did have a monetary theory, derived (I suppose) from Hayek, or (more justly) from the Hayekian atmosphere in which I was working. Later on, when I no longer held that theory, I wrote it out quite explicitly. It appears as the *classical* theory in my article "Mr. Keynes and the Classics".[4]

[1] Above, p. 266.   [2] Above, p. 306-7   [3] Above, p. 212.
[4] *Econometrica*, 1937, esp. pp. 148-150.

I remember that when Keynes saw that article, one of the (rather few) criticisms that he made of it was that he did not recognise the *classical* theory as I had set it out. There, of course, he was quite right. Keynes's *classical* theory is that of Marshall and of Pigou, a much more sophisticated affair than the crude thing which I was summarising. My "classical" theory is a caricature of that which was really held by the deeper Quantity theorists;[1] but it is pretty much what I had myself held when I wrote *The Theory of Wages*.

It goes like this. The Quantity of Money (M) and its income-velocity (V) are *entirely* determined by monetary causes, which are quite separate from the real causes which determine relative prices. It follows that the money value of total income, since it equals MV, is also entirely determined by monetary causes. It then further follows that when we are considering the working of the real system, this money value can be taken as given. It may indeed be changing during the time when our real processes are working out, but it will be changing for other reasons than those with which we are concerned. In "real" analysis, changes in money income may therefore be neglected.

As I observed, so long as this sheet-anchor holds, one may admit all the other relations which play so important a part in Keynes's system, and yet they leave one's "classicism" entirely unperturbed. Saving, for instance, might depend upon "income" if "income" were variable; but since "income" is not variable, this relation is of no importance. The rate of interest must therefore be determined by saving and investment—

[1] I have tried to formalise what I now think they did hold in a paper that pretends to be about Patinkin ("A Rehabilitation of Classical Economics?", *Economical Journal*, 1957).

by *propensities* to save and to invest. And if the diminishing marginal productivity of labour is admitted (or anything of that sort is admitted) real wages and money wages must go together. As I put it in 1937:

"So far we have assumed the rate of money wages to be given; but so long as we assume that (income velocity) is independent of the level of wages, there is no difficulty about this problem either. A rise in the rate of money wages will necessarily diminish employment and raise real wages. For an unchanged money income cannot continue to buy an unchanged quantity of goods at a higher price-level; and unless the price-level rises, the prices of goods will not cover their marginal costs. There must therefore be a fall in employment; as employment falls, marginal costs in terms of labour will diminish and therefore real wages rise. (Since a change in money wages is always accompanied by a change in real wages in the same direction, if not in the same proportion, no harm will be done, and some advantage will perhaps be secured, if one prefers to work in terms of real wages.) . . .

"Admittedly it follows from this theory that you may be able to increase employment by direct inflation; but whether or not you decide to favour that policy still depends upon your judgement about the probable reaction on wages, and also—in a national area—upon your views about the international standard."[1]

If, that is to say, the wage that is being demanded (say by Trade Unions) is a real wage, not a money wage—and this I still think to be a perfectly reasonable question to put to one's theory—they can get it at the expense of a certain amount of unemployment, but they cannot get it by inflation, which simply raises all money values.

The complete dichotomy on which this theory rests

[1] *Op. cit.*, p. 150.

will of course be modified as soon as we take account
of the effect of income-distribution upon income-
velocity; but it is at the touch of liquidity preference
(establishing a link between income-velocity and the
rate of interest) that the picture changes decisively,
and we pass into a Keynesian world. The existence of
that link destroys the old dichotomy between real and
monetary theory; for at the least there is the rate of
interest which belongs on both sides. It is nevertheless
possible (as Keynes discovered[1]) to impose a new
dichotomy. Here it is not the money value of income,
but the rate of interest, which is thought of as determined by monetary causes; the remaining real elements
in the system, including the level of employment, have
then to fall in with this rate of interest. If all prices,
including wages, are determined by supply-demand
equations, relative prices are determined in the "real"
sector, but money prices are left undetermined; thus
in the Keynesian system (the evolution of which may
not unfairly be represented in this manner) money
prices are only anchored if there is not full employment:
if, that is to say, there are some *sticky* prices (such as
wages) which are *not* determined by supply-demand
equilibrium.

It then becomes natural to say that the effect of
a *simple* change in money wages (a uniform change in
money wages throughout a closed system) is just to
raise prices in the same proportion as wages have risen;
leaving employment unchanged and real wages unchanged. The problem which I was considering, in the
later chapters of *The Theory of Wages*, is accordingly
denied to be a real problem; for it becomes impossible
for any authority (Trade Union or other) merely by

[1] Like Wicksell before him,

acting upon money wages, to affect real wages. Real wages only change as a result of changes in the real elements of the system, changes in productivity and the like; changes in money wages are not *real* changes. Rises in money wages can only have inflationary consequences; they cannot affect real wages (or employment) at all.

There is, of course, no question that this presentation of Keynes's (the essential features of which I have been baldly summarising) gives a much better *simple* picture of reality than was given by any form of "classical" theory; its power, as a simplification, has been abundantly illustrated by experience during the quarter-century since 1936. But there is a question (a question that was indeed raised without delay both by unfriendly and friendly critics) whether the admission of Liquidity Preference *necessitates* so drastic a change. The theory of money wages that has just been summarised is not a necessary consequence of the abandonment of the old dichotomy; it is a consequence of the new dichotomy which has been introduced to replace the old. If, when money wages rise, things are to work out in this Keynesian manner, it is necessary that the rate of interest should remain unchanged; but to assume that the interest rate is constant is theoretically just as extreme an assumption as the "classical" assumption of constant money income. If there is to be a general rise in money wages, and the rate of interest is to remain unchanged, additional money (to finance the enhanced money value of social output) must be forthcoming from somewhere; even though, in practice, it very frequently (if not usually) is forthcoming, the condition is one that deserves to have attention drawn to it. When attention is drawn to it, the Keynesian theory may not look so unlike the classical theory after all. For if money wages rise, *and* the supply of money is increased, "classical" theory would agree that the Keynesian effects would follow; real wages would not rise, employment would not fall, and (incidentally) the rate of interest would remain unchanged. But what do we then say about what then seems to be the more interesting case—that in which the supply of money is not increased, and the state of Liquidity Preference is not such that the additional money is made available by the dishoarding of idle balances; so that there is not enough money to finance the money value of total income, as it would be if the Keynes process were carried through? This is the problem—a problem of some practical interest, since it is a part of the practical problem of the ability of monetary policy to cope with wage inflation—to which the reader is now invited to turn his attention.

The orthodox Keynesian answer to this problem is, of course, very well known. If there is not enough money to support full employment at the enhanced level of money wages, the rate of interest will rise, employment will *therefore* fall, and (probably) real wages will rise, since a smaller volume of labour is being applied to an unchanged capital stock.[1] This is not so very far away from the classical analysis of the same problem; after all, it is a rather "classical" problem, with which classical theory ought to be better able to cope. Both are agreed that the rise in money wages will now lead to a rise in real wages and

[1] See, for instance, the "IS-LL" version of the Keynes theory which I gave in my 1937 *Econometrica* article and which has since passed into so many textbooks. On the last point, whether the real wage would in fact rise, many Keynesians would have doubts; some light may be thrown upon this point as we proceed,

a fall in employment. We seem to be in sight of some degree of reconciliation.

There remains, however, an essential difference. To the Keynesian the fall in employment comes about through a *rise* in the rate of interest; but on the classical theory (at least in the form that was given to it in *The Theory of Wages*) there should not be a rise in the rate of interest. There should be a fall in interest. Keynes's unemployment equilibrium comes about because the shortage of money pushes up the rate of interest; whereas in mine the high level of real wages pushes the rate of interest down.

Which is right? It was my view, for many years, that Keynes was right, and that *therefore* I had been wrong. I was fortified in this opinion by some work which I myself had done just before I read *The General Theory*, and which is reprinted here[1] (the "Bread" paper I may call it for ready reference). In that paper I constructed a simple economy without money (the single consumption good—Bread—being taken as a standard of value), and put it through a form of analysis which (as it turned out) was very like that used by Keynes. In such an economy the only kind of rise in wages which could be "engineered by Trade Unions" would be a rise in real wages. I examined the effect of such a rise, and the effect on interest which I seemed to get was the same as Keynes's. The rise in real wages would raise the rate of interest.[2] That was why I then said that Chapter IX. should be withdrawn.

It is only rather recently that I have realised that

[1] Above, pp. 268-285.

[2] Thus I could not find an escape by supposing that Keynes was talking about a money rate of interest while I was talking about a real rate (corrected for changes, or expected changes, in the price-level of consumption goods). The trouble was still there if one kept to the real rate of interest.

this will not quite do. Once again, one got different answers because (without realising it) one was discussing different problems. What was being discussed in the "Bread" paper (and also what was being discussed by Keynes) was a short-period, or impact effect. But that, quite certainly, is not what I was discussing in *The Theory of Wages*. All I was doing there (all that I could be doing with the tools that were then at my disposal) was to examine how things would work out in the long run. It is only in this sense that there can be anything in what I was saying in those chapters. To what extent they can be rehabilitated if taken in that sense is the question to which I now turn.

WAGES, INTEREST AND GROWTH

What used to be called the theory of long-period equilibrium has turned, in modern economics, into the Theory of Growth. The expanding economy, in which everything is growing at a constant rate over time, turns out to be a more useful setting for exhibiting long-period relations, than the old *stationary state*, which was all that was at my disposal when I wrote *The Theory of Wages*. It is nevertheless formally true that the Stationary State is a special case of a Growth Model, got by setting the growth rate equal to zero; things which are generally true in a Growth Model should therefore remain true in the Stationary State also. One may, therefore, sometimes perceive by stationary analysis some of the properties which are also important in growth theory. That, it now seems, what is I have done in these chapters; so they are, in the end, not so much wrong as out of place. They do not really belong in *The Theory of Wages*; where they belong is in the Theory of Growth.

There is an argument which makes its appearance, in one form or another, in most growth models. When it is looked at in isolation, it bears a striking resemblance to the argument of my Chapters IX.-X. It is set in different contexts by different authors, but out of context it will always take something like the following form.

Consider a uniformly expanding economy, in which all elements remain in the same proportion to one another, as time goes on. Labour employed increases in the same proportion as physical capital, and all outputs keep the same proportions. Every element has then the same growth rate (g). Granted these assumptions, there is no reason why relative prices should change; so we may take it that they do not change. Accordingly, if we take any good (or labour itself) as a standard of value, we may say that absolute prices remain unchanged over time. It can be readily shown that these conditions are not consistent among themselves, unless the growth rate g (the common growth rate of all elements) itself remains constant over time.

One of the elements in the economy which will grow at this constant growth rate (granted the constancy of absolute prices) is the *value* of the capital stock (which I will call K). The increment in this value, over any period, is gK; and this must equal the saving of the period. If r is the rate of interest (or profit—we do not here distinguish), the net profit that is earned in the period must equal rK. Now if we assume that all saving comes out of profits (a simplification indeed, but one which can be modified in moderation without affecting the trend of the argument), and if s is the proportion of profits that is saved (which must be constant over time, like all other elements in the system), if follows at once that $gK = srK$ or $g = sr$. Some such relation as this seems to be a necessary characteristic of any fixed proportions growth model.[1]

One of the things that can be done with a growth model of this kind is to use it for *comparative* purposes, just as is done with the static model in *comparative* statics.[2] Consider two such expanding systems, with similar technology and similar in all other respects, save that in one the rate of real wages is higher than in the other. (It must be emphasised that the real wage rate, being one of the relative prices of the system, is constant in each system over time. All that happens, in the course of expansion, is that more labourers are taken on at this given wage.) It can hardly be doubted (and is not, I think, in dispute) that in the system where the real wage is higher the rate of growth will be less. But then, since the equation $g = sr$ must hold in each system, if s is the same in each system, r must be lower in the system where the real wage is higher. The rate of interest must be lower in the system where the real wage is higher—just as I said in my Chapters IX.-X.!

I have deliberately set out the foregoing argument in a very "pure" and so unrealistic form, in order to sharpen the issue. The conclusion which is reached is nevertheless so definite that it could hardly be changed altogether by considerable relaxation of the assump-

---

[1] Thus for instance in the von Neumann growth model, where all profits are saved, $s = 1$, and therefore $g = r$.

[2] Mr. Kaldor's distribution theory is the theory which is appropriate to this model.

tions. We must, for instance, surely get the same answer if we merely assume that there is a greater propensity to save out of profits than out of wages. That higher real wages means a lower rate of profit, *and* a lower rate of growth, must surely remain valid for much less extreme assumptions than those which have just been made.[1]

The way in which I got to this result, in my Chapters IX.-X., was certainly different, but it was by no means inconsistent with what has just been said. A bridge can perhaps be built in the following manner. Suppose we think of all production being carried on in a giant firm, which also owns the truck-shop at which workers spend their wages; suppose that wages are paid in tickets which command a certain volume of goods, so that no prices can go up without other prices going down in terms of these tickets. The wages that are fixed are therefore real wages. It surely stands to reason that if the real wage were higher, the profit of the firm would be lower—the *rate* of profit would be lower—since the part of gross production which would have to be paid out, before capital could even be replaced, would be increased. And it is equally clear that unless the propensity to save out of wages were greater than that out of profits (an assumption so peculiar that it would change the whole character of the model), the proportion of net production that was invested would be lower, so that the rate of growth would be lower. Thus, so long as we stick to the *comparative* problem, comparing one state of steady growth equilibrium with another, we are bound to come to the old conclusion: that the rate of profit

[1] It must however be emphasised, most strongly, that this depends upon *given* saving-properties; a rise in s will pull g and r together, normally (therefore) raising g and diminishing r.

will be lower, and the rate of growth will be lower, when the real wage is higher.

It further appears, when we argue in this way, that as soon as there is any choice of techniques, higher real wages make for "substitution" of capital for labour. The economy with the higher real wage will use techniques with a higher proportion of (physical) capital to labour; and will increase its production of goods with a relatively high capital content relatively to its production of others. This substitution will diminish the fall in the rate of· profit that would otherwise have been necessary, and will accordingly diminish the fall in the rate of growth that would otherwise have been necessary. But it will diminish the employment of labour, relatively to capital stock, at each stage of the growth process.

All this is pretty much what I said in my book, except for the emphasis that must now be laid upon the *comparative* nature of the analysis. Without doubt, that makes a very great difference. So long as we are comparing one state of steady growth with another, things do work our pretty much as I said. But that still leaves us with the problem which I did not begin to face: how can an economy (and in particular a money-using economy) get from one such state of steady growth to another? How indeed can real wages rise?

Any proper discussion of this problem—one of the main problems of economic theory which still remain to us—would lead me far beyond any reasonable scope of this Commentary. It would however be intolerable to leave it without some further remarks.

We can, I think, begin to perceive the possibility of a reconciliation if we start by postponing the question of money, and begin by straightening out the "barter" problem. Here it will be useful to look back at the "Bread" paper. It was there shown that the impact effect of a rise in real wages was (in all probability) a rise in the (real) rate of interest. That, I still think, was perfectly correct; but closer examination would have shown that the force of the argument is based upon *lags* in adjustment. The full effect on employment does not exert itself at once; the full effect in reducing capitalists' consumption does not exert itself at once; thus while output is declining, there may well be a shortage of "bread", which, on the principles of that paper (quite correct principles, I still think them) would be reflected in a *rise* in the "bread" interest rate. If, however, one had taken the story further (to "Monday week" and after), the point would surely have come when the lags would not have worked in this way. It is certainly possible that some curious things would happen (the spectre of Cycle Theory with its accelerators and multipliers is standing at one's shoulder); but it is not ruled out that there would be a convergence to equilibrium, and it is now clear that in the final equilibrium, and therefore upon the path to equilibrium, the interest rate would have to fall.

This "barter" analysis is not very good for the Trade Union case, which I thought I was considering in the chapters now under discussion; but there do exist some genuine problems to which it could be applied. The expanding economy, which can draw unlimited labour at a constant real wage-rate, is not a bad model for the case of a new country, which is drawing immigrants from outside its borders; so that the real wage-rate is (approximately) fixed, at the rate which has to be paid to the new immigrants in order that they should come in. It might then genuinely happen that as a result of changes taking place abroad, without any change occurring in the country itself, the real wage-rate had to rise; and the result which would now follow from our analysis—that after an awkward period of adjustment, the rate of profit in the expanding country would have to fall, and its rate of growth would have to slow up—seems eminently sensible.

But now—what about the monetary reaction? It must clearly be supposed, in order that the original growth equilibrium should be sustained, that the supply of money is expanding *pari passu* with other elements (in the absence of technical improvements—financial inventions—which make a given supply of money go further). For it is a condition of the growth equilibrium that the rate of interest should remain unchanged; the supply of money must be increasing sufficiently for that to happen. If money prices are to remain reasonably steady, and the steady growth is not to be upset by monetary disturbances, the supply of money must be increasing sufficiently for the rate of interest, required by Liquidity Preference, to keep in line with the rate of interest that is required by the real wage-rate.

Now suppose that the real wage-rate rises—and (to fix the ideas) suppose that it rises for the reason that has just been mentioned, better opportunities for earning in the world outside. Instead of flowing in, labour begins to flow out. The first result of the labour shortage may well be that there is increased competition for labour, and a tendency to rising money wages; if unchecked this would simply lead to inflation. What is there to check it? There are two possibilities, which it is most important to distinguish.

It is possible, on the one hand, that a lack of money, to finance the higher level of money wages, may lead to a *rise* in the rate of interest. For the moment, this will (or may) save the situation; though some labour leaves, being unable to get employment, the remainder can get the higher real wages, which are needed to induce them to remain. But this is still only the "first Monday"; if the high rate of interest is maintained, and the high real wage is maintained, the rate of interest would be above its equilibrium level (in Wicksell's language, the money rate of interest would be above the natural rate) so that contraction must continue. If the contraction is to stop, and the economy is to resume its growth—the more modest rate of growth which is all that it can enjoy, now that labour has become more difficult to get—the rate of interest will have to come down. There is, indeed, a way in which it might come down without deliberate policy, if there was no inflation; for the contracted economy would require less money to finance it than was required before the supply of labour was checked. But this is a little fanciful; there is in general no automatic mechanism whereby the right reduction would occur at the right time. To adjust to this real change, as to any other major real change, without undesirable repercussions on the monetary side, must be expected to be a delicate matter.

That is one way in which things may work out; but there is another way also, which theoretically is perhaps more interesting. Suppose that there is no monetary check, so that there is no rise in the interest rate; then, on Keynesian principles, prices will rise

Bb*

freely, but real wages will not rise. But this is a situation which (on our assumptions) cannot continue. It will
be impossible to hold labour at the old level of real
wages; so there must be a real contraction in employment and output, whatever happens to money wages.
With the contraction in employment, there must (if
not at once, then after a lag) be a diminished demand
for the products of industry; this diminished demand
will itself make it impossible for prices to be pushed
up freely, as we have hitherto supposed them to be.
With an elastic money supply (constant interest rate)
the level at which prices will finally settle is of course
quite indeterminate; it is perfectly possible that if this
monetary policy (for that is effectively what it is) is
pursued, there will be a large rise in prices before the
effects of the disturbance can be worked out. But the
important thing, for our purposes, is that by this route
also there can be a convergence to the real equilibrium
that has been identified above.

In these terms we may perhaps find a partial
solution[1] for the problem of growth theory which has
been vexing us: how it is possible for a money-using
economy to get from one steady growth path to
another, when the rate of real wages changes. But
what bearing has this upon our "Trade Union"
problem? Very little; for we must still say (and can
indeed say with greater confidence) that in a money-
using economy, a simple rise in the general level of
money wages cannot be effective in raising real wages,
at least in the long run. What has now been shown
(in a particular case, but it looks as if it would prove

---

[1] It is not a complete solution, for it throws no light at all upon the
hardest part of the problem; how it is possible for the capital stock which is
appropriate to the one growth rate to be transformed into that which is
appropriate to the other. It may, however, be enough for present purposes.

to be a representative case) is that this is consistent
with the possibility that there may be a rise in real
wages, not only because of a change in productivity,
but because of some independent (exogenous) cause.
The fundamental difference between the two situations
has at last begun to come clear.

In the former instance, where wages are simply
put up by "Trade Unions", there is no effective check
to the supply of labour; in the latter, where the supply
of labour is elastic at a given real wage, there is a
check. If real wages are not raised, the supply of labour
will be reduced. This is the difference; we have simply
to point out that labour "monopoly" that does not
control the supply of labour—like any other "monopoly" that does not control supply (but not for quite
the same reason)—is likely to be ineffective.

Having reached that point, it will be well to look
back for a moment at the question of sectional wage-
pressure. As was previously observed,[1] there is a
Keynes type argument which would attribute, at least
in principle, the same effect to a sectional rise in money
wages as to a general rise. If there is full employment,
and if (a big if!) wages in all other sectors rise at once
in direct response to demand pressure, any attempt
to substitute B-labour for A-labour (along any channel)
will lead to a rise in B-wages, which will remove the
incentive for substitution. I do not myself think very
highly of this argument (it would be a fine tail that
could wag the dog in this way!) for, as explained, I do
not believe that the labour market works like that,
and I much doubt if the economic system, even of a
single nation, is *ever* in full employment in the drastic
sense which would be needed if this proposition were

[1] Above, p. 329.

to be even approximately true. All the same, it is interesting to observe that even if this proposition is granted, we are not obliged (at the point we have now reached) to follow it up with the paradoxical conclusion that might seem to follow from it. We can admit that Trade Unions are able to raise the wages of their members relatively to the wages of workers who are ununionised, or organised in weaker unions. What we should have to say is that they do this mainly by retrictive practices (control over the supply of labour in the widest sense), not by the direct negotiation of favourable wage-contracts. I would myself (for the reasons stated) be reluctant to jump to any such conclusion; there may, however, after all be something in it.

The question of "Hours and Conditions", to which I came in my last chapter (XI.), is a part of this question of the control of the supply of labour. It is understandable, in view of what has just been said, that it is not much damaged by the troubles which beset its immediate predecessors. As always, there are things in it which I would not now put as I put them then; but the qualifications which I should make are rather obvious, and I do not think that I need trouble my present reader with them. I have given him (and his predecessor) quite enough trouble on more important matters.

NOTES ON THE ELASTICITY OF SUBSTITUTION

I *The Two Definitions*

It may be as well to set down a formal proof of the identity of the two definitions of the elasticity of substitution, which I will write, for the moment, as σ_R and σ_H respectively. Putting x_a, x_b for the marginal products of factors a and b, in terms of product x, we have (from constant returns to scale)

$$ax_a + bx_b = x \quad \ldots \quad \ldots \quad \ldots \quad (1).$$

Differentiating partially with respect to a and b,

$$ax_{aa} + bx_{ab} = 0, \quad ax_{ab} + bx_{bb} = 0 \quad \ldots \quad (2).$$

Then

$$\frac{1}{\sigma_R} = -\frac{d \log (x_b/x_a)}{d \log (b/a)} = \frac{(dx_b/x_b)-(dx_a/x_a)}{(da/a)-(db/b)}$$

$$= \left(\frac{x_{ab}da + x_{bb}db}{x_b} - \frac{x_{aa}da + x_{ab}db}{x_a}\right) \Big/ \left(\frac{da}{a} - \frac{db}{b}\right)$$

But from (2)

$$a\left(\frac{x_{ab}}{x_b} - \frac{x_{aa}}{x_a}\right) = \frac{ax_{ab}}{x_b} + \frac{bx_{ab}}{x_a} = \frac{x_{ab}}{x_a x_b}(ax_a + bx_b)$$

$$= \frac{xx_{ab}}{x_a x_b} = (1/\sigma_H)$$

and similarly

$$b\left(\frac{x_{ab}}{x_a} - \frac{x_{bb}}{x_b}\right) = (1/\sigma_H)$$

so that

$$\frac{1}{\sigma_R} = \frac{1}{\sigma_H}\left(\frac{da}{a} - \frac{db}{b}\right) \Big/ \left(\frac{da}{a} - \frac{db}{b}\right) = \frac{1}{\sigma_H}$$

and the two definitions are proved identical.

II *The Elasticity of Derived Demand*

The formula for the elasticity of derived demand, given on p. 244, is unquestionably correct; but it is not written in what proves, in the light of later work, to be the most instructive form. It is better to begin by taking it in the special form to which it reduces when e (the elasticity of supply of the second factor) is infinite; this is evidently

$$\lambda = k\eta + (1-k)\sigma \quad . \quad . \quad . \quad . \quad (3).$$

which is at once suggestive of a similar formula in the theory of consumer's demand. (This is of course as it should be, for η the elasticity of demand for the product, is playing the same part here as the income-elasticity in consumption theory; both of them come in as "scale" components. The elasticities of substitution, though here it is factor substitution, there product substitution, are playing the same part in each case.)

Corresponding to this is the other special form that is taken when $e = 0$; it is

$$\lambda = \frac{\sigma\eta}{k\sigma + 1 - k\eta} \text{ or } \frac{1}{\lambda} = \frac{k}{\eta} + \frac{1-k}{\sigma} \quad . \quad . \quad . \quad (4).$$

so that the same relation which previously held between the direct elasticities (of quantity against price) now holds between their reciprocals (elasticities of price against quantity). This is the kind of thing which we should nowadays expect, for it is an example of the *duality* which extends throughout the greater part of economic theory.

Once this is seen, it will be more convenient to write the general formula as

$$\lambda = \frac{\sigma\eta + e\,(k\eta + \overline{1-k}\sigma)}{(k\sigma + \overline{1-k}\eta) + e} \quad . \quad . \quad . \quad . \quad (5).$$

which makes clear that it is a *mean*, weighted by the elasticity of supply of the second factor (e), between the two preceding formulae. This is a way of regarding the general formula which will be useful to us later on.

It is further apparent, once we split up the problem in this way, that the theory can be completed by formulae for cross-elasticities. In the case where e is infinite, we shall have the formula that is given by Mrs. Robinson[1]

$$\mu = k\,(\eta - \sigma) \quad . \quad . \quad . \quad . \quad . \quad (6).$$

where μ is the elasticity of the quantity demanded of B against the price of A. The dual to this is equally valid

$$\frac{1}{\mu'} = k\left(\frac{1}{\sigma} - \frac{1}{\eta}\right) \quad . \quad . \quad . \quad . \quad . \quad (7).$$

but $(1/\mu')$ is now the elasticity of the price of B against the supply of A, when the supply of B is fixed, so that μ and μ' are not identical.

In both cases, however (and it can readily be shown that this is true in all cases[2]), we find that $\eta > \sigma$ is the condition for an increase in the *supply* of factor A to increase the *demand* for factor B. It would have saved much trouble if I had pointed this out in my 1932 Appendix.

III *The Marshall Rules*

For the way in which I there used my formula for λ was to make a test of the four celebrated rules about the elasticity of derived demand that were given by Marshall (p. 242 above). All were confirmed, except the second,[3] to which I found an exception. "Even if we concern ourselves only with cases in which e is positive (η and σ must be positive) the second rule is only true as long as $\eta > \sigma$; so long as the elasticity of demand

---

[1] *Economics of Imperfect Competition*, p. 259.

[2] The general relation between μ and μ' is given by
$$\mu\mu' = -(d\log b/d\log p_a)\,(d\log a/d\log p_b)$$
$$\quad\;\; = -(d\log a/d\log p_a)\,(d\log b/d\log p_b) = \lambda e.$$
The general formula for the effect on the other factor may therefore be written in two alternative forms. We may write it as
$$\eta = \frac{k(\eta - \sigma)e}{(k\sigma + 1 - k\eta) + e} \quad . \quad . \quad . \quad . \quad (6').$$
if we are interested in the effect of the price of A on the employment of B—this reduces to (6) when e is infinite; or we may write it as
$$\frac{1}{\mu'} = \frac{k(\eta - \sigma)}{\sigma\eta + e(k\eta + 1 - k\sigma)}, \quad . \quad . \quad . \quad (7').$$
which reduces to (7) when $e = 0$.

[3] In Pigou's numeration. As I have been reminded by Professor Bronfenbrenner, in Marshall's own numeration it is the third.

for the final product is greater than the elasticity of substitution" (p. 243). No explanation was given of this exception, and it has (naturally) been something of a puzzle to many of my readers.[1] It was only lately, when the matter was brought up again by Professor Bronfenbrenner of Minnesota, that I saw a way of putting the point in economic terms, which I ought to have seen long ago. It is the above-mentioned property of the cross-elasticity which is the key. I quote from my reply to Professor Bronfenbrenner:[2]

"It is ordinarily not easy to envisage a process of production with two factors only, such that one is highly substitutable for the other. For we usually think of one factor as employing the other, and the mechanics of substitution at the expense of an employing factor (when carried to an extreme) may seem a bit mysterious. Let us. however, think of the two factors as two sorts of labour, and suppose (for the present) that there is no other factor used. Let us call them Black Labour and White Labour, which can easily be thought of as close substitutes in one set of conditions, and much less close substitutes in other conditions, very much as we like.

"Suppose that White Labour gangs up and raises its wage-rate (in terms of general purchasing power). At a constant wage of Black Labour, the cost of the product is raised and the amount to be produced falls ($\eta > 0$). The demand for White Labour falls, and (if there is no substitution) the demand for Black Labour falls also. But if σ is positive, there are two forces affecting the demand for Black Labour, the diminished demand for the product tending to diminish it, the substitution tending to increase it. Either may be dominant.[3]

"First consider the ordinary case, where the elasticity of demand for the product is dominant, so that the rise in the wages

[1] See, for instance, D. H. Robertson, *Lectures on Economic Principles*, vol. 2, p. 31.

[2] *Oxford Economic Papers*, October 1961. See also the contributions by Bronfenbrenner and Robertson in the same issue.

[3] So far I am assuming that the wage of Black Labour (in terms of the same general purchasing power) remains constant, so that I can simply apply formula (6). But the condition $\eta \gtrless \sigma$ determines whether the demand *curve* for Black Labour moves the one way or the other, so that it also determines whether the wage of Black Labour rises or falls, when the supply of Black Labour is less than perfectly elastic. This is confirmed by the other formula (6'-7').

of White Labour is bad for Black Labour. It is then maintained that the demand for the White Labour will be more elastic, the larger is its share (k) in the total costs of production: the traditional 'Marshall' view. For White Labour sustains its higher wage, partly at the expense of the consumer, partly at the expense of Black Labour. It is intelligible that White Labour can more easily increase its aggregate wage, the more easily Black Labour can be squeezed. If k is large, $1-k$ (the share of Black Labour) will be small; a relatively small increase in the share of White Labour means a relatively large decrease in the share of Black Labour, which will only come about with difficulty. Thus it is confirmed that in this case it is 'important to be unimportant'.

"Now consider the other case, when the elasticity of substitution is dominant. Here, when White Labour pushes up its wage, there is a gain to Black Labour. Some part of what White Labour squeezes out of the consumer has to be handed over to Black Labour. It is now intelligible that if k is large, so that Black Labour's initial share is small, a considerable relative expansion in the total accruing to Black Labour will do relatively little harm to White Labour. That, I think, is what my mathematics were really trying to say.

"In order to make sense of my 'paradox', I have had to construct a rather artificial example. That, of course, is why it has so long remained paradoxical. But having got so far, it is easy to notice that it could easily have been made less artificial—by introducing a third factor. I will not go into the mathematics of that—the idea of doing so is rather terrifying; as usual, they can be avoided. For suppose that there are three factors in our industry —White Labour, Black Labour, and Capital as well. In theory, we can split the process of production up into two stages, in one of which White Labour is combined with Black Labour to make Grey Labour, while in the other Grey Labour is combined with Capital to make the Product.[1] The theory which has been elaborated above can then still be used, but must be used twice: once to derive the demand for Grey Labour from the demand for the Product and the supply of capital, once to derive the demand for White Labour from the demand for Grey Labour and the supply of Black Labour.

[1] If the three-factor production function exhibits constant returns to scale, the intermediate product (Grey Labour) can evidently be defined so that both of the partial production functions will exhibit constant returns to scale also.

It still remains true that the demand for White Labour will be more elastic the larger is k, if $\eta > \sigma$; less elastic the larger is k, if $\eta < \sigma$. But η is here the elasticity of derived demand for Grey Labour, σ is the elasticity of substitution between White Labour and Black Labour, k is the proportion of White Labour costs to total *labour* costs, not total costs including capital costs.

"I do not see why the "paradox", in this latter form, should not be acquitted of its paradoxicality, and become quite reasonably useful."

IV. *Multiplicity of Factors*

In view of what has been said in the passage just quoted, I shall be careful to abstain from writing out an "elasticity of substitution" theory for more than two factors; nothing is to be gained by littering the page with determinants of second derivatives, the meaning of which it would be hard to disentangle. There is in fact just one property of the many-factor production function which we do require;[1] a proof of that property can be given here, which springs directly from the ideas that have been used in the preceding sections of these notes.

What we want to do is to compare the two cases in which the "other" factors (B, C, D . . .) can be treated *as if* they were a single factor. This can be done, as has been explained, *either* if the ratios between the quantities of these factors remain unchanged when the input of A varies; *or* if the ratios of their prices (that is to say, of their marginal products) remain unchanged. In each of these cases the two-factor theory will apply, in the sense that the increase in A will increase its relative share if the elasticity of substitution (of A against the complex) is greater than unity. But the meaning of the elasticity of substitution will be different in the two cases; what we want to do is to compare the two elasticities.

In either case we can use the regular definition (or definitions) of the elasticity of substitution, with a suitable interpretation of the "quantity" of the "other" factor. There is

---

[1] See above, p. 339-40.

however yet a third (equivalent) definition, which for the present purpose is rather more convenient than either of those which have become familiar. We have, using the notation of (I) above,

$$ax_{aa} + bx_{ab} = 0$$

so that

$$\sigma = \frac{x_a x_b}{x x_{ab}} = -\frac{b x_a x_b}{a x x_{aa}} = \frac{b x_b}{x}\left(-\frac{x_a}{a x_{aa}}\right) \quad . \quad . \quad (8).$$

so that σ is $(1-k) \times$ the elasticity of the marginal productivity curve of the factor A, along which the "quantity" of the "other factor" is of course taken as given.[1] The comparison in which we are interested may then be made as follows.

It will be convenient to rename our factors, calling the first factor A as before, but instead of calling the others $B, C, D \ldots$, let us call them $B_1, B_2, B_3. \ldots$ We may then, as in the last section, introduce an "intermediate product" B, which is made by the combination of $B_1, B_2 \ldots$, only. Our two cases can then be expressed as (i) that in which the quantities of the inputs of $B_1, B_2 \ldots$, are fixed, (ii) that in which the prices[2] of these inputs are fixed, while the total value of all B inputs (at these prices) is fixed; we are to consider the effect of a change in A-input on these two assumptions.

We start from a position in which the input of factor A is a (0), while the inputs of the other factors are b_1 (0), b_2 (0). . . . The given prices of the B-factors are such as to be proportional to their marginal products, when the quantities of all inputs are as stated; so that the initial position is an equilibrium position, whether it is factor-quantities or factor-prices that are fixed.

Now suppose that the input of factor A is increased, from a (0) to a (1). On the factor-price-fixed assumption, the quantities of B-factors that are used can be varied, subject

[1] Alternatively, we may proceed from formula (4) above, setting $(1/\eta)$ equal to 0, since the "price" of the "product" can be regarded as fixed, now that we are interested in relative shares.

[2] It is obviously immaterial in what standard of value these prices are to be reckoned.

to the condition that their total value, at the fixed factor-prices, remains unchanged. From the various quantities of B-factors that are available as inputs, subject to this restraint, there will be a number of different quantities of the intermediate product B that can be produced. But if the *specification* of the intermediate product is given, there will be one of these quantities that will be larger than any other; it will be that quantity of B which will be the equilibrium quantity, regardless of the input of factor A. There is however no reason why the specification of the intermediate product should be given. There will then be a choice between different patterns of B-production, available under the same restraint (of fixed prices of the B-factors, and given expenditure on them). In terms of intermediate products, the factor-restraint is transmuted into a restraint which limits B-production to *either* so much of the intermediate product B^1, *or* so much of the intermediate product B^2, or . . . In the initial situation, it was one of this set of alternatives (B^0 say) which was selected. But when the supply of A is increased, it is not necessary that the same B^0 should be chosen. It may (and in general will) be more productive to substitute for B^0 one of the alternatives to it, say B^1. B^1 will in general require a different set of inputs than were required by B^0.

This deals with the case in which factor – price ratios are to be kept constant; but the other case, in which factor-quantities are to be kept constant, fits at once into the same scheme. If it is the quantity-restraint which is to be operative, there will again be a choice between intermediate products B^4, B^1, B^2 . . . ; and it is again not necessary that the same alternative should be chosen when the input of factor A is at a (1) as was chosen at a (0). It is nevertheless clear that all of the alternatives that are open in this second case are alternatives that were also open in the first. It would have been possible, subject to the price-restraint, to keep quantities unchanged; but it was not necessary to do so. The price-choice is wider than the quantity-choice.

If B^{1*} is the alternative that is selected under the quantity-restraint, it is possible that B^1 will be the same as B^{1*}, but if they are different, B^1 must be an alternative that requires a different set of quantities of inputs, so that it is an alternative that is not available under the quantity-restraint. Thus, under the price-restraint, B^{1*} is rejected in favour of B^1; the total product X must therefore be larger with B^1 than with B^{1*}

We started, it will be remembered, with a position (0) in which the two restraints gave the same equilibrium position. The supply of A was then increased from a (0) to a (1); it has been shown that the total product (X) will be greater, after that increase, if the B-factors are limited by a price-restraint than if they are limited by a quantity-restraint. The increment of product must therefore be greater, so that the marginal product of the factor A is greater; the marginal productivity curve of A will be more elastic. Using formula (8) for σ, we have proved that the elasticity of substitution (of A for the other factors) will be greater when the inputs of those other factors can adjust themselves to relative demands; which is what we set out to prove.

V. *Multiplicity of Products*

It may be well to conclude by giving a proof of the formula for commodity elasticity of substitution between factors, which is given in a footnote of the "Revised Version"[1] without being proved. The general character of this commodity substitution comes out more clearly if we proceed from the Samuelson inequalities, as I did in an earlier section of this Commentary.[2] But the formula itself is of some interest; and I can hardly allow it to appear again without justifying it.

The system which is now to be considered is one with many products (X_r) but only two factors (A and B). Since we are not here concerned with direct technical substitution between the factors, we may suppose, for present purposes, that technical coefficients are fixed. I shall write a_r, b_r for the amounts of the factors needed to produce a unit of product X_r; reserving

---

[1] Above, p. 298.   [2] Above, p. 325.

A, B, for the total supplies of the factors. Prices of factors will be written w_a, w_b; prices of products p_r and outputs x_r. (Since we shall only be concerned with *relative* prices, prices may be fixed in any standard.)

We have the usual (Walrasian) equilibrium equations:

$$\Sigma a_r x_r = A, \quad \Sigma b_r x_r = B, \quad w_a a_r + w_b b_r = p_r \quad \text{(all } r\text{)}$$

What we wish to calculate is the elasticity of substitution $d \log (B/A) \,/\, d \log (w_a/w_b)$, when the only demand effects that are taken into account are substitution effects. We have

$$AB\, d \log (B/A) = A\, dB - B\, dA = \Sigma_r\, (Ab_r - Ba_r)\, dx_r$$
$$= \Sigma_r[(Ab_r - Ba_r)\, \Sigma_s\, (\partial x_r/\partial p_s)\, dp_s]$$

Now if we only take account of the substitution effect, we have $(\partial x_r/\partial p_s) = x_{rs}$ (in the notation of *Value and Capital*[1]), where $x_{rs} = x_{sr}$ and $\Sigma_s\, p_s\, x_{rs} = 0$. So that

$$\Sigma_s\, (\partial x_r/\partial p_s)\, dp_s = \Sigma_s\, p_s\, x_{rs}\, (dp_s/p_s)$$
$$= \Sigma_s p_s x_{rs} \left(\frac{dp_s}{p_s} - \frac{dp_r}{p_r}\right);$$

and it follows at once, from the Walrasian price-equations, that

$$p_r dp_s - p_s dp_r = (a_s b_r - a_r b_s)\, (w_b dw_a - w_a dw_b)$$
$$= (a_s b_r - a_r b_s)\, w_a w_b\, d \log (w_a/w_b)$$

Substituting back, and dividing through by $d \log (w_a/w_b)$, we have for the elasticity of substitution

$$\sigma = (w_a w_b/AB)\, \Sigma_r\, [(Ab_r - Ba_r)\, \Sigma_s\, (a_s b_r - a_r b_s)\, (x_{rs}/p_r)]$$

But $x_{sr} = x_{rs}$, so that this is the same as the double sum, taken over all *pairs* of commodities X_r and X_s,

$$(w_a w_b/AB)\, \Sigma\Sigma \left[(a_s b_r - a_r b_s)\, x_{rs} \left(\frac{Ab_r - Ba_r}{p_r} - \frac{Ab_s - Ba_s}{p_s}\right) \right]$$

---

[1] *Value and Capital* (either edition), p. 309.

Again using the Walras price-equations, the last bracketed expression reduced to

$$(1/p_r p_s) (a_s b_r - a_r b_s) (w_a A + w_b B)$$

so that finally

$$\sigma = (w_a w_b / AB) (w_a A + w_b B) \Sigma\Sigma (a_s b_r - a_r b_s)^2 (x_{rs}/p_r p_s)$$

By appropriate grouping of terms, this reduces to the formula that is given in the footnote on p. 298 above. For if $Y = w_a A + w_b B$, which is the value of the total product, and H_a, H_b, H_r are the relative shares of the factors and of the individual product X_r in Y, we have

$$H_a H_b \sigma = (w_a^2 \, w_b^2 / Y) \Sigma\Sigma [(a_s b_r - a_r b_s)^2 (x_{rs}/p_r p_s)]$$
$$= \Sigma\Sigma (k_{ab} k_{br} - k_{ar} k_{bs})^2 (p_r p_s x_{rs}/Y)$$

where $k_{ar} = w_a a_r / p_r$, the cost-proportion of factor A in the production of X_r. Nothing more is now necessary than to notice that $k_{ar} + k_{br} = 1$, and to define (perhaps arbitrarily) the *partial* elasticity of substitution (in demand) between X_r and X_s so that

$$(1/Y) \, p_r p_s x_{rs} = H_r H_s S_{rs};$$

and we have

$$H_a H_b \sigma = \Sigma\Sigma (k_{ar} - k_{as})^2 H_r H_s S_{rs}$$

which is in effect the formula that I have here set out to prove.[1]

It will be observed that in this formula the double sum is taken over all pairs of commodities X_r and X_s in which s and r are different; all terms where $s = r$ will have vanished. Thus if there is no complementarity (in the *Value and Capital* sense), all S_{rs} (or x_{rs}) will be positive, and σ must clearly be positive. That was as far as I had got in 1936; and I was still stuck at the corresponding stage when I did the first edition of *Value and Capital* a couple of years later. But from the general substitution theorem (which I did not get clear until the

---

[1] Any definition of a partial elasticity of substitution must satisfy the two requirements: that it is a pure number (independent of units) and that is symmetrical.

second edition),[1] we have that $\Sigma\Sigma\lambda_r \lambda_s x_{rs}$ (over *all* r and s) is necessarily <0, for any λ's. it follows that

$$- \Sigma\Sigma k_{ar} k_{as} H_r H_s S_{rs}$$

is invariably non-negative; while the remaining terms in the formula for σ will vanish, when they are taken over all r and s, since $\Sigma_s H_s S_{rs}$ vanishes, from the vanishing of $\Sigma_s p_s x_{rs}$. Thus the commodity elasticity of substitution is non-negative, without exception.

As stated,[2] the total elasticity of substitution is the sum of the commodity elasticity of substitution and the technical elasticity within the "industries". It should perhaps have been stated that the latter is now a weighted average of the technical elasticities within the individual industries, as may readily be confirmed by a similar method. If σ_r is the technical elasticity of substitution in the production of X_r, it can readily be shown that

$$(da_r/a_r) = - k_{br} \sigma_r d \log (w_a/w_b)$$
and
$$(db_r/b_r) = k_{ar} \sigma_r d \log (w_a/w_b)$$

It then follows that the technical component σ' is given by

$$H_a H_b \sigma' = \Sigma_r H_r k_{ar} k_{br} \sigma_r$$

which is the kind of thing we might expect.

[1] *Value and Capital*, 2nd edition, pp. 311, 329.
[2] Above, p. 341.

INDEX

Absolute share, of non-increasing factor, 115–6, 246–7, 293
Adding-up problem, 233, 334, 337–8
Allen, R. G. D. (and J. R. Hicks), "A Reconsideration of the Theory of Value", 286, 289, 298–9, 374
Arbitration, 148–151

Balance of payments, 330–1
Barone, E., 18
Beveridge, W. H., 44, 68, 316
Blacklegs, 161–2, 165
Böhm-Bawerk, E. von, 190, 201, 268–9, 283, 314
Bowley, A. L., 130, 335
"Bread" paper, 268–85, 361, 367
Bresciani-Turroni, C., 215
Bronfenbrenner, M., 375–6

Cannan, E., 113
Capital, theory of, 17–20, 187–207, 296, 342–9; physical and fund concepts, 342–9; unemployment of capital, 347
Capital-labour ratio, 13–14, 187–8; Shove's comment, 264–6
Capitalistic, more and less capitalistic industries, see Capital-labour ratio
Casual labour, 63–9; "casual co-efficient", 67n.
Champernowne, D. G., 286, 293
Circulating capital, in relation to marginal productivity, 17; in relation to wage-policy in depression, 53
Clark, Colin, 335
Clark, J. B., 116, 235, 268
Clay, H., 80, 86, 232, 316
Coefficients of production, 237; and elasticity of substitution, 117n.
Combination laws, 163
Common rule, 164
Complementarity, between factors, 293–4; in consumption, 298n., 383; intertemporal complementarity, 280n.
Conciliation, 147–8
"Conditions" of labour, 110, 226

Constant returns to scale, 236, 241, 288
Cost-of-living scales, 211–2
Cross-elasticity, 291n., 374–5

Dalton, H., 113, 119, 247
Demand for income, in terms of effort, 98
Demand for labour, theory of 1–22, 321–31
Depreciation, 20, 297, 347
Dichotomies, 357–9
Distribution, see Relative shares
Dobb, M. H., 103
Douglas, P. H., 303, 312–3

Edelberg, V., 268, 275
Edgeworth, F. Y., 5, 26, 235, 306
Efficiency of labour, differences in, 28–32; and efficiency of employers, 34–6; effect of wages on, 94–7, 207–10
Elasticity of substitution, 117, 286–92, 373–84, 245–6; the two definitions, 245, 290, 373; consumers' demand affects, 118, 120, 298; historical guesswork about, 131–2; in relation to hours of labour, 222; partial elasticities, 294n.; combined elasticity, 298, 384
Employers' associations, 166, 168
Employer's concession curve, 141–2, 154–8
Evasion, 229
Expectations, 60, 71–2, 83, 201–2, 274–80
Exploitation of labour, in Pigou's sense, 82–6, 258–9, 295, 332

Factory legislation, 107, 110
Fair wages, 80–2
Fairness and efficiency, 73, 317
Foresight, 58–60; in relation to fluctuations, 50–2; see also Expectations
"Free" capital, 19, 25
Full employment, 328–9, 371–2

"Good" and "bad" employers, 55–6, 102, 164, 167, 169

385

DATE DUE